DATE DUE

#47-0108 Peel Off Pressure Sensitive

Disciplining

Music

Disciplining

Music

Musicology and Its Canons

Edited by

Katherine Bergeron

and

Philip V. Bohlman

The University of Chicago Press   *Chicago and London*

Katherine Bergeron is assistant professor of music at Tufts University.
Philip V. Bohlman is assistant professor of music at the University of Chicago.

ML
3797.1
.D5
1992

The University of Chicago Press, Chicago 60637
The University of Chicago Press, Ltd., London
© 1992 by The University of Chicago
All rights reserved. Published 1992
Printed in the United States of America
01 00 99 98 97 96 95 94 93 92   5 4 3 2 1

ISBN (cloth): 0–226–04368–1

Library of Congress Cataloging-in-Publication Data

Disciplining music : musicology and its canons / edited by Katherine
    Bergeron and Philip V. Bohlman.
        p.   cm.
    A collection of essays which grew from a conference at Cornell
University in Feb. 1986, and from the 1987 New Orleans meeting of
the American Musicological Society.
    Includes bibliographical references and index.
    ISBN 0-226-04368-1 (cloth)
    1. Musicology.   2. Ethnomusicology.   3. Music—Theory.
I. Bergeron, Katherine.   II. Bohlman, Philip Vilas.
ML3797.1.D5   1992
780'.7—dc20   91-37836
                                                                    CIP
                                                                    MN

To William W. Austin
and to the memory of Edward P. Morris

Contents

         Richard Cohn and Douglas Dempster

10   A Lifetime of Chants   182
         Katherine Bergeron

11   Epilogue: Musics and Canons   197
         Philip V. Bohlman

       Contributors   211

       Index   213

Preface

Disciplining Music started as a conversation among friends and colleagues at Cornell University during 1985–86. Stimulating our conversation was, in fact, our interdisciplinary background—that is, the diverse perspectives on music emerging from our diverse interests and professional turfs. Cornell's Society for the Humanities, with its interdisciplinary agenda, provided the ideal forum for this conversation, and the spirit of intellectual exchange that attracted scholars from other fields into conversations in Cornell's Music Department eventually led to a mini-conference devoted to the study of the study of music, or the disciplining of music. Philip Bohlman, a Junior Fellow at the Society for the Humanities, hosted the conference (with a little help from his friends) on a Friday afternoon and evening in February 1986. The point of departure for most of the papers and responses was Joseph Kerman's *Contemplating Music* (Harvard University Press, 1985), though it was obvious that the pressing question of the day was how the individual scholar took a stance vis-à-vis something called "music." Did music as some sort of phenomenological reality determine the "disciplines," or did we somehow do the disciplining, rendering music perhaps slippery and elusive but bringing it into a conversation many could share?

The conversation at Cornell continued long after the mini-conference, and we were particularly pleased when the late Edward Morris, Professor of Romance Languages at Cornell, expressed interest in editing the papers as a special issue of a journal of literary criticism for which he was an advisor. We liked the idea but decided that first we would prefer to invite a few others to contribute to the interdisciplinary theme, initially at a special session at the 1987 New Orleans meeting of the American Musicological Society. All along, we had inflected the interdisciplinary questions with issues from outside the field of musicology; and the more we worked on organizing the AMS session, the more we appreciated the range of theoretical positions on the subject. Presenting papers at the AMS panel (entitled "Disciplining Music") were the editors of this volume, together with Richard Crawford, Don Randel, and Daniel Neuman, who served as chair.

During the days and months that followed, conversations about the topic proliferated, and new questions entered the fray. Recognizing the need to broaden our project—to include concerns that our panel had neglected—we invited authors from other musical fields to contribute. We make no claims, however, that this book represents every area of musicology and every route to the scholarly study of music; by its very nature, the subject of this book invites additional perspectives. It is the goal of *Disciplining Music* not to leave these out, but rather to provide their advocates with new portals to musicology. Indeed, we regard the book as a beginning, or rather an extension of the conversation among friends and colleagues that began five years ago.

♪

We owe a debt of thanks to many for making this project possible. Surely, we would not have begun without the support and stimulation of many friends and colleagues at Cornell, especially William Austin, Lenore Coral, Jonathan Culler, the late Edward Morris, and Don Randel. And without the panelists on the AMS "Disciplining Music" session we would not have enjoyed the the wide-ranging discussion of musicology's canons at one of the central forums for the field; we wish to thank Don Randel and Richard Crawford for their contributions on that day, and Daniel Neuman for guiding the discussion.

As for the book itself, Katherine Bergeron wishes to express gratitude to her colleagues at Tufts University, and especially to Jane Bernstein, whose moral support and innumerable practical suggestions over the past two years helped to bring this project to fulfillment. Wye Allanbrook, David Cohen, Marilyn Ivy, Roger Parker, and John Pemberton offered important ideas and criticisms that helped to shape her Prologue as it was being written; her brother Michael Bergeron discovered the *Laymen's Music Book* in a New York City bookstore and had the good sense to send it to her. Philip Bohlman benefited from the reactions of students in his proseminar on the history of ethnomusicology in the fall of 1989 and from the students in all subdisciplines of music at the University of Chicago, who generously shared in the discussion of the issues in this volume, issues which they willingly accepted as their own. As always, Christine Wilkie Bohlman, who disciplines music so beautifully as pianist and pedagogue, reminded Philip Bohlman of several issues that he might well have left out of this project, which we eventually came to know simply as "the canons book."

This collection, of course, would not exist at all without the careful and patient work of the scholars who have contributed the essays in the following pages. Heartfelt thanks to all of them for including their thoughts and ideas in this conversation about the discipline we all share.

Katherine Bergeron
Philip V. Bohlman

ONE

Prologue: Disciplining Music
Katherine Bergeron

Music is the art of measuring well.

Augustine

In Paine Concert Hall at Harvard University, the names of great composers from Monteverdi to Tchaikovsky are painted in fine, Roman capitals. They line the ceiling and look down on the chairs, capturing listeners in a permanent, austere gaze. Our musical Fathers stand in gold leaf, protected, enshrined, preserved (as Frank Kermode would say) in a continuous state of modernity: Beethoven is front and center, flanked by Mozart and Schubert; the rest fall in like so many ranks of troops. It is the Canon at a glance; a solemn spectacle of the disciplining of music.

The essays in this volume explore the ideological and social practices that inform the disciplining of music—understood in terms of our scholarly "disciplines" of historical musicology, music theory, and ethnomusicology—and the connection such practices have to that valued space we call the canon. Authors in some cases propose alternatives to the canon (as the plural in the volume's title suggests); they raise questions about the nature of its exclusions, about the music that gets in, and the music that stays out. In all the essays, however, a distinct relation obtains between the concepts of canon and discipline, a relation that orders the behavior of social bodies (our scholarly "societies") and the individuals within them. It may be useful to spell out this alliance in some of its manifestations.

໌

Let us begin, as our music teachers advised, with scales. If, as we learn from Foucault, discipline is the ordering of bodies, then the scale represents one of its elementary units. For the performer, certainly, practicing scales is the first (and last) measure of instrumental discipline, the source of "tech-

1

nique," the training of the body into an orderly relation with itself in the production of music. Such training involves a physical partitioning: the hand, the arm, the fingers, the spine are all marked, positioned, according to separate functions. The Suzuki class (perfect model of discipline) playing in unison demonstrates the eerie power of the ordered body.

But playing scales presupposes another, more primary discipline—that of tuning, or playing "in tune." This also implies an ordering of the body, a disciplining of the ear, so to speak; for to play in tune is to make judgments, to mark precise distances between sounds in the act of producing them. Indeed, such a marking of difference points to one of the earliest senses of the word *canon*, whose etymology (from the Greek *kanon*, meaning "rod," "bar," "ruler"; and *kanna*, meaning "reed") refers to a sort of measuring stick, a physical model that both embodies a standard of measure and makes possible its reproduction. The canon is, in this sense, an ideal of order made material, physical, visible.

In the scale, of course, such order is also audible, materialized as a finite set of intervals, perfectly tuned by mathematical calculation, by the ratio—the numerical representation (as the term would suggest) of order, "reason." So compelling, in fact, is this model of rationality—the scale—that it appears in Plato's *Timaeus* as a symbol for the original act of creation in the universe, the "tuning" of the *psyche*, the world soul. Later, in the *Sectio canonis* ("segmentation of the canon") attributed to Euclid, we find the same model scaled down to comprehend the set of distances available on the simplest of instruments, the monochord. Tuned on the single string (a miniature universe), each ratio yields a precise section, a measurement that marks, or "rules," the space, producing the divisions that are the canon's values. The operation thus reveals the essential link between canon and discipline: the tuned scale, or canon, is a locus of discipline, a collection of discrete values produced out of a system that orders, segments, divides.

The canon symbolized on the ceiling of Paine Hall, however distant from Euclid, could be described in similar terms. It, too, represents a scale of values. The Great Men inscribed there are the chosen ones, plucked from a long history of music like perfect notes from the monochord. Students of this history, attuned to its values, learn to reproduce them: to segment in the same way, according to the discipline. This, one could say, is the social impact of the canon. Indeed, once a principle of order is made into a standard, it becomes all the more accessible; translated into a "practice," its values can be internalized. The well-trained monochordist finds the right intervals, certainly, because he practices: he models his behavior after the canon he is attempting to reproduce. The "fact" of the canon thus implies a type of social control—a control that inevitably extends to larger social bodies as individual players learn not only to monitor themselves but to keep an eye (and an ear) on others. To play in tune, to uphold the canon, is ultimately to interiorize those values that would maintain, so to speak, social "harmony." Practice makes the scale—and evidently all of its players—perfect.

A very different, though significant, example of this same disciplinary logic turns up in an introductory music textbook written in the 1930s by the pianist Olga Samaroff, the first wife of conductor Leopold Stokowski. The third chapter of her *Laymen's Music Book* offers a lesson in music history that underscores, tellingly, the socializing effects of the canon just described. It begins innocently enough, presenting a general account of the scale through the Greeks, then goes on to conclude—abruptly—that "not one" among thirty thousand children who had studied music in New York schools during the previous twenty-five years "had ever been brought before a juvenile court for delinquency" (Samaroff Stokowski 1935:62). This unexpected report is amplified with further evidence drawn from the author's own "survey of penal institutions in the United States." It is the bandmaster of the Southern Illinois Penitentiary who has the last word:

> There is not one member of our band to-day who ever played a note of music before coming here. Of the many band men who have been paroled, but one has been returned on either a new charge, or for parole violation.
>
> I would not urge musical training as a crime preventive, but the fact remains; trained musicians do not commit crimes, and men who receive musical training in penal institutions stay out when released. (Ibid:64)

All this in a chapter entitled "Why Scales?"

The apparent leap of logic that takes Samaroff from the scale to the prison, in a single bound, may owe something to popular Platonic wisdom concerning the moral character of the modes, and the benefit of music to a free society—ideals that are predictable enough given a context of the democratic music-appreciation "movement" that burgeoned in the United States between the wars.[1] But this testimony to low rates of recidivism among trained prisoner-musicians also tells another story. Indeed, to consider the prisoners' rehabilitation within the penitentiary band is to discover something like the musical equivalent of Bentham's Panopticon, that revolutionary model of eighteenth-century discipline whose primary power, as described by Foucault, lay in the ability to maintain inmates under a constant (and centralized) surveillance. Power, as Bentham himself maintained, "should be visible and unverifiable." Hence prisoners knew of their potential to be seen at all times by an agent stationed in a central tower, while never knowing the exact moment of being seen. The effect of this disciplinary technology, in which the observer remained invisible to the observed, was radically to extend the power of the gaze. "He who is subjected to a field of visibility and who knows it," Foucault explains, "assumes responsibility for the constraints of power . . . he inscribes in himself the power relation in which he simultaneously plays both roles" (Foucault 1979:202).

Like any large instrumental ensemble, the band relies on the same sort of panoptical arrangement: players are seated (out of convenience, we say) in curved rows around a central podium, completely visible to the conductor who stands above. Yet the discipline of the band is not so much visual as aural: the conductor *listens*. Here the player is entrapped by an acoustic constraint; he cannot escape his own audibility. And, as with the Panopticon, he never knows precisely the moment when the conductor—this master of acoustic surveillance—may be listening to *him*, picking out his instrument from the dense ensemble of musical sounds. The effect, as we all know, is to cause players to assume more and more responsibility for their own performance: to play in tune, at tempo, on cue, controlling their part both individually and in relation to the whole. Inmate-players learn to conduct *themselves*, so to speak, according to the canons of performance they share.[2] As a field of audibility, a type of acoustic enclosure, the band thus implicates the musician in a network where acts of mutual surveillance serve to maintain the musical standard.

≀

The scholarly "fields" represented by authors in this book are, of course, enclosures in very much the same sense, distinguished from one another principally by the nature of the conduct they foster. A field is, in other words, a site of surveillance, a metaphorical space whose boundaries, conceived "panoptically," are determined by the canon that stands at its center. As Foucault's model suggests, it is not really the watchman in the prison's central tower (nor, by analogy, the conductor of the band or orchestra) that maintains order among those enclosed, but rather what such figures, seen or unseen, *stand for:* a "higher" authority, a "standard" of excellence, all ideals embodied in what we call the canon. It matters little whether we conceive of this canon as a scale, a body of law, or a pantheon of great authors and their works; the effect in every case is the same. The canon, always in view, promotes decorum, ensures proper conduct. The individual within a field learns, by internalizing such standards, how not to transgress.

"Trained" scholars know this all too well. Like rehabilitated prisoners (bleak thought), they learn how to negotiate their field of scholarship—how not to commit crimes—by yielding to the law of that field, measuring their activity accordingly. In this sense the canon remains (as its etymology implies) a "measuring stick" for a discipline, a guide that keeps the scholar well within scholarly limits. Don Randel plays on this sense of the term as he explores the "canons," or range of instruments, contained within the scholar's "toolbox," his metaphor for the standard working methods of all fields of musicology. Such tools, fashioned from the discipline itself, serve to maintain its limits, ensuring "standards" within the standard repertory. Among the most prevalent of these measuring devices, as Randel suggests, are notation, which fixes the musical text as a permanent value, and biography, which predicates those texts upon the figure of the composer, subsuming all value under the sign of his name—an operation Bruno Nettl ponders in more detail through a critique of two principal figures of Western musical culture.

Yet the limits of the field—the boundaries that, by marking an "inside," signify the presence of order—indicate also an exterior, a space beyond the enclosure where values can no longer be measured. Two essays in the collection address figures positioned on the margins of the discipline, writers whose work has openly challenged such limits. Robert Morgan considers some of the more dissonant voices from the margins in his treatment of Busoni, Cowell, and—most significantly—John Cage, by whose example he proposes a restructuring of the canon to account for the pluralism of contemporary musical life. Ruth Solie hears another sort of voice in Sophie Drinker's *Music and Women,* a work "alien to the musicological tradition" that nonetheless sought a place for women in that tradition by revising not musicological method but the very concept of "music" and its function in society. Solie interprets Drinker's resistance to discipline (evident in the "unorthodoxy of her methods") as a resistance to history, particularly the music history of the 1940s—a reading that causes her to consider the alternative disciplines in which a women's music might be inscribed.

Philip Gossett and Gary Tomlinson demonstrate a similar concern for music on the margins—for musical works that have been denied a place in histories—in examining the status of works within an individual composer's canon. Gossett addresses this question more or less directly, as he critiques the apparent "facts" of history that have marginalized Rossini's Neapolitan operas. Through analysis of individual works, he clears a hypothetical space for Rossini's *Napoletana* in the canon of Italian opera, while questioning the very conditions under which such spaces are assigned value. The "facts," he contends, demand a revaluation of the processes by which histories are written and of the canons that come with them. Tomlinson's essay considers the problem the other way round, in a sense, as Miles Davis becomes a sort of pretext for a broader meditation on the nature of canon formation—a meditation inspired by, among other things, recent criticism of African-American literature and theories of culture. He invokes as a central concept the notion of "signifying," the rhetorical figure of the "double-voiced" in African-American discourse, in order to illuminate the peculiarly double nature of Davis's jazz-rock fusion. His purpose, however, is not so much to secure a central place for this supposedly marginal music as to imagine an entirely different sort of canon: one whose values would be (like those of "fusion" itself) contingent, discursive: determined through a continuous dialogue among a plurality of voices.

This imaginary "canon" would require, of course, a reorientation of the discipline that it is supposed to represent. With "dialogue" the central activity, it is no longer a question of maintaining fixed limits, of segmenting according to well-established rules, but of constantly negotiating and renegotiating these boundaries. The locus of surveillance, so to speak, moves from the center to the margins in this alternative discipline; there is not a single canon constantly in view, but rather a continually changing idea of what that canon might be. Indeed, the canon, quite contrary to its nature, becomes an open question. The theorists Richard Cohn and Douglas Dempster entertain a similar logic of reversal in their examination of music-theory canons—although their essay radically shifts the focus, moving us from the notion of a canon that governs a general field (the set of works that embody value) to the related idea of an individual canon, or "rule," by which such value is specifically measured and controlled within a discourse. They examine the rule of "unity" that governs theoretical discourse about tonal music, while focusing attention on what they consider to be "the most sophisticated and powerful account of musical structure," namely, Schenkerian theory. In proposing a revised model of tonal unity Cohn and Dempster obviously affect a different stance from that of other authors in this book: their critique, it would seem, comes not from without, but from within the system; they seek not so much to reject as to refine a discipline whose self-evident "power" remains intact. This refinement could be described as an attempt to reconsider the Schenkerian gaze, to turn away from Schenker's fundamental structure (which, to quote the master himself, monitors the middleground and the foreground "as a guardian angel watches over a child") in order to contemplate the surface of the musical work. In other words, Cohn and Dempster attempt to relocate "surveillance" (to use our term) within the Schenkerian discipline itself. Their alternative yields a new metaphor for musical structure: the composition becomes a "network" rather than a strict (and more problematic) "hierarchy"; hence, analytical readings are no longer fixed, but pluralistic, located in an activity analogous to Tomlinson's dialogues—a "shuttling between the surface and underlying compositional parameters."

By redefining this relation of center to margin, by shifting value away from some putative deep structure toward the complex surface of a musical work, their model functions not just to revise Schenkerian theory, but, in fact, to preserve for future music theorists the canonicity of Schenker and, by extension, the very notion of the masterwork. My own essay offers a kind of historical critique of this phenomenon of canon preservation—though again from a very different perspective—in the story of the nineteenth-century revival of Gregorian chant by the Benedictine monks of Solesmes. Most significant for this story is the decentering of Rome as the sole locus of authority for the Gregorian canon, through the institution of a marginal "school" at Solesmes whose purpose it is to control the chant repertory—what we might call, by analogy, its complex "surface," as presented by the manuscripts. Such control is maintained by a rigorous counter-discipline involving a whole range of scholarly expertises: grammar, philology, paleography, photography. My essay essentially shows how this new interpretive discourse, resistant to Vatican authority, saves the canon by reinvesting it with "modern" values.[3]

But the essay also points to a significant moment in the history of musicology as a discipline, a time during which the scholarly technology that Randel describes is perhaps first developed and tested. That this marginal "field" eventually becomes central is implied, of course, by the very title (and theme) of our collection. Philip Bohlman refers to this centrality from another viewpoint in his own historical essay, which takes us through one more transformation of the field: the emergence of ethnomusicology as a bona fide discipline in the 1950s. The "challenge" of this new discipline can be construed, once again, as a shifting of the locus of surveillance. Yet this shift has as its goal neither the dismantling nor the preserving of an established canon (such as the canon of Western art music), but rather a concern for the ways such canons—and the very notion of "music"—are constituted by a discipline. A certain self-consciousness is thus written into this new discipline: what is to be preserved, scrutinized, evaluated, is, as Bohlman argues, not a body of music (the masterworks of the world, as it were) but the body of writing that constitutes the ethnomusicologist's discourse about that music—a music whose status within its own culture has little to do with such writing. This scrutiny within the discipline fosters a sort of hyper-surveillance, in which the disciplined is always reflecting back on itself. The modern ethnomusicologist cannot act simply according to an established "standard," since, for her, that standard is itself a question about what should constitute the standard for a given culture. To submit to this discipline is thus to be trapped in a gazed-at gaze, enclosed in something like a hall of mirrors.

This condition of modern ethnomusicology emerges, perhaps, as a natural consequence of having rejected the values of another discipline—indeed (to return to our opening discussion for a moment), of having rejected the scale itself. For, not accidentally, it was the scale, in all of its possible manifestations, all of its tunings, that formed an essential point of departure for the ancestors of the discipline, the so-called comparative musicologists. Figures such as Hornbostel, Ellis, and Stumpf reserved a space in music scholarship for the diverse (and exotic) musical cultures of the world first of all by defining their scales, and then by showing how they related to those of Western music (see Blum 1991 and Schneider 1991); they attempted, in other words, to measure "other" musics against the standard set by European music. Yet this was precisely the attitude the later generation of scholars turned against in the 1950s, in their desire to examine music of the "other" on its own terms. Modern ethnomusicology comes into being at the moment the scale is brought into question.

A similar sort of questioning is evident among the essays in this book. Certainly, the condition of music in a "post-tonal" age, as discussed by Morgan, implies the denial of a clear musical standard—a rejection, it could be said, of the complacency associated with the scale. Sophie Drinker, too, adopts a comparable stance as she attempts to meet women's music on its own terms, to resist the impulse to judge it against standards established for men's music, men's history. To resist the scale in this way is, then, to question its values; at the same time, however, it is to imagine another world of values that might reside in between—to squint, as it were, into those unmarked spaces in order to discover what the discipline has *not* accounted for. The present volume can be read as an attempt to bring such spaces into sharper focus.

NOTES

1. Samaroff's book was written exclusively for her Laymen's Music Courses, Inc., in New York City and includes, as suggested study aids, a list of RCA Victor recordings at the end of every chapter. See Horowitz 1987 for a recent study that evaluates this movement in light of one of its principal heroes, Arturo Toscanini.

2. Foucault notes that Bentham himself had tried, though unsuccessfully, to include such a means of acoustic surveillance in his elaborate architectural model. The system was to be "operated by means of pipes leading from the cells to the central tower. In the *Postscript* he abandoned the idea, perhaps because he could not introduce into it the principle of dissymmetry and prevent prisoners from hearing the inspector as well as the inspector hearing them" (Foucault 1979:317 n. 3). The prison band, in fulfilling this project, becomes in effect the "Panacouston" Bentham couldn't quite imagine.

3. See Kermode 1985:67–93 for a discussion of similar incidents of canon preservation within literary and Biblical criticism.

WORKS CITED

Blum, Stephen. 1991. "European Musical Terminology and the Music of Africa." In Bruno Nettl and Philip V. Bohlman, eds., *Comparative Musicology and Anthropology of Music: Essays on the History of Ethnomusicology,* 3–36. Chicago: University of Chicago Press.

Foucault, Michel. 1979. *Discipline and Punish: The Birth of the Prison.* Trans. Alan Sheridan. New York: Vintage.

Horowitz, Joseph. 1987. *Understanding Toscanini: How He Became an American Culture God and Helped Create a New Audience for Old Music.* Minneapolis: University of Minnesota Press.

Kermode, Frank. 1985. *Forms of Attention.* Chicago: University of Chicago Press.

Samaroff Stokowski, Olga. 1935. *The Laymen's Music Book.* New York: W. W. Norton.

Schneider, Albrecht. 1991. "Psychological Theory and Comparative Musicology." In Bruno Nettl and Philip V. Bohlman, eds., *Comparative Musicology and Anthropology of Music: Essays on the History of Ethnomusicology,* 293–317. Chicago: University of Chicago Press.

T W O

The Canons in the Musicological Toolbox

Don Michael Randel

In the hefty tome titled *Inside Macintosh: Volumes I, II, and III,* copyrighted by Apple Computer, Inc., a section of the first chapter is headed "The Toolbox and Other High-Level Software," and it begins as follows:

> The Macintosh User Interface Toolbox provides a simple means of constructing application programs that conform to the standard Macintosh user interface. By offering a common set of routines that every application calls to implement the user interface, the Toolbox not only ensures familiarity and consistency for the user but also helps reduce the application's code size and development time. (Apple Computer 1985, I:9)

We could perhaps transpose this to the domain of musicology as follows:

> The Musicologist's Toolbox provides a means of constructing dissertations and scholarly articles that conform to the standard Musicological interface. By offering a common set of techniques that every dissertation and scholarly article employs to implement the Musicological interface, the Toolbox not only ensures familiarity and consistency for the scholar but also helps reduce the time and effort required to produce the scholarly product.

Each of us shows up for work lugging a toolbox, and the contents of this toolbox have a great deal to do with what kind of work we can do and what the work will look like when we are finished. Apple Computer, Inc., designed and made available their Toolbox precisely so as to ensure that pro-

This paper draws together and expands on remarks made at the annual meetings of the American Musicological Society held in New Orleans in 1987 and in Baltimore in 1988 as well as in a lecture given for the Society for the Humanities at Cornell University in 1986 and subsequently published (Randel 1987).

was largely lost in the musicological shuffle and that the application of foreign tools did not in this case illuminate a subject, as scholarship claims to do, but rather falsified it.

The question is, once again, whether this constituted merely an expansion of the canon or a case of attempted appropriation and domination. The expansion of the canon is more like a struggle for empire. It is a political move as much as an aesthetic one, for it serves first of all to incorporate foreign goods into the economy of the academy.

The struggle over the canon shows itself most clearly not with respect to non-Western music (which may be thought of as attractively exotic) or jazz (which can be made to behave like Western art music), but in the domain of Western popular music—the music that by any quantitative measure overwhelms all other kinds in our society. Here the traditional Musicological Toolbox seems destined primarily to continue to keep the musical riff-raff out rather than to broaden the horizon of our investigations. The study of this kind of music will require a bigger and more varied set of tools. But some of these tools will enrich the study of our more traditional subjects, too—including some of the subjects that we have admitted to our canon under false pretenses.

Popular music forces some issues to which we have paid only lip service and some others that threaten musicology's most ingrained habits. In this domain, "the work itself" is not so easily defined and certainly not in terms of musical notation. The composer/author is not always clearly identifiable and does not leave the kind of paper trail that our tools can investigate readily. Rhythm, timbre, and performance styles, for which we have only primitive vocabularies, tend to overwhelm harmony and counterpoint as significant elements, with the result that traditional musicological discourse quickly takes on a dismissive cast with respect to popular music. Producers, engineers, and marketing people may rival our traditional subjects—composers and performers—in their contributions to the character of "the work itself," whatever that turns out to be. Popular music aims at specific audiences, and those audiences, both as groups and as individuals, use popular music as a means of identifying and defining themselves in society (Frith 1987). In this way, popular music forces the study of social context at a level sometimes talked about—but rarely undertaken—with respect to Western art music. Finally, popular music foregrounds its own temporality. It claims importance only for the here and now, and thus is bound to threaten an academic community that represents and justifies itself as preserver and transmitter of enduring values.

We might content ourselves with the view that popular music is simply an underdeveloped specialty: in an age of specialization, it is simply not what we musicologists do, and not doing it does not constitute a fault of the profession. But popular music represents only the extreme case of something that we do do a lot of the time, and in this sense it ought to be at least a lesson to us. Even in the domain of Western art music, we can think of repertories that "don't look like much on the page," that rely for their effectiveness on the particular circumstances of place, audience, and performance and that have in consequence often been (to put it gently) undervalued in our profession.

We should not abandon the strengths that flow from the formalist character of some of our traditional tools. But as we increasingly recognize the contingent status of even our favorite notated masterpieces and at the same time approach repertories in which "the work itself" and "the composer" may not be readily definable, the focus of our energies must inevitably move in the direction of the listener: away from the process of composition and toward the process of hearing; away from the presumably autonomous text and outward to the network of texts that, acting through a reader or listener, gives any one text its meaning. This shift will open the way to—indeed, will demand—kinds of musical criticism and analysis that have not yet made contributions as significant as we should expect: Marxist, psychoanalytic, and feminist, for example.

Feminist criticism has a particularly important role to play in our discipline, for it confronts directly the issues of canon formation described above and invites the collaboration of Marxist and psychoanalytic studies. That women composers are almost wholly absent from the canon of Western art music is clear enough. The reasons for this are of two general types, though the two are not easily disentangled. The first type results from women's historical condition as an oppressed class without equal access to political or economic power in society. It lends itself to analysis in Marxist terms. The second type derives from beliefs about the nature of sexual difference and from the dominance of male-produced and male-centered constructs in Western thought. It lends itself to analysis in biological, psychoanalytic, and psychosocial terms. But what can any analysis of the reasons suggest about a proper response to the gender-related facts of the canon? This is to ask, "What should the agenda of a feminist musicology be?"—a musicology that, in at least some of its aspects, might be practiced by both men and women.

First there is, of course, the labor of discovery and exposure. The names and hitherto-silent voices of women composers of all periods must be re-covered for the benefit of teachers, students, and ordinary listeners alike. But a great deal more must be done as well. However great and important the labor of historical research and recovery, we should not be content to address only access to power and to prominence through a kind of affirmative-action program that does not take some account of gender difference and that does not question the gender-related implications of what has enshrined the canon that we propose to expand. Rather than make well-intentioned exceptions to a criterion of excellence that we claim to find embodied in the canon, we must challenge that traditional criterion. For this criterion, which is formulated only vaguely if at all, has been the ultimate weapon—not least because of its very vagueness—in the male-produced, male-dominated arsenal that has so long kept women out. Until we have asked, "Excellence according to whom?" we should remain suspicious of any canonizations that take place in its name.[1]

Two issues come into play here. The first is traditional musicology's traditional imperialism. I have claimed that musicology's canon has been determined largely by the methods with which musicology has studied its objects. Musicology has typically added repertories to its domain by a process of colonization that imposes traditional methods on new territories. After years of regarding Italian opera as peripheral, if not frivolous, we discovered that it too had sources and even sketches to study and edit and that it too could be investigated in terms of large-scale formal coherence. We appropriated jazz not because of what was most interesting or characteristic about it, but because it too presented us with a body of source material and variants to classify.

Music by women composers occupies, in this respect, a position precisely analogous to that of, say, most French and Spanish music of the nineteenth century. It was composed by (and perhaps for) people different from—foreign to—those who officiated at the canonizations that have dominated us. We cannot expect to understand any new repertory other than the traditional ones if we are not prepared to invent new methods appropriate for its study. The canon of Western art music as we know it was formulated by a body of specific individuals, all of whom happen to have been men. Until we interrogate that fact—and them—we cannot suppose it either an accident *or* a phenomenon of dispassionate nature that this canon includes only the works of men.

The second issue in play here derives from the ways in which traditional notions of canon rest on certain traditional notions of the work of art. And this is where we must begin our agenda. Music—precisely because it is so manifestly not a single universal language—lays bare the respect in which the work of art is a function of the reader/listener. The author/composer is powerless in the absence of a reader/listener who can situate the so-called work in an appropriate matrix of the other texts/compositions on which it depends for its meaning. Once we recognize the status of the reader/listener in the production of the work of art, we necessarily confront differences among readers/listeners, of which gender is surely the most inescapable. We undermine a certain brand of pious humanism in which great works reveal great and eternal truths, and we validate the process of reading/listening as a woman alongside the reading and listening that we have been taught by men.

With respect to gender, two approaches to the canon are thus opened. First, how does a woman listen to the traditional (male-dominated) canon? And second, how might listening as a woman expand that canon, specifically to include those works that are the product of composing as a woman?[2] These questions raise the spectre of yet another canon that is less often mentioned but even more thoroughly male dominated. This is the canon of music theory (and, one might add, even criticism). Our present difficulty in naming canonical women composers is surely exceeded in considerable measure by our difficulty in naming women contributors to that body of theoretical writing that surrounds and thus largely defines the canon.[3] This is not because the existing body of theory has exhausted what we all know to be prominent features of musical works.

Listening as a woman implies writing about music as a woman, whether the music in question is composed by a man or by a woman. Even if we decline to import in their entirety French feminist criticism's notions of *écriture féminine*,[4] we need to recognize the possibility that gender might be expressed in ways of writing about music as well as in ways of writing music. This possibility bears on what I have called the canon of acceptable dissertation topics in musicology, which is simply our way of imposing on the young and powerless our own canonical tendencies.

If we foreground sexual difference in our approach to canon formation, we confront the need to address the nature of that difference. Feminist literary criticism has shown something of the variety of terms in which this difference might be framed and their consequences for the project of such criticism. Feminist musicology should not settle for any less variety in its theoretical orientation or in its practical projects. Above all, it should not cede to inherited male authority the theoretical frame in which its discourse is inscribed.[5]

There is one more set of tools that deserves mention here because of its widespread use in our thinking about most everything and because of the particular marks that it has left on our writing about history. This is the whole set of binary oppositions in which we frame so much of our discourse: high culture and popular culture, sacred and secular, constraint and freedom. The list is very long. Of these, constraint and freedom is surely the opposition at the heart of the master trope of music-historical writing—the trope in terms of which we have rewritten every story in history. It is the story of freedom won through throwing off the constraints (or worse) of the sacred, the courtly, of some form or genre, of convention, tonality, the barline, the work itself. And the freedom won by one generation quickly becomes the constraint against which the next generation will struggle to win its own freedom.

This opposition is just another version of the opposition between good and evil. And it is, as Fredric Jameson observes in the wake of Nietzsche, rooted in turn in the opposition between the self and the Other: "What is good is what belongs to me, what is bad is what belongs to the Other" (Jameson 1981:234). In the Western democracies since the late eighteenth century—but particularly in the United States of the twentieth century—the version that opposes freedom to constraint has risen to unequalled status. And *we* occupy the pole of so-called freedom. Our study of history is then a search for people like ourselves—people defined in the struggle of freedom against constraint, good against evil, the self against the Other. This is the story in terms of which we have fashioned our period labels, for "period formulations always secretly imply or project narratives or 'stories'" (ibid.:28). The Renaissance is only the most striking case of a period defined as being inhabited by people who were in certain essential ways like us. The same story can be told in one way or another for what marks the end of the Renaissance, or for the Romantic period, or at the level of generations or genres or individual composers.

How does this narrative device affect what we study or how we study it or what is admitted to our canons? It functions by identifying certain periods, composers, and works (not always the same ones, depending on the particular story being told) with constraint, evil, the Other, while identifying others with freedom, good, the (our)self. And as Derrida shows, in all such oppositions, one term is the dominant one, the other marginalized: "In a traditional philosophical opposition we have not a peaceful coexistence of facing terms but a violent hierarchy. One of the terms dominates the other (axiologically, logically, etc.), occupies the commanding position" (quoted in

Culler 1982:85; see also Jameson 1981:114). Our study is thus framed in terms that undermine the means by which we claim to arrive at our results: the objective, dispassionate study of "the evidence." We *systematically* undervalue certain periods, composers, and works and privilege others because of the very nature of the conceptual and narrative tools that we apply.

It might be supposed that our formalist tools will save us. Sooner or later we must answer to the notes, and they are not so easily made to lie. But the danger in calling our formalist analyses to witness for a historical narrative is not that it may not work, but rather that such a maneuver will always work. The formalist analysis will itself always bend to the narrative strategy that motivates it. The wish to find freedom in one piece and constraint in another will always succeed unless the deck is outrageously stacked.

Our narrative tools, relying as they do on certain binary oppositions (or perhaps on only one), may be the most powerful forces at work when we as historians construct the canon. Freedom (that word again) from these forces will require the unmasking of the supporting oppositions—the reversal of their polarities, their deconstruction.

}

As we use our tools, we constantly remake them. Recent years have seen the remaking of a good many scholarly tools and the forging of some new ones. Those of us who have participated in this effort ought to feel a bit uneasy. To the extent that our product succeeds in defining and describing our subjects and the methods by which our discipline has studied those subjects, it is likely to become another one of those tools that limits subjects for future study and constrains the ways in which those subjects will be studied. Either that or it will continually threaten to undo itself—to undo what we claim to know by questioning the bases on which we claim to know it. In the end we can only hope to be honest in our account of the canons of the past—and of the forces that created and maintained them—without, however, restricting their expansion in the future.

Notes

1. With respect to literary studies, Chris Weedon puts the matter as follows: "Traditionally the social and educational function of the critic has been not merely to produce 'true' readings but to constitute and maintain certain criteria of literariness. Feminist criticism has attempted to show how these criteria have been implicitly patriarchal, marginalizing gender and rendering women passive recipients of culture rather than its producers, a role compatible with hegemonic norms of femininity outside literary discourse" (Weedon 1987:143–44).

2. Elaine Showalter writes about literary studies as follows: "Feminist criticism can be divided into two distinct varieties. The first type is concerned with *woman as reader*. . . . The second type of feminist criticism is concerned with *woman as writer*" (Showalter 1985a:128).

3. Literary theory has been much debated in feminist studies generally and much resisted in some quarters on the grounds that it is by its nature patriarchal. Rita Felski's view of the matter might prove most useful to musicology: "I suggest in contrast that it is impossible to speak of 'masculine' and 'feminine' in any meaningful sense in the formal analysis of texts; the political value of literary texts from the standpoint of feminism can be determined only by an investigation of their social functions and effects in relation to the interests of women in a particular historical context, and not by attempting to deduce an abstract literary theory of 'masculine' and 'feminine,' 'subversive' and 'reactionary' forms in isolation from the social conditions of their production and reception" (Felski:2).

4. See, for example, Jones 1985.

5. Jonathan Culler puts the matter with respect to literature in ways that might serve musicology as well: "The task of feminist criticism . . . is to investigate whether the procedures, assumptions, and goals of current criticism are in complicity with the preservation of male authority, and to explore alternatives. It is not a question of rejecting the rational in favor of the irrational, of concentrating on metonymical relations to the exclusion of the metaphorical, or on the signifier to the exclusion of the signified, but of attempting to develop critical modes in which the concepts that are products of male authority are inscribed within a larger textual system" (Culler 1982:61).

WORKS CITED

Apple Computer, Inc. 1985. *Inside Macintosh: Volumes I, II, and III.* Reading, Mass.: Addison-Wesley Publishing Company.

Culler, Jonathan. 1982. *On Deconstruction: Theory and Criticism after Structuralism.* Ithaca: Cornell University Press.

de Man, Paul. 1982. "The Resistance to Theory." *Yale French Studies* 63:3–20.

Felski, Rita. 1989. *Beyond Feminist Aesthetics: Feminist Literature and Social Change.* Cambridge, Mass.: Harvard University Press.

Frith, Simon. 1987. "Towards an Aesthetic of Popular Music." In Richard Leppert and Susan McClary, eds., *Music and Society,* 133–49. Cambridge: Cambridge University Press.

Gates, Henry Louis, Jr. 1986–87. "'What's Love Got to Do with It?': Critical Theory, Integrity, and the Black Idiom." *New Literary History* 18:345–62.

Jameson, Fredric. 1981. *The Political Unconscious: Narrative as a Socially Symbolic Act.* Ithaca: Cornell University Press.

Jauss, Hans Robert. 1982. *Toward an Aesthetic of Reception.* Trans. Timothy Bahti. Minneapolis: University of Minnesota Press.

Jones, Ann Rosalind. 1985. "Writing the Body: Toward an Understanding of *L'écriture féminine.*" In Showalter 1985b, pp. 361–77.

Randel, Don Michael. 1987. "Defining Music." *Notes* 43:751–66.

Showalter, Elaine. 1985a. "Toward a Feminist Poetics." In Showalter 1985b, pp.125–43.

———, ed. 1985b. *The New Feminist Criticism: Essays on Women, Literature, and Theory.* New York: Pantheon Books.

Weedon, Chris. 1987. *Feminist Practice and Poststructuralist Theory.* Oxford: Basil Blackwell.

THREE

Sophie Drinker's History
Ruth A. Solie

Knowledge has a very sly way of accumulating in odd places where it is
with difficulty perceived.

Paul Henry Lang

My endeavor here is a meditation on the question of in what circumstances an alternative may arise to the historiographic paradigm current in a
discipline. In particular, I want to ask what it would take—how canonic
practices and values would have to be different—in order for the participation and experience of women to appear in the history of Western music. My
exercise focuses on *Music and Women,* published in 1948 by Sophie H.
Drinker, as an exemplar of such an alternative practice. The book provides
an occasion for asking both "What is history?" and, more specifically, "What
is music history?" During the period of its writing, as it happens, these were
questions that much occupied practitioners of both disciplines. What sorts of
questions should history ask, what are its data, how does it properly conduct
its research?

The Drinker name is familiar to most musicologists from acquaintance
with Sophie's husband, Henry, a lawyer and passionate amateur musician
who became known for his English translations of cantata and lied texts, as

This essay is dedicated to Vernon D. Gotwals. I would like to express my gratitude
to Dr. Henry Drinker of Northampton, Massachusetts for providing me with a copy of
his grandmother's unpublished memoir; to Susan Grigg and the staff at the Sophia
Smith Collection (Smith College) and to Eva Moseley of the Schlesinger Library
(Radcliffe College) for their assistance in working with Sophie Drinker's papers; to
audiences at Duke University, the University of Pennsylvania, Notre Dame University, and Rutgers University for their sympathetic but probing responses to an earlier
version of this paper; and to Philip Bohlman, Philip Gossett, and Leo Treitler for particularly astute and detailed help.

well as for the extensive Drinker Choral Library that he assembled and circulated to college and university choral organizations (Drinker 1965:119–32). The social context in which both Harry (as he was known to his friends) and Sophie found themselves is of considerable significance in understanding their musical activities. The Drinker family were Main Line patricians who had been in Philadelphia for generations, many of them famous and all distinguished.[1] The Hutchinson family, from which Sophie came, similarly began to "play a conspicuous part in the life of Philadelphia" as early as the seventeenth century (ibid.:26). Typical of her generation and social class, Sophie had no formal education beyond finishing school; but equally typical was the passion for self-improvement, the dedicated and quite serious amateurism, and the striking sense of entitlement that marked all of her and Harry's undertakings.

A decade or two into their marriage, in 1928, Harry and Sophie Drinker built a new house in Merion with a large music room, in which they hosted monthly gatherings of musicians—more than a hundred at a time—to sing and play.[2] They were apparently familiar to the entire musical establishment of the area, pursued musicology as well as performance as an amateur interest, and even lent their music room for chapter meetings of the American Musicological Society.[3] One of Sophie Drinker's favorite activities was a women's chorus that met in her home, and it was the effort of finding music for the women to sing that led her ultimately to the writing of *Music and Women*. For, as she says in her foreword, "I was both surprised and shocked at the type of choral literature offered by the music publishers. It was childish, trivial, far too sentimental for these intelligent women." She also discovered that little or none of the music available was composed by women.

> Women musicians are experts in performing vocal and instrumental music, but rarely do they play or sing music that they themselves have composed. Why do they allow themselves to be merely carriers of the creative musical imagination of men? Why do they not use the language of music, as they use gesture and speech, to communicate their own ideas and feelings? (xi)[4]

She embarked upon twenty years' worth of research and writing to find answers to this question. The result is a surprising, even eccentric, book in terms of conventional music-historical practice both then and now. It combines what are customarily considered separate disciplines—musicology, anthropology, classical archaeology, sociology, folkloristics—and combines them so creatively and fruitfully that one is inclined to be grateful that she knew no better. She read voluminously and hired people to translate for her, using research sources in five languages. She did a great deal of her research by correspondence, simply writing to an expert when she needed the answer to a particular question; an astonishing number responded.[5] Out of it all came a book of extreme originality and a wealth of information that was not then (and, for the most part, is not now) available anywhere else. Somehow the unorthodoxy of her methods, along with the unprofessionalized clarity of her mind, allowed her access to those "odd places" where Lang says that knowledge lurks. In particular, she unearthed unfamiliar information because she asked unfamiliar questions.

Perhaps predictably, though, *Music and Women* remained virtually invisible to the musicology community, despite the fact that it was very widely reviewed—in the daily newspapers of many major cities including Philadelphia, Chicago, Cleveland, and San Francisco; in the Sunday book-review sections of both the *New York Times* and the *Herald Tribune;* in *Newsweek, The New Yorker,* and *The Saturday Review,* and in music journals covering the spectrum from *The International Musician* to *Notes* and *The Musical Quarterly.* (*JAMS,* which was in its first year of publication in 1948, did not run a review.) Surprisingly, not one reviewer of the book questioned the research underlying the work, and indeed virtually all credited it with sound scholarship and a rich contribution to knowledge.[6] There was bemusement that so much material about women and music even existed; and, most interesting to feminist historians, a virtually obligatory opening paragraph assured readers that the book was nothing like what its title might suggest. One expects, even searches for, condescension from these writers, but in fact very little is discernible.

Partly this is because in the United States, history, more than most other academic disciplines, had a long tradition of amateur participation. Indeed, it had become professionalized only at the end of the nineteenth century;[7] and during the 1930s and 1940s, when Drinker was writing, publication of historical works in this country was still fairly evenly divided between those who wrote history for a living and those who wrote as a hobby or from personal interest. One notes as well that these amateur American historians had for generations come almost exclusively from the well-to-do classes, and this is the point at which Sophie Drinker's patrician background links her clearly to a long-standing tradition.[8] The writing of history was perhaps a form of *noblesse oblige* for members of this group; for instance, their work characteristically took the form of local history, involved with their own genealogies and the history of family property. The point to be made, however, is that as an activity it had a recognizable place within the American tradition of historiography.

Such was not the case, however, in musicology, passed on from German hands already acclimated to the academy, but struggling for intellectual and professional respectability in the United States during these decades. Indeed, as Charles Seeger noted in 1946, American scholars were explicitly engaged in defending the term *musicologist* from encroachment by amateurs (Seeger [1946] 1977:216). In a strikingly anxious comment, Curt Sachs declined the title altogether: "Any girl that manufactures a newspaper article by transcribing Grove's Dictionary without too many misspellings presents herself as a musicologist." He preferred the term *music historian,* no doubt for the security of its association with an older and more firmly established field (Sachs 1945:78).[9]

For whatever reason, no musicologist felt then—or has felt since—any need to come to grips with Drinker's book, to contend with it, or to incorporate either its data or its argument into business-as-usual musicology. It was not treated in the manner we have learned to expect for "controversial" works (which it surely was) because it was not recognized as a participant in musicological discourse at all. Its alien quality as music history is capsulized in a question raised in Barzun's review—"What has all this to do with the history of art?"—and in Drinker's response, in a letter to Barzun, that "it has to do with the relation of women to music, which is quite enough for one book."[10] The near-miss of this exchange is typical of the whole relation of Drinker's book to American musicology, in ways which I will now go on to detail.[11]

In doing so, I want to be clear that it is not my purpose to advocate *Music and Women* as a model for current scholarship, despite its provocative challenges and its salutary reminders of how extensive is the uncharted terrain in the landscape of music history. But its eccentricities are real—and not all of them charming—and its methods are, finally, too unschooled to enter into productive dialogue with other modern modes of study. Rather, my intent is to use Drinker's book as a lens through which to examine canonic musicological practice, both as it was in her day and as it has since come to be. I believe that the refractive properties of her work can help us to see habit and arbitrary custom where we once saw necessity and scientific exactitude.

≀

To begin, I want to argue that the book bore the imprint of American historiography rather than that of still-Germanic American musicology—in particular that school of democratic, economically oriented history called "progressive"—at least in part because of Drinker's association with Mary Ritter Beard. Charles Beard, Mary's collaborator on several books and sharer of her liberal philosophy, was a leader in this particular historiographic movement in the early decades of the twentieth century (see Hofstadter 1968). Mary Beard corresponded with Sophie Drinker over a period of many years, gave her a good deal of advice on the writing of *Music and Women,* and worked with her later on an abortive project to establish a national archive of women's history.[12] Among other similarities in their work is a common interest in what the Beards called "long history"—a notion espoused both in American progressivism and in the French historiographic school that emerged in 1929 in the journal *Annales.* The world of musicology was heading in a different direction during the 1930s and 1940s; the long-history perspective had not been common since the nineteenth century, and even when occasionally practiced—for instance, by Curt Sachs—it tended to locate itself not within the discipline of historical musicology but in musical ethnography, or what was then called comparative musicology.[13] For Drinker, however, the consideration of long history followed naturally from her rather prescient understanding, fixed now in feminist theorizing, of the cultural structuring of gender roles and their tendency to persist over long periods of time.

Another way, of course, in which a discipline can recognize and acknowledge a scholarly project is to approve and share its apparent goals. In 1970 Vincent Duckles wrote that "the object of the historiography of music is the mind of the learned musician, whether he be historian, theorist, aesthetician, critic, or pedagogue" (Duckles 1970:76). His comment describes a practice familiar to us as professionals: ours is a discourse among peers, each scholarly piece of it intended as grist for the mill of another scholarly purpose. By contrast, Sophie Drinker's goals are explained in her foreword, "I present my message, therefore, in the hope that it will remind every woman—and especially my own little granddaughters . . . that they have deep, and as yet in our world, untapped reservoirs of imaginative power" (xv). This is history not for the disengaged contemplation of other historians, but with the intention of doing political "consciousness-raising" work among its readers. She addresses a general public rather than Duckles's "learned musician," and she implicitly rejects that academic fetish, disinterested objectivity.[14]

So Drinker's book is both broader in historical scope and more personally engaged in style and intent than contemporary musicological work. There

are other, more fundamental differences as well, differences that go to the
heart of historiographic method: first, the definition of the subject that is under investigation; and second, the principles of historical explanation that
are invoked.

≀

The first issue, then, is "What is music history about?" If the question
seems oversimple, reflect that it took the discipline about one hundred years
to change its mind the last time, to abandon its old commitment to the lives
of great composers. At just about the time Drinker was writing, Manfred
Bukofzer observed that

> the strange emphasis on biographical writing reflects very clearly
> the hero worship characteristic of the nineteenth century. What
> is even more amazing is the fact that the life of a composer fre-
> quently received a more thorough treatment than his musical
> works. . . . As a reaction against the overemphasis on the per-
> sonal aspect, a shift of emphasis has occurred in musicology that
> has brought a concentration on the music itself. (Bukofzer
> 1946:51)

This concentration is very firmly established in the profession at the moment. In his famous plea for a rigorously reasoned history of music in 1961,
Arthur Mendel commits himself absolutely to the achievement of a history
of works, despite the fact that there is nothing in his allegiance to positivism
that entails such a commitment; indeed, it creates problems, since it hopelessly entangles the apparently "objective" facts of history with the imponder-
ables of aesthetic judgment. It is a mark of the strength of this commitment
that it persists under such circumstances. Carl Dahlhaus's *Foundations of Music History* wrestles for pages with this dilemma—how to view the musical
work double, as simultaneously an aesthetic experience and a piece of historical data—but he too comes out in the same place: the goal of music history, for him, is a history of works. So it is with the *New Grove* definition of
musicology: "The prime object for the historian is the individual work of
art." Within the last decade or so we have begun to see evidence that the
discipline is restless and may wish to change this definition again; we are
reminded that the question is a charged one by the intense discussion the
recent English translation of Dahlhaus's *Foundations* has provoked.

One might also ask, "*Whom* is music history about?" Until a fairly recent
date, historians of art in the West have been concerned largely with the production of individual members of societies; these are individuals of such cul-

turally atypical skills that it is difficult to be sure how we may posit a connection between their works and the cultural backgrounds from which they are said to "arise." This focus on exceptional individuals has not been absent from general history either, and was particularly characteristic during the 1930s and 1940s, when Sophie Drinker was writing. In a lecture entitled "The Situation of History in 1950," Fernand Braudel described this historical school with dissatisfaction:

> To the narrative historians, the life of men is dominated by dra-
> matic accidents, by the actions of those exceptional beings who
> occasionally emerge, and who often are the masters of their own
> fate and even more of ours. And when they speak of "general his-
> tory," what they are really thinking of is the intercrossing of such
> exceptional destinies. . . .[They have] a vision of too narrow a
> world, a world made familiar by dint of having been so much ex-
> plored and evoked, a world in which the historian may delight in
> consorting with princes. (Braudel 1980:11)

Whether or not Braudel was aware of it, there could hardly be a better description of the contemporary work of music historians. Warren Allen re-
minds us that the tradition of individualism is particularly strong in
Germanic historiography—indeed, he remarks that German scholarship in
the 1930s saw "communalism" as a Mediterranean, Oriental, and Semitic
trait (Allen 1962:163)—and so it is understandable that musicology as a discipline has adopted it as its principal mode. There is a more important reason: if what you are interested in is a history of works of art—that is, "great
works"—then of course this individual focus is inevitable and, indeed, quite
appropriate.

But it should be immediately clear that an individualistic focus will never
surface much about the history of women. Because Sophie Drinker was entirely aware of the various phenomena of history and of cultural organization that combine to render women's activities invisible, she focused her
work on communal, socially based musical production. Hers is a history not
of works but of musical activities, of cultural practices. Her chapters concern
themselves with the nature of participation in music-making, as differenti-
ated in various types of social structures; with the effect on this participation
of changes in religious thought and in attitudes toward women; and, most
importantly, with the links between such participation and women's sense
of power and authority within their given cultural frame. Indeed, insistence
upon these links was the aspect of her book that most surprised and impressed many of its reviewers, some of whom had apparently never thought

of music in this way at all. For *The Musical Quarterly* Doris Silbert noted that
the book "sounds the fundamental tones of social and spiritual forces from
which all artistic expression emanates" and Karl Geiringer commented, in
his review for *Notes,* that her message—"not to think of music as a matter of
technical proficiency possessed only by a few, but as a natural form of expression and a vital force in the lives of everyone"—was "well worth heed-
ing" (Silbert 1948:285; Geiringer 1948).

Curiously, the same point—that Drinker had in effect turned her back on
individual accomplishment—was understood, though differently inter-
preted, by Jacques Barzun. He objected to this stance and to the political purpose he clearly recognized as underlying her systemic view: "Mrs. Drinker
does not see that women's liberation was not exclusively, collectively, politically, from men, but from a network of once useful social relations. This is
proved by the fact that men, too, had to fight for individual rights and are still
doing so." Barzun does not ask *to whom* those social relations were once so
"useful," a question that might have prompted him to see that gender roles
are societal and systemic, not a matter of individual negotiation. I point out
Drinker's political interestedness here because in her work it had to play
against a kind of class loyalty that was otherwise characteristic of her, of the
amateur historical investigations (and other amateur activities) of the
Drinker family taken together, and indeed of American amateur history-
writing as a social phenomenon.[15]

While *Music and Women* for the most part concerns itself with the musical
expression of collectivities of women—often hypostatized as "woman"—
Drinker is nonetheless aware of the problematic effects of this commitment.
As one seriously interested in music and deeply moved by the familiar
masterworks in her own life, she understands the need to think about the
emergence of individual genius and what it tells us about the health of a musical culture as a whole. What might have suggested a paradox thus becomes
instead an opportunity for interrogating social structures. Her discussion of
Sappho—of whom she says, "Hers was the last perfect flowering of thou-
sands of years of women's song" (107)—exemplifies an explanatory gesture
that is repeated many times in the book and, indeed, summarizes its whole
thrust:

> Here in this tiny island city-state of Lesbos, women had the high
> social, political, literary, and religious status then common in the
> Aegean world. They owned their own property and were free to
> come and go as they pleased. Well educated, especially in poetry
> and music, they enjoyed the companionship of both men and

other women, taking part, as a matter of course, in political and
literary discussions. As priestesses in the temples of Lesbos, they
served especially Hera, Aphrodite, Demeter, and Artemis. . . .
[In] this environment Sappho was born, matured, and asserted
her leadership. (104)[16]

Thus cultures as a whole must answer for the failure of female talent to
appear in substantial quantity, for, as she says of a later period of history,
"what was yielded to an individual woman of genius or charm was not
yielded to women collectively and as a right" (238). This particular formulation of the dichotomy between individual and collective musical production
calls up another one that disciplinary musicology has long taken for
granted—the distinction between amateur and professional musician. I
have spoken above about the Drinkers' deep and serious commitment to
amateur musicianship; in the crucible of their intensive home music-
making, it flowered into a full-scale philosophy of life, and it is not surprising
that Sophie Drinker's history is marked by it as well. Although she acknowledges the appropriate leadership role of those who are especially gifted (and
specially educated), she writes with skepticism of the modern ethos of performance by professionals before "masses of nonparticipating spectators"
(137), and she dwells feelingly on the desirability of "using music as a
normal activity" (261).

Disciplines that expend their energies primarily upon canonic works and
individual achievement also tend, for obvious reasons, to focus on those
groups and social classes that produce and consume—pay for, in short—
those works and achievements. Here the situation of women in history is
particularly interesting, since we belong, of course, to all socioeconomic
classes and might be expected to be differentially affected by the invisibility
traditional historiography has inflicted upon non-elite groups. Strangely,
such has not been the case, as conventional musicology is largely silent even
on the subject of the considerable influence upper-class women have often
had, through patronage, on the development of musical styles and genres.
Apparently class as such is not an issue. But from the point of view of an
interested and politically candid historian like Drinker—and one not particularly concerned with "high culture" as social practice—women share a
structural position that is somewhat castelike, if not classlike; their role is cul-
turally constructed, marked by generalized characteristics attributed to them
by others, and birth-determined. Castes exist in order to exemplify and enforce hierarchical status, and they do not permit of individual mobility from
one to another—caste, like anatomy, is destiny—but by the same token they

provide a locus of identification for their members and do not set up expectations of change achieved through individual effort. It is for this reason, as
Drinker saw it, that a history of "music and women" was a viable project.[17]

{

I would like to turn now to questions of explanation, beginning with
matters of large-scale historical organization. Historiography in the Western
tradition has for a long time been dominated by one or another of the available models based on revealing and explaining the "progress" of civilization.
Since the nineteenth century, the favored language for discussing this progress has been evolutionary. There has been a good deal of disputation on
this point, at first in general history and then, more recently, within musicology. It has been common for some time now to decry the practice, but as Leo
Treitler's review essay "The Present as History" reminded us, this manner of
historical organization was still prevalent in the 1960s (Treitler 1969).

Such a form of organization, though it must have appeared so familiar as
to seem "natural" in 1948, could not have served for a project like Drinker's
because she knew then what women's historians take for granted nowa-
days: that what is sauce for the gander has not always been sauce for the
goose. Women do not always thrive when "civilization" progresses; in fact,
the reverse is often true.[18] Drinker's attitude toward this hard reality—
which, remember, she discerned from her evidence without benefit of the
pool of theorizing that exists now—reflects some personal ambivalence. She
did believe in the onward march of civilization or, at least, in some related
theory that enabled her to distinguish "levels of culture" in the old comparativist manner; but she pointed out that male historians failed to acknowledge that women had, through long history, paid for this "progress"
by relinquishing their power. Because she could not imagine herself having
to live without such products of Western high culture as her beloved
Brahms, she wrote conventional evolutionary accounts of Western music,
such as "Creative musical imagination was . . . stimulated to proceed along
the modern line of harmony and counterpoint" (215). Because, on the other
hand, she understood what Brahms had cost us in terms of the fundamental
orientation of cultural values, she wrote such phrases as "China was thus
'civilizing' itself, by repressing women's rites and music" (129).

Drinker chooses to model her history not on "progress" but on phases of
the moon, a figure that has been associated with the female from time imme-
morial and in many cultures. This image is, of course, every bit as dependent
upon notions of natural necessity as evolutionary history ever was. She de-

scribes the matrix of values with which her book is concerned as "three mighty facts of nature" originally enfolded within representations of the great goddesses:

> One was the waxing and waning of the moon . . . The second was the fact that, in nature, death is the prelude to new birth . . . And the third was the kinship of the woman—in all those biological details that distinguish her from the male—to the moon cycle and to something that gives birth throughout all nature. (109–10)

Her diachronic historical structure is thus borrowed from a synchronic nexus of cultural meanings that she takes (problematically, but characteristically) to be universal. This model allows her to do a number of things at once: to insist that what she called the "patriarchal culture pattern" had not always prevailed but came into existence at a specific historical moment; to write a book that is, although very angry, optimistic at the end—the moon is again on the wax, she believes; but at the same time to argue that for the last two thousand years or so women have lived through a very dark time. And the inescapable conclusion her structure suggests is that the world has been living in an "unnatural" condition since the period roughly twenty-five hundred years ago when the Jews, Chinese, Greeks, and Indians simultaneously developed patriarchal societies that deprived women of their naturally ordained cultural functions in music, in religion, and in healing—or the management of life and death.

That is, because Drinker took this naturalized view of gender, her understanding of the dark time, the waning phase of the moon, has to do with the usurpation of women's proper roles and forms of artistic expression by men or by "unnatural" women fashioned according to men's interests and fantasies. She sees such male appropriations as perverse, even morbid, just as she does the distortion of women's art into "*seductive* music, rather than . . . a genuinely *feminine* expression."[19] Thus neither the male nor the "unnatural" female speaks for (or sings for) womankind. What happened in history, Drinker writes, is that "for the mother-musician, singing naturally in rituals of her own making, out of the fullness of her own vital experience, they substituted young boys, castrated males, and the courtesan" (140). Elsewhere she speaks scornfully of "men in skirts," her term for priests.[20]

Her sexual politics are somewhat conventional, then, acknowledging gendered roles in music as in social life: what she wants from long history is not for women to wear the pants, but only to get the skirts back. Nor is her essentialism simply metaphysical. The angriest portion of her book, and a pillar of her argument as a whole, dwells on her belief that the Church—and thus all subsequent formative institutions in Western music history—discriminates against women precisely and explicitly on biological grounds. She speaks of motherhood as the essential distinguishing feature of women, and goes on: "for no other reason, God, who is male, will not have a mother stand and speak at the altar. The door of the holy of holies, with its symbols of regeneration derived from her own function as life bringer, is closed to her, who brings the child into the world" (266). And then, further: "Withal, the real core of the matter is not woman's failure to have created great music. It is what that failure, when analyzed, reveals of the constitution of our society and the deep denial of life on which it rests" (281).

The agenda of *Music and Women*—what it is a "history of"—can now be more clearly seen. As part historian, part anthropologist, Drinker wants to know: in what kinds of societies can there be women musicians? (Which is to say, in what kinds of societies do women have approximately the same power and status granted to music?) As my account of her appropriation of the moon-phase model suggested, the book has a certain synchronous quality that is enhanced by her universalizing assumptions about the nature of women. From scholars of an earlier generation she adopted what anthropologists call the "contemporary-ancestor" theory, now discredited but not yet entirely supplanted in the 1940s: she took current cultures, especially nonliterate ones, to be exemplars of hypothetical human ancestors in cultures whose artifacts are no longer available for study. This belief informs the overall structure of the book as well. The opening "Full Moon" section explores a putatively timeless and "natural" relationship of women to music (and to men), illustrated cross-culturally and cross-historically; the notion of culture as such enters the narrative only at the fourth chapter, which broaches the idea of "taboo" to explain the arbitrariness of cultural variation; finally, in the fifth chapter, history (diachronicity) arrives on the scene.[21]

𝄞

Drinker's book differs from standard histories of music on a more local scale as well as with respect to long-term models. What marks music-historical epochs? Here, too, there has been methodological discussion among musicologists, and there has also been change over the last century or so. Music history used to be defined by the life spans (or career spans) of "great composers"—a habit which, as Philip Bohlman has recently pointed out, worked against any inclination to study music history on a worldwide or multicultural scale (Bohlman 1987:155). It was apparently Kiesewetter in 1834, naming epochs after their most important composers, who started us on this path, although he was at the same time one of the voices calling for the inclusion of non-Western musics within Western musicology.

By the turn of the century, though, a different version of music history had already begun to emerge—particularly in the work of Riemann and Adler—which focused on the emergence of musical forms and styles as more or less autonomous representations of culture, to be considered and understood together with a range of other cultural products. Such a work is Hugo Leichtentritt's 1938 textbook *Music, History, and Ideas,* in whose chapter titles epochs are identified by cultural traits: "reformation," "rationalistic traits," "classical tendencies," and so forth. No doubt the impulse is related to Heinrich Wölfflin's famous call for "history without names."

This practice rests absolutely, of course, on the underlying notion I have discussed above: that what one wants to understand in music history is the works that have been produced—and in particular those that have, as we say, "survived." But we have already seen that Sophie Drinker will not be interested in a history of works or in music-historical epochs named for compositional styles, much less for great composers. She believes, and wants her history to demonstrate, precisely that women have been prevented by social arrangements and the structural features of civilizations from becoming the names of epochs, or from leaving behind those works that led Arthur Mendel to remark that in music history the documents themselves *are* the deeds (Mendel 1962:14). Not so, says Drinker: most of women's musical deeds were never destined for posterity, have no *Wirkungsgeschichte,* but were deeds of human and musical significance nonetheless. She will not, that is, define historical "importance" either in terms of the survival, the "presentness" to us, of certain works or in terms of their influence on later generations of composers; music's importance, on the contrary, is for Drinker a matter of its spiritual and expressive function for human beings, not an occasion for musical analysis. There is no critical discussion here, and so far is she from autonomous-aesthetic values that she is inclined to take them as pernicious; her caption for a photograph of Martha Graham's ballet "Primitive Mysteries" comments that "while the Sherbro women *live* their rituals, these dancers merely *act* them on the stage" (plate 62, facing p. 232). The book as a whole is flavored with the assumption that highly aestheticist values are a sort of usurpation of the general artistic power of a people.[22]

So her history builds its epochal framework around social structures, expectations, the uses to which music is put. Thus she says, for instance, "The cultural pattern in which women as musicians function today was set at the beginning of the seventeenth century. At that time modern society, with new and revolutionary uses for music, began to take form" (228). The twelfth century is described in terms of social changes having to do with the relation of women to music; among them, for example, Drinker mentions "the limitation of the woman to the position of being the object of men's music, instead of the creator of music of her own" and "the exaltation of the woman as the inspirer and sponsor of men's music" (211). In a similar gesture, she remarks that "the romantic movement sounded the death knell of artificiality" (233–34), thus defining the period in terms of one of its most characteristic psychological traits, which gave women new and unheard-of musical opportunities because its ideology required emotional authenticity.[23]

♩

Music and Women departs from standard music-historical practice not only in its methods of organizing time periods, but also in its sense of what we might call the "mechanisms" of history. Efforts during the last century and a half to make history "scientific," and the more recent debates about the appropriateness of those efforts, entailed at the same time a debate about whether and how causality may operate in history, which is to say a debate about whether history may be explained in terms of general laws.

General history in the United States fought its battle with positivism early on, at the turn of the twentieth century (Herbst 1965:53ff.). By 1946 R. G. Collingwood was able to claim that its program had failed, that positivist history had fulfilled the first part of its mission—the collection of facts with what he called "infinite scrupulosity" and a vast increase in the sheer amount of information amassed—but that it had more or less given up on the possibility of ever reaching its further goal, the formulation of general historical laws (Collingwood 1946:127).[24] In a 1946 report by the Committee on Historiography of the Social Science Research Council, J. H. Randall and George Haines found that by the 1920s the critics of "scientific history" had won their battle and were "free to write the kind of history they wanted, economic interpretations, social and cultural history, intellectual history" (Randall and Haines 1946:27). And, writing about this issue in 1944 from his cell in the Nazi prison in Lyon, Marc Bloch warned against the tribe of historiographic Beckmessers: "Are we then the rules committee of an ancient guild?" (Bloch 1962:21). But, as Joseph Kerman has reminded us, musicology lagged behind this development, and it was not until well after World War II—after Drinker had completed her nearly twenty-year project—that it became clear that positivist influence would no longer dominate (Kerman 1985:40; also see Treitler 1989). It was to be expected, then, that the strong sense of historical causality would persist longer in musicological writing, particularly in its focus on style transmission and influence and on histories of form positing "inner laws" of musical evolution.

Drinker's notion of causality, however, is markedly different. Causes, for her, lie in spiritual and psychological factors, in the relations of individuals to their communities and their deities, and of course in the relations of women and men. It is worth noting that such an explanation of causality is a far cry from the familiar, abstract account in which musical compositions and whole genres may appear to give birth to one another almost without the intervention of human beings; on the contrary, Drinker's sense of historical explanation is explicitly political, organizing itself around the location and exercise of human power. In *Music and Women,* social change creates musical change, as when the development of capitalism altered the nature of people's spiritual relation to music and hence the kinds of music they made (229–30) or when the advent of Protestantism enhanced the participatory role of the congregation in liturgical singing (266).

Given the large-scale framework Drinker uses, with its cyclic waning and waxing of the moon, it stands to reason that she will be interested primarily in the causes of decline—the loss of women's power and their music-making—and in the causes of the regeneration she saw beginning. With regard to the former, her understanding of human spirituality as an essentially holistic force underpins the argument. "For creative expression in music," she writes, "there must be a free flow between the plane of daily experience and the plane of thought and fantasy. One must be able to transfer into universal and ideal terms one's vital personal experience" (108). This opportunity for idealization was once available to women, she argues, before the formulation of the patriarchal religions restricted them to "a single male god." Her comment on the subject is telling: "From the psychology of the Jews came the omnipotent Father-God of our own religion today, with no daughter, no mate, and even no mother" (143). That is, a kind of psychosis about women underlies the whole Judaeo-Christian tradition.[25]

Particularly interesting is the playing out of this idea later, in Drinker's account of the resurgence of women's musical authority. She predicts the arrival of something that sounds like what we know as New Age spirituality, something she describes as a holistic sense appearing in science and culture.

"Belief in the unity of all life is itself a rebirth for women," she writes (284), especially since at the same time it emphasizes "the primitive use of music as an affective power for a specific occasion and purpose" (287). It would seem, in other words, that Drinker expected an end to Western high culture's insistence on art as autonomous and transcendent, and that she read that development—as an essentialist naturally would read it—as tending toward the incorporation of female sensibility.

> Now music is reattaining its primeval value, which in no way interferes with the value of concert giving and virtuosity. Music, which produces an inner harmony, is being introduced into homes, schools, colleges, moving pictures, and theaters, and especially into hospitals for its direct power over emotionally disturbed people (287).[26]

{

It may seem, since Drinker's book is finally so alien to the musicological tradition, that an interrogation of ethnomusicology and its history would be a surer route to the sources and the natural disciplinary home of *Music and Women*. It seems clear that many of the book's presuppositions—about communal values, about caste and class, about the embedding of musical expression within culture—will appear considerably more familiar to scholars of anthropological bent than they do to Western musicologists. Drinker certainly considered her work to be at least partially anthropological, as she explains in her foreword.

I would raise the question, though, what we would know about ourselves if we learned that Drinker's book *does* sit more comfortably there than in musicology: that women have an anthropology but no history? And that that difference, perhaps, is part of what it means to be the quintessential Other? (It was more or less on grounds of "otherness" that history and anthropology divided their terrain in the first place.) More to the point, what would we know about the discipline of musicology? I suspect that Drinker's methodological ruptures will remain salient no matter through what disciplinary lens her work is examined. That is because her study of women required that, time and time again in her book, she confront "one of those perplexities in men's scholarship and writing of history that baffles a sincere woman's mind" (263–64).

NOTES

1. There is a collective biography, *Family Portrait*, by Henry's youngest sister, Catherine Drinker Bowen.

2. A list of all the guests over a thirty-year span has been published (Drinker and Drinker 1960); it includes the names of many prominent musicians and musicologists among its distinguished company. The singing parties are described in Drinker 1965:111–16; Bowen 1979, chap. 11; and Waln 1951.

3. "Dr. Edmund H. Fellowes lectured . . . to a group at our house. . . . Others came in connection with the Musicological Society. On several occasions, we had the members' meetings and a supper at our house. Dr. Edward J. Dent was one of the important [lecturers] who came. Dom Hughes was another. Dr. George Herzog still another" (Drinker 1965:107).

4. Note that Drinker's assumption here is that women's "own ideas and feelings" are not the same as men's, that the expressive medium of music would be used differently in women's hands. At present this essentialism is a much-debated point in feminist critical scholarship, and is for the most part regarded skeptically by Anglo-Americans; but Drinker's belief in such an innate gender difference was typical of her generation and is a crucial foundation of all her work, as will become clear further on.

5. Much of the correspondence has been transcribed into the sixteen volumes of notes for *Music and Women*. Copies are located in the Sophia Smith Collection, Smith College, and at the University of Pennsylvania Library, Special Collections.

6. This holds true even of the two negative reviewers, James Lyons for the *New York Times* and Jacques Barzun for the *Herald Tribune* (the latter will be discussed below).

7. Ernst Breisach observes that this professionalization was signaled by the discipline's espousal of Leopold von Ranke's principles; the "divorce" of professional from amateur history writing also meant, then, the eclipse of old-fashioned, narrative history and of "history with a direct public purpose" (Breisach 1983:287–88). While the amateur history-writing tradition was unlikely to address the grand themes Drinker takes on here, it did tend to concern itself, as she does, with the common life of people (Bell 1972; Blegen 1947).

8. Among her own immediate family there is little evidence of any history-writing proclivity; perhaps she absorbed it from the Drinkers, nearly all of whom wrote history in one form or another—or, in the case of their aunt, Cecilia Beaux, painted it in portraits.

9. This meddlesome girl is, of course, the only female referred to in Sachs's talk; the "music historian" is described as "he." Philip Bohlman has reminded me that Sachs also sought to sharpen the distinction among the three branches of *Musikwissenschaft*, but that concern does not appear to be a factor in the present context.

10. Sophie Drinker to Jacques Barzun, 27 February 1948, copy in Sophie Drinker Papers, Addendum, box 1, folder 85-M53, Schlesinger Library, Radcliffe College. Quoted by permission.

11. Barzun, of course, is not strictly speaking a musicologist, but he has functioned as one and shares most of the presuppositions of the discipline. For a sense of the intellectual environment at the time Drinker's book appeared, in the disciplines that most closely concern us here, consider the following contemporaneous books. In general history we have R.G. Collingwood, *The Idea of History* (1946); Theodore Blegen, *Grass Roots History* (1947); Morton White, *Social Thought in America: The Re-*

volt against Formalism (1949) and Karl Jaspers, *The Origin and Goal of History* (1949). In anthropology and ethnomusicology Melville Herskovits's *Man and His Works: The Science of Cultural Anthropology* and Curt Sachs's *Our Musical Heritage: A Short History of World Music* were exact contemporaries (1948). In historical musicology, 1947 saw the publication of Alfred Einstein's *Music in the Romantic Era,* Manfred Bukofzer's *Music in the Baroque Era,* and Karl Geiringer's *Brahms;* Ernst Toch's *The Shaping Forces in Music* and Eric Walter White's *Stravinsky* appeared in 1948 and Einstein's *The Italian Madrigal* in 1949.

12. I am grateful to Cynthia I. Mucha, archives assistant at DePauw University, for her generous help in locating relevant correspondence in Mary Beard's papers.

13. It should be borne in mind that in this period historical musicology and eth-nomusicology were still in the process of formation as separate disciplines, gradually dividing between them custody of the various aspects of musical knowledge, much as anthropology and history had done about a century before. This situation appears poignant from the vantage point of the early 1990s, when so much of the talk in both divorced couples is of reconciliation.

14. As for Drinker's particular political engagement, the reactions of her reviewers are instructive; only two object to her feminism. One of these writes anonymously in *The New Yorker* of February 1948; the other, James Lyons in the *New York Times,* adopts a disingenuous tone, complaining that Drinker proves "what no intelligent person disputes anyway: that women are the artistic equals of men" (Lyons 1948). Marion Bauer, on the other hand, makes a point of assessing the book as "without too much militant feminism"; since Drinker's feminism *is* in fact rather militant, Bauer's comment suggests a greater tolerance than we have typically attributed to the 1940s—or, for that matter, to Marion Bauer.

15. It has been pointed out that the gradual professionalization of history within the academy produced, among other changes, a noticeable shift in the class back-ground and interests of historians—resulting eventually in changed notions of how history should be written (Hamerow 1987). For Drinker, some notion of gender soli-darity partially overcame, or interfered with, the tendency to speak from one's class position.

16. Drinker here anticipates the argument later used with great power by Linda Nochlin in 1971 in her influential essay "Why Have There Been No Great Women Artists?" (Nochlin 1988).

17. The vagaries of current usage suggest that confusion persists about how to consider women as a group: women are sometimes spoken of as a "minority," al-though we are not; alternatively, one hears the phrase "women and minorities," as though racial and ethnic minority groups did not also include women. What, after all, is a gender?

18. The classic study of this phenomenon is Kelly [1977] 1984. Again, Drinker's formulation is prescient.

19. Sophie Drinker to Marjorie Greenbie, 20 September [1946], Sydney and Mar-jorie Greenbie Papers, Special Collections, Knight Library, University of Oregon. I am grateful to the Knight Library staff for assistance in finding materials and for permis-sion to use them.

20. Catherine Bowen offers a further example: "How, Sophie asked furiously,

could Mary's joyful words [i.e., the *Magnificat*] be pronounced before the altar by little boys in surplices?" (Bowen 1979:181).

21. For discussion of earlier examples of such comparative-method music histories and their implications, see Solie 1982. An organizational feature Drinker's book has in common with many of its predecessors is a comparative, global beginning that gradually narrows to a Western focus by the end. According to this familiar trope, only the West is "modern" or has a present.

22. An important influence on Drinker—and apparently a personal friend—was Kathi Meyer, whose *Bedeutung und Wesen der Musik* (1932) Vincent Duckles characterized as "among the few studies that have been devoted to the cultural meaning of music" (Duckles 1972:34). But "meaning" is a slippery business, and paradoxes abound in this area. Melville Herskovits (1948), writing just contemporaneously with Drinker, attaches great importance to music in the study of culture, seeing it as a structural system analogous to language in the kind of information it can provide. As a result, his anthropological commitment, rather than embedding the music in culture, yields up another reason for formalist analysis.

23. Nineteenth-century naturalism had, in this view, an ironic outcome in twentieth-century musical institutions. While it created opportunities for women performers in areas like opera and ballet, where they were needed *as women,* it did nothing to overcome the barriers (and indeed may have led to their reactive fortification) in organizations like symphony orchestras, where their sex gave them no obvious advantage. See Drinker, chapter 15, especially pp. 238–40.

24. At just about the same time, Melville Herskovits noted that the comparative method in anthropology had failed by virtue of producing too many facts torn out of context, so that their meaning was not intelligible (Herskovits 1948:475).

25. It is particularly interesting to note how many of Drinker's reviewers grasped and accepted this link between art and spirituality without demur. This suggests a striking change in cultural beliefs between the 1940s and the 1990s, and perhaps indicates a lingering trace of the nineteenth-century sacralization of art described, for instance, in chapter 2 of Levine 1988.

26. I doubt that she would have retained this faith had she lived to see the ubiquity of "elevator music" and the commercial triumph of Muzak and its clones. Like many who pin their hopes on communitarian values, Drinker gave little thought to the politically totalizing aspects of imposed public music.

WORKS CITED

Allen, Warren Dwight. 1962. *Philosophies of Music History: A Study of General Histories of Music, 1600-1960.* New York: Dover Publications.

Barzun, Jacques. 1948. "Only a Bird in a Gilded Cage." Review of *Music and Women. New York Herald Tribune Weekly Book Review* 24 (22 February):4.

Bauer, Marion. 1948. "A Viewpoint of Women in Music." Review of *Music and Women. Musical Digest* 29:30–31.

Bell, Whitfield J., Jr. 1972. "The Amateur Historian." *New York History* 53:265–81.

Blegen, Theodore C. 1947. *Grass Roots History.* Minneapolis: University of Minnesota Press.

Bloch, Marc. 1962. *The Historian's Craft.* Trans. Peter Putnam. New York: Knopf.

Bohlman, Philip V. 1987. "The European Discovery of Music in the Islamic World and the 'Non-Western' in Nineteenth-Century Music History." *Journal of Musicology* 5:147–63.

Bowen, Catherine Drinker. 1979. *Family Portrait.* Boston: Little, Brown.

Braudel, Fernand. 1980. "The Situation of History in 1950." In *On History,* Trans. Sarah Matthews, 6–24. Chicago: University of Chicago Press.

Breisach, Ernst. 1983. *Historiography: Ancient, Medieval, and Modern.* Chicago: University of Chicago Press.

Bukofzer, Manfred. 1946. "Historical Musicology." *Music Journal* 4:21, 51–52.

Collingwood, R. G. 1946. *The Idea of History.* Oxford: Oxford University Press.

Dahlhaus, Carl. 1983. *Foundations of Music History.* Trans. J. B. Robinson. Cambridge: Cambridge University Press.

Drinker, Henry S., and Sophie H. Drinker. 1960. *Accademia dei Dilettanti di Musica.* N.p. (published by authors).

Drinker, Sophie H. 1965. Untitled memoir typescript. Copy in Sophie Drinker Papers, Addendum, box 1, folder 84-M182. Schlesinger Library, Radcliffe College.

———. 1977. *Music and Women: The Story of Women in Their Relation to Music.* Washington, D.C.: Zenger. Originally published 1948.

Duckles, Vincent. 1970. "Patterns in the Historiography of Nineteenth-Century Music." *Acta musicologica* 42:75–82.

———. 1972. "Musicology and the Mirror: A Prospectus for the History of Musical Scholarship." In Barry S. Brook, Edward O. D. Downes, and Sherman Van Solkema, eds., *Perspectives in Musicology,* 32–49. New York: W. W. Norton.

Geiringer, Karl. 1948. Review of *Music and Women. Notes,* 2nd ser., 5:234–35.

Hamerow, Theodore S. 1987. *Reflections on History and Historians.* Madison: University of Wisconsin Press.

Herbst, Jurgen. 1965. *The German Historical School in American Scholarship: A Study in the Transfer of Culture.* Ithaca: Cornell University Press.

Herskovits, Melville. 1948. *Man and His Works: The Science of Cultural Anthropology.* New York: Knopf.

Kelly, Joan. 1984. "Did Women Have a Renaissance?" In *Women, History, and Theory: The Essays of Joan Kelly,* 19–50. Chicago: University of Chicago Press. Originally published 1977.

Kerman Joseph. 1985. *Contemplating Music: Challenges to Musicology.* Cambridge, Mass.: Harvard University Press.

Levine, Lawrence. 1988. *Highbrow/Lowbrow: The Emergence of Cultural Hierarchy in America.* Cambridge, Mass.: Harvard University Press.

Lyons, James. 1948. "Esthetic Dynamics of the Female." Review of *Music and Women. New York Times Book Review* 97 (4 July):6.

Mendel, Arthur. 1962. "Evidence and Explanation." In Jan LaRue, ed., *IMS: Report of the Eighth Congress,* 3–18. Kassel: Bärenreiter.·

Nochlin, Linda. 1988. "Why Have There Been No Great Women Artists?" In *Women, Art, and Power and Other Essays.* New York: Harper & Row. Originally published 1971.

Randall, John Herman, Jr., and George Haines IV. 1946. "Controlling Assumptions in the Practice of American Historians." In *Theory and Practice in Historical Study: A Report of the Committee on Historiography,* 17–52. New York: Social Science Research Council.

Sachs, Curt. 1945. The Music Historian." *Music Educators' Journal* 31, no. 6 (May-June) 1945: 78–79.

Seeger, Charles. 1977. "Music and Musicology in the New World 1946." In *Studies in Musicology, 1935–1975,* 211–21. Berkeley and Los Angeles: University of California Press. Originally published 1946.

Silbert, Doris. 1948. Review of *Music and Women. Musical Quarterly* 34 (1948): 285–88.

Solie, Ruth A. 1982. "Melody and the Historiography of Music." *Journal of the History of Ideas* 43:297–308.

Treitler, Leo. 1969. "The Present as History." *Perspectives of New Music* 7:1–58.

———. 1989. "The Power of Positivist Thinking." *Journal of the American Musicological Society* 42:375–402.

Waln, Nora. 1951. "The Sunday after Korea." *Atlantic Monthly* 187:23–26.

FOUR

Rethinking Musical Culture: Canonic Reformulations in a Post-Tonal Age

Robert P. Morgan

In a recent issue of *Critical Inquiry* devoted to "Canons," Joseph Kerman opened his excellent contribution by noting that, for musicians, the word "means something else. 'Wir haben ein Gesetz'" (Kerman 1983:107). We think of "canon" first as a compositional procedure, based on a rule of strict imitation; with regard to the kind of canons the editors of *Critical Inquiry* had in mind, we prefer to speak of "repertories." Kerman provides convincing reasons for this, mainly concerning music's "evanescence"—its status as a "program of action"—and its relatively recent acquisition of a sufficiently precise notational system to ensure permanent documentation.

Kerman does not mention, however, that these two meanings of *canon*—a body of exemplary works drawn from the past and a law, or rule of conduct, for musical construction—are in fact inseparably joined. For an essential function of the canonic repertory is to provide models—thus also "rules of imitation"—for compositional practice. The canonic work is thus both a model for creation and a standard against which creation is measured. It too is a law, or "subject," obeyed by "canonic imitation"—not slavishly, perhaps, but essentially, in conformance with the aesthetic and technical assumptions it embodies.

It is the conjunction of these two senses that lends the word *canon* a more general meaning that seems particularly applicable to music and that throws a revealing light on our current musical situation. Western music has been characterized not so much by the existence of a particular collection of classics (a relatively recent arrival in its history—a "legacy from early Romanticism," as Kerman notes) nor by a particular compositional procedure based on strict imitation (though remarkably persistent, hardly a constant feature), as by an idea that has given life to both: that music constitutes a well-formed and coherent "language" based upon commonly shared formal and expressive assumptions.

The history of Western music theory, including both its speculative and practical branches, is deeply rooted in this conviction. Whether conceived as an effort to demonstrate that the essential musical relationships are drawn from "nature," and thus sanctioned by God's law (reflecting the simplest mathematical-acoustical ratios and ultimately the very harmony of the spheres) or, somewhat less comprehensively, as an effort to formulate "universal" principles regulating harmonic combination and linear progression, music theory has clung to the conviction that there is a right way of understanding and of realizing musical relationships, and correspondingly a wrong way as well. Music is not simply what one wants it to be. It has an essence, dictated by a transcendent power and preserved by an equally transcendent tradition.

Within the dynamic context of Western cultural history, this preservation has had to be tempered by some latitude for change, at times quite extensive. Yet these changes have tended to be defended either as superficial adjustments, beneath which the essential principles persisted, or as necessary corrections of previous digressions that had diverted music from its true course, distorting its essential nature. A classic instance of the former is Christoph Bernhard's mid-seventeenth-century justification of the freer dissonance of the *seconda pratica* as being logically derived from the strict counterpoint of the *prima pratica*. And Richard Wagner's mid-nineteenth-century ruminations on the wayward course of previous operatic history provide a famous (or notorious) example of the latter. In either case, the belief in an unchanging eternal order surpassing time-bound stylistic transformations remains intact.

In this larger, more general sense, then, Western music has always had a canon, a belief that there is a "proper" mode of musical conduct. It is this, more than any particular conception of what that mode of conduct might be, that has traditionally given our music a common core, despite its highly unstable and developmental history. Underneath the momentarily transient qualities of its variegated surfaces, Western music was considered to preserve a more permanent substructure; despite all stylistic heterogeneity, it was based upon an enduring structural foundation. It had, in short, a grammar— a system of relatively stable constructive principles providing a basis for meaningful utterance. Even the most acrimonious disputes in the critical and theoretical literature rested upon this assumption, without which, indeed, they would have been meaningless.

Although these principles evolved, they did so sufficiently slowly—not unlike those of the grammar of a verbal language—to preserve their underlying integrity. If at first it appeared that some particular stylistic transformation had impaired the old order, a new generation would demonstrate that what was essential had not in fact been abandoned at all, but only cast in a new light (thanks to which, it was often felt, it could be fully understood for the first time). These principles provided an essential measure for all musical statements. If one wished to be understood, to avoid speaking musical nonsense, one had to conform to them (although the more richly the music was able to exploit them, the more it tended to be favored). The essential canonic idea in Western music, whether textually or orally transmitted, was thus the belief in a communal musical language, prevailing underneath a wealth of superficial, time-bound stylistic transformations.[1]

Although this conception of canon as language has maintained a consistent hold throughout most of Western music history, it has been seriously undermined by musical developments during the present century, resulting in a transformation of our historical and cultural perceptions of unprecedented scope. These developments were rooted in the gradual erosion of "common-practice" tonality, which led to the so-called atonal—or, perhaps better, "post-tonal"—revolution of the first decade of this century.

Some music historians have been inclined to view this moment as one among several major turning points that have marked Western music and shaped its overall course, likening the musical events of about 1900, say, to those of about 1600, when there was a shift from an essentially modal, intervallic, and polyphonic conception to one that was tonal, harmonic, and homophonic. If one traces the history of the demise of common-practice tonality, there would seem to be considerable support for this view. Like the developments leading to the end of the musical Renaissance, those responsible for tonality's ultimate collapse emerged slowly and gradually; and they did so in direct response to the dynamic possibilities contained within the dominant musical system itself. The tonal system, that is, was undermined largely from within, its own grammatical potentialities being ever more deeply explored until, pushed to their limits, they reached a breaking point.

Given this evolutionary background, one might well assume that the twentieth-century revolution would turn out to be like previous ones—that out of the ashes of the old musical order a new one would emerge, exhibiting attributes that would eventually prove to be just as logical as those of earlier Western music, even essentially compatible with them. Continuity, as well as evolution, would be preserved.

This has not proved to be the case, though it has taken us some time to realize it. It now seems evident that with the end of common-practice tonality music entered a fundamentally new phase. It is impossible to say just when this occurred, for tonality was under siege from many different directions throughout the nineteenth century—indeed, one might argue, throughout its entire existence. But the appearance of Schoenberg's first nontriadic, nontonal compositions in 1907 provided—following an extended death rattle—a sort of symbolic pronouncement of its ultimate demise.

Of course in some sense tonality remained, and still remains. It was, and is, available for any composer inclined to use it. But once its possibilities were widely perceived as exhausted, incapable of further expansion, tonality lost the traditional basis for its expressive force. And without general acceptance, it surrendered perhaps its most essential attribute: its "universality," its status as a common language.

What set this musical turning point off from previous ones was not that an old system expired (which was hardly unprecedented), but that no analogous new one offered itself as a replacement. This had not only enormous psychological consequences for the composer, but a decisive impact upon the very meaning of music and musical culture. Suddenly left empty-handed, composers were confronted with a seemingly limitless array of compositional possibilities. With the old grammar gone and no new one to take its place, nothing was either prescribed or forbidden. As if in a single stroke, anything and everything became possible.

Given the extreme nature of this change, it is hardly surprising that during the first half of the century most composers concentrated upon minimizing its effects. Almost without exception, the response was to seek new constraints and to reestablish ties with the past. One can accordingly view the history of earlier twentieth-century music, above all that of the interwar years, as a series of conscious, individually devised stratagems designed to check the chaos threatened by tonality's collapse. Whether viewing their work as a direct, logical continuation of a still-viable and ongoing tradition (the Viennese twelve-tone composers), or as a rapprochement with some bygone stage of music history (Stravinsky), or perhaps as both (Bartók), the major figures sought order and coherence through links with the past.

Although these links now had to be forged by conscious, personal decision, rather than through the mechanisms of a transcendent tradition, a great deal of twentieth-century music thus maintained much in common with earlier Western music, especially of the eighteenth and nineteenth centuries. The dynamic shape of the music—the way it breathed, developed, and moved forward in time—shared unmistakable affinities with music of the common-practice period. The new music produced a decidedly distorted image of that music, to be sure, but an image nonetheless, and one whose formal coherence and expressive effect depended explicitly upon recognition of points of contact with the past.

In this connection, it should be remembered that all of the major compositional figures of the first half of the century, those responsible both for passing beyond tonality and for staking out the new post-tonal terrain, belonged to a generation nurtured entirely within a musical culture accepting tonality as a necessary and universal force. They acquired instincts that assured that the new music would significantly mirror the old. Yet there was a critical difference in this music: what had formally been shaped through the operations of an "internal" grammar was now passed through some "external" musical filter determined by conscious choice (e.g., Bartók's folk-music-derived tonality and symmetrical pitch constructions, Stravinsky's polar tonality, and Schoenberg's twelve-tone system). This perhaps explains, at least in part, the "heroic" character that so many find in the music of the leading figures of the generation that reached maturity around the turn of the century. We hear these composers, the last masters of the "great Western tradition," struggling against seemingly insurmountable odds to preserve something of the goal-directed continuity and logical coherence, as well as individualized expressiveness, of the music of the past.

From our present perspective it seems increasingly evident, nonetheless, that however one may value the music of this generation (it ranks very high on my list), there is an arbitrary aspect about it, stemming from its dependence upon highly conscious and individually made choices regarding both musical material and structural limitations imposed upon the material. Whatever decision a composer made, it was necessarily personal rather than public. The balance between the particular and the universal, between transience and continuity, had shifted irrevocably.

≀

Though the radical consequences of post-tonality were to some degree obscured by the various neo-classicisms evident in the main line of earlier twentieth-century music, indications of the fundamentally altered compositional context began to appear almost immediately. Limited in scope and largely ignored at the time, they assume far greater historical significance from our current vantage point.

There was, for example, a sudden and unprecedented questioning of what could properly constitute musical material. During the tonal period, when connections between the musical system and the material it governed were fixed, such questions did not, and could not, arise. Since the tonal system made no provision for structuring such literally "nonmusical" content, unpitched "noise," including purely percussive sounds, was incorporated, if at all, only as an essentially decorative element. After tonality there was no necessity for this prohibition: with the absence of a prescribed governing system, any sonic material at all could theoretically be used as long as it lent itself to temporal arrangement.

Since most early-twentieth-century composers preferred to disguise the discontinuity of the historical situation by constructing new musical systems that preserved analogies with tonality, the pitch repertory of traditional twelve-tone tempered tuning was almost universally preserved. Yet at almost exactly the same time as Schoenberg's first atonal works announced the passing of tonality, certain composers began to question previous notions of musical material as well. Among them was Ferruccio Busoni, who in his pamphlet *Sketch of a New Esthetic of Music,* published in 1906, complained that "our whole system of tone, key, and tonality, taken in its entirety, is only a part of a fraction of one diffracted ray from that Sun, 'Music'" (Busoni 1962:91). Busoni called for an expansion of the available resources to encompass, among other possibilities, microtonal subdivisions, and he praised attempts to create electronic instruments that would be able to produce them. The significance of Busoni's appeal, coming from one of the most prominent musicians of the age (both as composer and pianist), was considerable; and his proposals elicited widespread and heated (if mostly negative) discussion.

Busoni's suggestions were not widely translated into practice, either by Busoni himself or his contemporaries; but a notable exception appeared in the Italian Futurists, who some four years later began issuing manifestos expressing similar concerns. The most consequential formulation of their position is found in Luigi Russolo's 1913 pamphlet *The Art of Noises,* in which the author attacked the poverty of "pure musical sound" (i.e., pitched sound), arguing that music should encompass all possible types of noise:

> Musical sound, a thing extraneous to life and independent to it
> . . . has become to our ears what a too familiar face is to our eyes.
> Noise, on the other hand, which comes to us confused and irregular as life itself, never reveals itself wholly but reserves for us innumerable surprises. . . . The Art of Noise . . . will reach its

greatest emotional power through the purely acoustic enjoyment
which the inspiration of the artist will continue to evoke from
combinations of noises. (Quoted in Slonimsky 1971:1301)

Though not himself trained as a musician, Russolo invented a series of
noisemaking instruments, called *intonarumori,* and composed a number of
pieces for them. Judging by the single page of score and one recorded fragment that have survived (the latter of extremely poor acoustical quality),
there is good reason to question the quality of his music. Moreover, since
Russolo was primarily a painter and sculptor, historians of music have
tended not to take him seriously. But here (as in the case of the dog who
walks on hind legs), what matters is not so much the quality of the act as the
sheer fact of its existence. Russolo's work embodied a radically new conception of what music might be; and the significance of his vision now seems
considerable, as it served notice that, beyond tonality, the boundaries of
compositional possibility could be fundamentally redrawn.

Indeed, given the dates of his earliest activities, Russolo's lack of musical
training was probably a necessary condition for the formulation of his musical aesthetic. The attempts of professional musicians of the period (including Russolo's Futurist colleague Balilla Pratella) to explore the possibilities
of post-tonality were, by comparison, markedly timid. In any event, Russolo
occupies a prominent position in what can now be seen as a persistent, if
secondary, stream of musical exploration during the early post-tonal period,
encompassing microtonal tuning (Alois Habba, Ivan Vishnegradsky, and
Julián Carrillo), timbral expansions (Edgard Varèse and, especially, Henry
Cowell, whose *New Musical Resources,* published in 1930 but dating back to
the late teens, goes well beyond Busoni in advocating alternative musical
systems), and radical eclecticism (Charles Ives). Something new was in the
air, however diffuse its traces were at the time.

≀

    The full consequences of post-tonality have become evident only since
World War II; and the critical figure in their unveiling is John Cage. In 1937,
his twenty-fifth year, Cage already proclaimed (echoing Russolo by way of
Varèse) the need for instruments that could produce "any and all sounds that
can be heard." Since such instruments were still unavailable, alternative
sources for new sonic possibilities were explored: brake drums, thunder
sheets, primitive electronic equipment (manipulated phonograph recordings), and modified pianos, all of which appeared in Cage's works by the
early 1940s.

These early compositions addressed one of the important consequences of the new musical condition: the absence of a "given" material required by a preordained musical system. In response, Cage sought to construct, or "invent," a unique sound corpus for each composition. Moreover, he expressly stressed the "arbitrary" nature of his choices by avoiding any connection between the sounds chosen and the structures devised to contain them. In a rejection of traditional beliefs in the mutual interaction of form and content, Cage's materials had no influence on the structures that contained them, nor did his structures influence the materials. Form was reduced to a neutral receptacle, a sequence of empty durational lengths regulated by a set of numerical proportions. Individual segments were simply filled with sounds, alternated according to the same proportional relationships. The result was a succession of static juxtapositions of musical content, with no formal unit implied by the preceding one nor implying the one to follow.

In his pre-1950 works, Cage nevertheless gave each work a fixed identity, determining its form and material by conscious decision, no matter how capricious the choice (he once commented that the sounds used in his prepared piano compositions "were chosen as one chooses shells while walking along a beach" [Cage 1961a:19]). By mid-century, however, Cage's intentions had taken a crucial step forward: to "make a musical composition the continuity of which is free of individual taste and memory (psychology) and also of the literature and 'traditions' of the art"; and to "give up the desire to control sound, clear [the] mind of music, and set about discovering means to let sounds be themselves rather than vehicles for man-made theories of expression or human sentiments" (Cage 1961b:10).

This brought Cage to indeterminacy, which by relying on chance and random elements to determine musical materials and formal order represented the ideal image reflecting the artificiality of musical structure in the posttonal period. In indeterminacy the choice of form and content, of structure and material, becomes literally inconsequential. Between 1950 and 1952, Cage produced a series of works that fundamentally changed the meaning of music. In the piano piece *Music of Changes* (1951), he determined all aspects of the structure by reference to charts derived from the *I Ching*, chosen by tossing coins. Since the piece was for piano, however, the basic instrumental sound was still established by compositional choice. In *Imaginary Landscape No. 4* (1951) for twelve radios, Cage again determined the structure— including specifications for the frequency tunings of the radios, changes in tuning, dynamics, points of entrance and cutoff, etc.—by reference to the *I Ching;* but here the sonic material also remained entirely indeterminate, dependent upon such variables as what, if anything, happened to appear on a given frequency. Essentially everything relating to the composition as a sounding event had been taken out of the composer's hands, placed beyond his control.

Cage's best-known composition, the most heatedly discussed of all his works, followed: *4'33"* (1952), the score of which consists of the Roman numerals I to III, each followed by a duration (their sum equal to the title) plus the word "tacit." Since only silence is indicated, the "music" consists of whatever ambient sounds take place during a performance: air-conditioning hum, crowd noise, street sounds, etc. *4'33"* offered an ideal representation (a word that would no doubt make the composer uncomfortable) of the altered nature of twentieth-century musical constructions. Structure and material are totally severed from one another. Indeed, since the only material specified is silence, the piece actually consists *only* of structure, conceived as a series of empty durations. The dissociation of sound and syntax is absolute.

This critical phase of Cage's development discloses the implications of post-tonality in their most extreme form. The only musical development that might rival it in this regard is integral serialism, which emerged, not coincidentally, at almost exactly the same moment and which aspired to integrate all compositional elements through rational, precompositional planning. At first glance serialism seems diametrically opposed to Cage; yet it shares with him an attempt to arrive at compositional decisions through the mediation of an outside agent: in one case operations of a quasi-mathematical character, capable of generating compositions more or less automatically; in the other, operations of chance. And both reveal equally a quality of calculated arbitrariness, carrying to extremes the notion that, given the absence of a communal compositional language, new ones can be constructed at will.

Since the serialists normally limited themselves to traditional pitch material and instruments, however, Cage alone embraced the full range of post-tonal possibilities—or, expressed somewhat differently, accepted the absolute capriciousness of any kind of compositional restriction. More than anyone else, he reset the boundaries of musical art. This explains why he is, despite the extraordinarily controversial nature of his work, undeniably a major figure, not only in music but in the contemporary art world at large. Despite Cage's protestations of "purposelessness," moreover, his prominence did not happen "by chance." In the final analysis his music is immanently purposeful and ideologically slanted. It explores the absolute limits, or absence thereof, of what is possible within the contemporary compositional context.

Two characteristic features of Cage's work are especially revealing in this connection. One is a shift from an essentially subjective conception of musical composition (a consequence of composing with an "internal" language such as tonality) to an essentially objective one (as a consequence of composing with an "external" system such as the *I Ching* tables). Eschewing dynamic musical relationships, which seem to mirror human emotions, Cage favors passive structures that allow sound to be apprehended for its own sake, without distortion from human intervention.

The second characteristic is Cage's notion of music as pure process rather than a collection of musical compositions. Paradoxically, the objectivity of Cage's compositional processes destroys the objectivity of the compositional product. The rigid segregation of structural system from material content deprives the work of its traditional status as artifact. Since formal structures are "empty," they do not provide a stable, enduring set of relationships that can be designated "the piece." The latter—no longer a predetermined configuration of pitch and temporal relationships realized in performance only after the fact—becomes an ongoing event, often nothing more than a set of activity-oriented instructions that produces entirely different results in different realizations.[2]

The range of possible processes and the types of activities they involve are virtually unlimited. Cage's *Theater Piece* (1960) consists of actions worked out according to instructions with the intent of "arriving at a complex situation"; *0'0"* (1962) consists (in the composer's interpretation) of cutting up vegetables, mixing them in a blender, and drinking the result; and *4'33"* involves simply the passage of time. Music becomes indistinguishable from anything else; in Cage's words, "everything we do is music."

As Cage's work became increasingly less anchored in human memory, in cultural tradition and psychological reality, it thus became more and more closely allied with physical reality, finally becoming essentially indistinguishable from it. As the American composer Robert Ashley has commented: "Cage's influence on contemporary music . . . is such that . . . the ultimate result would be a music that wouldn't necessarily involve anything but the presence of people. . . . It seems to me that the most radical redefinition of music that I could think of would be one that defines 'music' without reference to sound" (quoted in Nyman 1974:10).

The "purity" of Cage's response to post-tonality has nevertheless carried with it something of a dilemma. As music approaches life (or as Cage might prefer to say, as life approaches music), there is ideally no longer a need for either composer or musical composition. Having shed its autonomy, "music" should dissolve into an integral, all-encompassing experience. By continuing to produce musical compositions that, paradoxically, are intended to render all compositions superfluous, Cage has had to ignore his own message.

There is thus an aspect of self-negation inherent in Cage's aesthetic position. Yet it would be shortsighted to say that he has "failed." It might rather be argued—and frequently has been—that his voice speaks most authentically for the contemporary musical situation. Certainly his ideas have had a significant impact on a wide range of his contemporaries, including musicians, visual artists, cultural historians, and philosophers; and his works are performed by both major musical ensembles and more specialized new-music groups with notable frequency. As these words are written, he occupies the Charles Eliot Norton chair of poetics at Harvard University, placing him with such distinguished company as Stravinsky and Hindemith. Whatever one thinks of Cage, he is clearly saying something about the nature of music today that a large number of people find compelling.

Viewed from the present perspective, what Cage is saying is that, deprived of a common "linguistic" base, each composer must reinvent music from the ground up. Musical choices become subjective, and thus arbitrary. Cage concludes that this renders choice meaningless and that therefore the most reasonable response is to avoid choice entirely (at least to the extent possible), submitting to the dictates of arbitrary systems. The more purposeless the mechanisms of the system, the more "authentic" the result.

Cage's conclusion is of course not the only one that can be drawn from the current state of music; and it is one that most composers (not to mention listeners) have rejected. Yet recent compositional developments in general, though by and large following a different course from the one taken by Cage, have reflected the new musical landscape with almost equal, if less pointed, clarity. Especially telling is the extraordinary eclecticism of recent music, surely its single most characteristic feature, which far exceeds anything previously known in Western music (including that of the first half of the present century). Recent music exhibits a range of stylistic and technical attributes that would be unimaginable if there were a common language underlying compositional practice. The absence of such a language has set composers free (or condemned them, as Sartre might have said) to make any choice they wish. And they often do so seemingly by whim, following a meandering course that, though producing quite different musical results, recalls Cage in its inconstancy and apparent willfulness.

The ubiquity of borrowing—making use of musical materials not actually one's "own"—is another telling sign. It takes many different forms. When quotation first emerged as a central compositional practice during the 1960s, the preferred source was tonal music of the common-practice period. The third movement of Luciano Berio's *Sinfonia* and Lucas Foss's *Phorion*, to name two of the most influential works of the time, draw upon Mahler and Bach respectively, subjecting the music to a range of post-tonal compositional procedures (including, in Berio's case, juxtaposition with quotations from other composers and periods). Traditional materials are thus treated according to the willed methods of post-tonal practice; the language of tonality is appropriated to represent its own dissolution.

This is especially evident in the Foss work, where the music of Bach (the Preludio from the E-major partita for unaccompanied violin) seems literally to come apart before the listener's ears, increasingly dissolved until it ultimately disappears entirely into the cacophonous din that brings the piece to an end. Taking its own musical past as content, *Phorion* faithfully retraces the historical evolution of Western music from integrated language to mechanistic construct.

The fascination with quotation, after attracting virtually every major composer of the late 1960s and 1970s (at least the younger ones), has largely subsided. But as a symptom of a new stage in musical evolution in which composers, having reached an acute awareness of the lack of native language, look "elsewhere" for points of departure, quotation proved to be remarkably prophetic. It has given way to an entirely new kind of musical culture, still in the making, that exhibits a pervasive and unfocused pluralism and in which the borrowings, though usually less literal than before, encompass a vastly wider range of sources. Cut free from a base of their own, composers appropriate whatever they want from whatever cultures they wish (often greatly distant in time or space). Current music thus makes open reference to the "other"—to earlier historical styles, popular and folk music, non-Western music, etc.; and more often than not, it mixes what it has borrowed so as to underscore the essentially foreign nature of the material.

To take a notion from recent literary theory, the "language" (if one may still use this term) of current music contains a "surplus of signifiers": it is full of evident designations that have no apparent referents. (Translated into musical-analytical terms, from the work of Leonard B. Meyer, it is full of implications that have no evident realizations.) There are no necessary "signifieds," only a seemingly unlimited play of references. Consequently, anything can be combined with anything else. Previously distinct musical cultures and subcultures become difficult to distinguish from one another, as does the musical present from the musical past.[3]

꜒

Contemporary music reflects historical changes of such overwhelming proportion that we are only beginning to be aware of their implications for such matters as our canonic assumptions. Since these assumptions were in the past firmly tied to a linguistic base, the uprooting of that base has had profound consequences. Take the matter of "repertories." The eclecticism that currently characterizes the musical scene is not confined to the specialized world of new music but extends to the concert world in general and to all media of musical dissemination, including radio and television. The volume and variety of music presented to the public today is unprecedented. The repertories of even such traditionally oriented institutions as symphony orchestras and opera houses are much more diverse than they were even a quarter of a century ago, and they encompass not only what we still somewhat anachronistically call the "classics," but also recent music, older music, and an ever broader sampling of secondary composers of the common-practice period.

Even more indicative than the chronological range is the variety of aesthetic (not to mention social and political) assumptions this repertory embraces. If one accepts the fact that a recent composition by John Cage represents something fundamentally different from one by Bach, Beethoven, or Tchaikovsky, or even by Webern, Ives, or Machaut (as surely one must, since Cage's work is designed to show the irrelevance of all such music), then there is something fundamentally different about a musical culture that supports the appearance of his compositions on its symphony-orchestra programs. Similarly, major opera houses throughout the world compete for performances of Philip Glass's most recent ritualistic ceremony, despite the fact that Glass's stage works stretch the conventions of the operatic genre to the breaking point (though seemingly less so with each new work). Our idea of symphonic and operatic repertory has expanded dramatically to allow for such a wide range of possibilities; and we are experiencing only the early phases of what promises to be an ongoing development.

New musical configurations are even more apparent in the mass media.

Radio and recordings now provide easy, instantaneous access to a world-wide compass of "musics," including a full range of Western art music from the medieval period to the latest generation of contemporary composers, a generous sampling of non-Western art music, and folk music and popular music from throughout the world. This ready availability has markedly increased the types of music about which we have direct (if not firsthand) knowledge and has made us "literate" (if not "native speakers") within a range of musical languages inconceivable even a short time ago.

This growing knowledge of such a wealth of different music has contributed essentially to the pluralistic cast of contemporary musical life, and it has altered—and continues to alter—our conception of musical culture in fundamental ways. Indeed, contemporary musical culture is fast becoming not a single, relatively focused entity, but a melange of conflicting subcultures that interact with one another in complex ways while still preserving considerable autonomy. These subcultures, moreover, cannot be viewed simply as satellites of a central culture; taken collectively, they are coming to constitute that culture themselves. Earlier music (more often than not performed on original instruments), to take one example, increasingly rivals traditional symphonic music in importance. Similarly, as I have suggested, contemporary compositional style is most readily defined by an absence of unified style. The appropriate image for the current musical scene is no longer Tovey's "mainstream," fed by various tributaries; the tributaries have progressively taken over the main body, until the primary channel has become almost unrecognizable.

The inevitable consequence of the loss of a central musical language is that music speaks in many different tongues. Some of us may know several of these; but the more of them we know, the less fluently we speak and understand them. More importantly, we no longer have the ability to speak any musical language as natives. Within today's musical culture, all languages are more or less acquired, and to that extent artificial and foreign. They can therefore be exchanged and combined, and new ones invented, at will.

Although there has always been room for some degree of choice in Western music, never has the range of possibilities been so great as now. This stems not so much from the absence of a single constraining compositional system, something we have been living with for some three-quarters of a century, as from the much more recent acknowledgement that a new, comparable system is unlikely to emerge. This is perhaps the single most telling factor affecting the state of music today.

It would be an oversimplification, however, to say that the nature of the contemporary musical scene is explained in any comprehensive sense by the loss of tonality and subsequent absence of a common musical language. To do so would beg the more fundamental questions of why functional tonality has become part of history—still available for anyone who wishes to use it but no longer present as an unavoidable component of musical experience; and why it has not been replaced by a new common language. The answers are obviously not to be discovered exclusively in the changing complexion of music itself but must be sought in the transformations that have shaped the world at large, in which contemporary music has made its place. The loss of a central musical language is merely one symptom—though certainly a vivid and symbolically resonant one—of the increasing individualization and isolation of human experience in general. Our fragmented and dissociated manner of life, reflecting the loss of an encompassing social framework capable of ordering and integrating the varied facets of human activity, has received its faithful expression in the autonomy and particularization of the musical composition. The Western musical work, having since the Renaissance progressively severed its connections with "outside" institutions—first the Church and then various centralized political agencies (monarchical, aristocratic, and democratic)—now proclaims its isolation and independence from other musical compositions as well.[4]

Viewed in this wider context, the seemingly confused and directionless quality of recent music acquires a degree of focus. The plurality of styles, techniques, and levels of expression appears both plausible and meaningful in a world increasingly shedding its common beliefs and shared customs, where there is no longer a single given "reality" but only shifting, multiple realities, provisionally constructed out of the unconnected bits and pieces set loose by a world stripped of all attachments. If traditional tonality—with its highly developed notion of a musical "center," a focus according to which all pitches orient themselves—adequately reflected a culture characterized by a community of purpose and well-developed system of social order and interpersonal regulation, its loss, and the musical atomization that has ensued, reflects a fragmented and defamiliarized world of isolated events and abrupt confrontations where—as Yeats said some seventy years ago—"things fall apart; the centre cannot hold."

The traditional concept of culture as a unified complex of elements that work together to create an integrated, homogeneous whole has thus been abandoned in favor of one allowing for high levels of diversity and instability.

Culture is no longer perceived as a consistent order but as something in motion that focuses only momentarily, and diversely, to provide temporary frameworks. It is increasingly understood to be, in the words of anthropologist James Clifford, a "collective fiction." Referring to Mikhail Bakhtin's analysis of the "polyphonic" novel, cited for its "ethnographic"—i.e., relativistic and intentionalist—conception of language, Clifford remarks in terms especially relevant for the present discussion:

> For Bakhtin, preoccupied with the representation of non-homogeneous wholes, there are no integrated cultural worlds or languages. All attempts to posit such abstract unities are constructs of monological power. A "culture" is, concretely, an open-ended, creative dialogue of subcultures, of insiders and outsiders, of diverse factions. A "language" is the interplay and struggle of regional dialects, professional jargons, generic commonplaces, the speech of different age groups, individuals, and so forth. (Clifford 1988:46)

The artistic consequences of this new concept of culture were accurately described by Leonard B. Meyer some quarter century ago, when he characterized the contemporary period as one of "fluctuating stasis . . . a steady-state in which an indefinite number of styles and idioms, techniques and movements, will coexist in each of the arts" (Meyer 1967:172). Subsequent developments have only confirmed Meyer's view. Musical composition has increasingly become a matter of making selections from a sort of imaginary catalogue of unlimited musical items, capable of being fitted together at will in ever-changing configurations. The works that result are—to borrow Peter Burkholder's suggestive description—"museum pieces" (Burkholder 1983), but in a rather different sense from the one Burkholder had in mind in speaking (mainly) of the music of a somewhat earlier period: they are motley collections of cultural artifacts, including texts, styles, mannerisms, and conceits, acquired from a broad range of historical periods and geographical locations.

❧

No doubt this description of the current musical scene sounds pejorative in the extreme—and is so if that scene is measured by traditional notions of a unified cultural consensus founded on timeless virtues, giving birth to polished, "organic" works of art. Yet there is much to be said in its favor. It has enabled us to question the hegemony of a relatively small and limited body of music in setting absolute standards of acceptability. And it has enabled us to look anew at neglected repertories, indeed whole cultures of "other" music, previously relegated to the periphery and tolerated—if at all—as merely exotic seasonings enhancing an undisputed central tradition.

Now other traditions, often performance-oriented rather than text-based, are coming into their own. No longer measured against an absolute standard of "high" art, they participate on essentially equal terms, as full partners within an encompassing cultural mix. Indeed, if anything, Western art music now tends to be measured against folk, popular, and non-Western traditions (and more often than not found woefully deficient). This reflects the growing democratization of an ever more heterogeneous society, within which various minorities compete for equal status, demanding their own say in their own terms. Unified systems and hierarchies are distrusted, both on the level of political action and on that of artistic expression.

How does one orient oneself in such a free-flowing, unstable environment? Recent musical developments have not only altered our understanding of musical repertory but, as a consequence, significantly undermined the closely related belief in a canonic body of musical texts, invested with authority to provide standards for compositional practice. At first glance, it might appear that these developments have rendered obsolete the very notion of canonicity. Given the current musical situation, it is surely pointless and misguided (not to mention hopeless) to try to preserve a conception of canon closely corresponding to the traditional one. For how can absolute standards be maintained, and what would they represent if they could be (by fiat, say), when there is absolutely no broad consensus on what such standards ought to be? Perhaps the most reasonable response is a laissez-faire attitude: leave everyone to their own devices, each to do his or her thing, as the current saying symptomatically puts it.

This attitude has in fact gained considerable currency; and it is easy to understand its appeal, even to sympathize with its attractions, given the prevailing cultural flux. It proposes that the canon be opened up and enlarged, made more inclusive so as to encompass the varied types of music that intersect in present experience. Yet if this attitude is followed consequentially, the whole idea of canon is quickly eroded. For what does it mean to speak of a canon in which there is room for essentially everything? A canon is by nature exclusive as well as inclusive; it not only channels possibilities, it also sets limitations.

When all music becomes equally acceptable, then all standards become equally irrelevant. We are left in a world where, since everything is valued, nothing has particular value. Surely no culture before ours has ever adopted a position in which any musical activity at all is considered equally worthy of acceptance—or, what amounts to the same, in which no particular kind of musical activity is considered of sufficient value to serve as a model for emulation (and thus also exclusion).

If we are in the process of redefining our concept of culture, rather than doing away with it entirely, then the idea of canonicity will have to be preserved. In light of current musical developments, the canon as we have known it certainly requires demystification (a much-favored word in this connection), to be made more responsive to temporary differences in taste, to ethnic diversity, to considerations of gender, etc.; but it need not—and should not—be entirely abandoned.

What is required, then, is not one amorphous, all-encompassing canon but a set of multiple canons that, taken individually, are relatively precise in delineation. Of course such canons would frequently work at cross-purposes with one another; but they would also, and one hopes equally frequently, intersect in complex and fruitful ways. While this arrangement would allow for alternative canonic models for alternative subcultures, it would preserve the core of the notion of canonic authority. It would (to return once more to the notion of musical language) acknowledge a multilingual framework within which different subgroups speak different tongues, but in which any given tongue retains some sense of grammatical norm. Many musicians would speak several of these languages, perhaps not with equal ease but nevertheless with considerable fluency, and would quite likely mix them in polyglot combinations. And virtually everyone would understand, to some degree, more than one language. But no one would have full command of them all, and there would be no absolute arbiter controlling them all. Ideally, this framework would produce a culture of tolerance and broad understanding, but one in which differences still mattered and standards of excellence still applied.

Under such circumstances a pluralistic musical culture could flourish, offering adequate provisions for different and divergent lines of development; yet a place would be preserved for valuative criteria. The latter would not be immutable laws, of course, but would vary with time (as has always been the case, to a degree, with canonic standards); nor would they be universally applicable, but would apply to only certain types of music. Such criteria would above all have to shed their idealistic tinge, in acknowledging their status as pragmatically conceived constructs intended for specific contexts and limited purposes. As a basis for judging what music one values and finds worthy of cultivation, they would nevertheless fulfill a critical function.

Although it would be impractical, faced with the current musical land-scape, to try to maintain the canon as formerly conceived, it would be self-destructive to drop it entirely. Rather than being jettisoned, traditional canonic assumptions need to be rethought fundamentally in light of present-day musical and cultural pluralities. A multicanonic structure, though it may strike some as a middle-of-the-road accommodation (if not self-contradictory), seems the most realistic response to a world that we have on the one hand inherited (characterized by well-entrenched beliefs in tradi-tion and continuity) and on the other significantly reshaped in our own less certain image.

The question of the composition of such a multicanonic structure, of its actual constitution, is beyond the scope of this article and is, in any event, inherently resistant to precise and detailed formulation. Since a multicanon would involve many different types of music and would change complexion in response to different musical contexts, it could not be tied down in any authoritative way. Ultimately such a multicanon would perhaps be the re-flection more of a particular mental disposition, directed toward composi-tional excellence within infinitely variable contexts, than of a particular body of canonic masterpieces, or even of a set of general aesthetic and tech-nical principles.

The adherence to some such notion of canonic excellence, however elu-sive and loosely defined it may have to be, nevertheless seems imperative. There is without question a lot of good music still to be written; and one must not give up entirely the concept of "good," simply because it has lost its aura of universality. In any event, the aura was always only that.

Notes

1. This "linguistic" conception of canon is not peculiar to music but lies at the basis of any synoptic view of a universal cultural order. Though so fundamental as to be normally unspoken, it is not always so. In his essay "What Is a Classic?" T. S. Eliot places his conception of a central Western tradition firmly on a linguistic—as well as political and religious—foundation: "The Roman Empire and the Latin language were not any empire and any language, but an empire and a language with a unique destiny to ourselves; and the poet in whom that Empire and that language came to consciousness and expression is a poet of unique destiny." For Eliot this poet is Virgil, who, as a result of his "unique position in our history of the Roman Empire and the Latin language," has acquired "the centrality of the unique classic; he is at the centre of European civilization." But Eliot also takes pains to accommodate the stylistic and linguistic variety that has characterized post-Renaissance art in the West. He thus em-phasizes the vitality of vernaculars, while stressing that they acquire larger significance only through their associations with the Latin past, through "[their] place in a larger pattern, a pattern set in Rome." To be broadly comprehensible "local traditions" must

partake in a "common European tradition." There is thus a give-and-take between what is permanent, immune to momentary fashion, and what is transitory, responsive to changing historical contexts and shifting local conditions. Without a measure of the former, the work becomes "provincial"; without the latter, it lacks vitality and force (see Eliot 1957:53–71).

2. These compositional conditions are discussed further in Nyman 1974.

3. The evocation of literary theory raises the question of the degree to which what is being said about musical language here mirrors what literary critics, notably deconstructionists, have recently been saying about verbal language. They too have emphasized the arbitrary nature of linguistic signs and thus the purely subjective and unstable character of verbal meaning. But there is an important difference. Here the point is made with reference to a specific historical context—the breakdown of traditional tonality and its aftermath—whereas there it is applied to language in general. Of course it is possible, as some music theorists and critics are beginning to do, to subject the language of common-practice tonality to a "deconstructionist" analysis in an effort to show that here too the "grammatical rules" are purely conventional in nature and thus must ultimately be considered arbitrary and illusory. Even if accomplished, however, this would in no way affect how the contemporary composers themselves, and their listeners, conceived of musical language during the common-practice period—namely, their acceptance of the conventions of common-practice tonality as a lingua franca. And this point is essential in the present argument.

4. For a discussion of similar issues with particular reference to current concerns for "authenticity" in musical performance, see Morgan 1988.

Works Cited

Burkholder, Peter. 1983. "Museum Pieces: The Historicist Mainstream in Music of the Last Hundred Years." *Journal of Musicology* 25, no. 2:115–134.

Busoni, Ferruccio. 1962. "Sketch of a New Esthetic of Music." In Theodore Baker, trans., *Three Classics in the Aesthetics of Music.* New York: Dover.

Cage, John. 1961a. "Composition as Process." In *Silence,* 18–56. Middletown, Conn.: Wesleyan University Press.

——— 1961b. "Experimental Music." in *Silence,* 7–12. Middletown, Conn.: Wesleyan University Press.

Clifford, James. 1988. *The Predicament of Culture: Twentieth-Century Ethnography, Literature, and Art.* Cambridge, Mass.: Harvard University Press.

Eliot, T. S. 1957. *On Poetry and Poets.* New York: Farrar, Straus and Cudahy.

Kerman, Joseph. 1983. "A Few Canonic Variations." *Critical Inquiry* 10, no. 1:107–25.

Meyer, Leonard B. 1967. *Music, the Arts, and Ideas.* Chicago: University of Chicago Press.

Morgan, Robert P. 1988. "Tradition, Anxiety, and the Current Musical Scene." In Nicholas Kenyon, ed., *Authenticity and Early Music: A Symposium,* 57–82. Oxford: Oxford University Press.

Nyman, Michael. 1974. *Experimental Music: Cage and Beyond.* New York: Schirmer.

Slonimsky, Nicolas, ed. 1971. *Music Since 1900.* New York: Charles Scribner's Sons.

FIVE

Cultural Dialogics and Jazz:
A White Historian Signifies
Gary Tomlinson

Free of the white person's gaze, black people created their own unique
vernacular structures and relished in the double play that these forms
bore to white forms. Repetition and revision are fundamental to black
artistic forms, from painting and sculpture to music and language use. I
decided to analyze the nature and function of Signifyin(g) precisely because it *is* repetition and revision, or repetition with a signal difference.
Whatever is black about black American literature is to be found in this
identifiable black Signifyin(g) difference. That, most succinctly if ambig-
uously, describes the premise of this book. Lest this theory of criticism,
however, be thought of as only black, let me admit that the implicit
premise of this study is that all texts Signify upon other texts. . . . Perhaps critics of other literatures will find this theory useful as they attempt
to account for the configurations of the texts in their traditions.

Anyone who analyzes black literature must do so as a comparativist, by
definition, because our canonical texts have complex double formal antecedents, the Western and the black.

Signifyin(g) is the figure of the double-voiced.

The Signifying Monkey . . . seems to dwell in [the] space between two
linguistic domains.

(Gates 1988:xxiv–xxv, 105)

"Signifyin(g)" operates at three levels of increasing generalization and
importance in Henry Louis Gates, Jr.'s *The Signifying Monkey: A Theory of
African-American Literary Criticism*. It is a theme in certain African-American

This essay originally appeared in a somewhat longer version in *Black Music Research
Journal* 11, no. 2 (1991), published by the Center for Black Music Research, Columbia College, Chicago. Many people helped with the conceiving and writing of it,
among whom I would particularly like to thank Houston Baker, Jeffrey Kallberg,
Ronald Radano, and the cicerone of my jazz studies, Ralph Rosen.

literary works, a set of rhetorical strategies pervasively embodied in black American discourse, whether informal or formal, and "an indigenous black metaphor for intertextuality" all told (p. 59), a trope by which to represent black literary culture's vernacular theorizing of itself. In setting out to Signify on Gates and other recent theorists of African-American literature, I certainly do not presume to have expertise in the thematics of that literary tradition; neither do I pretend to deep insight into indigenous black rhetorics. Rather, I accept Gates's implicit invitation, in the first epigraph above, to gauge from a vernacular situation different from his the usefulness of his critical theory (and by extension that of other recent African-American theorizing). My Signifyin(g) and the theorizing that results from it will manifest my own vernacular as it intersects with other vernaculars. I make no presumptuous claim to blackness in my presentation, but at the same time, as will soon become apparent, I do not undervalue the potential dialogical richness of my interlocutions with African-American culture from a position outside it. The two most general aims of my Signifyin(g) will be to outline the ways in which Gates's and other black observers' theorizing defines with compelling clarity issues crucial to the whole realm of postmodern theorizing in the human sciences and to suggest the profits offered by theories like Gates's to students of black musical traditions, specifically jazz.

In informal black discourse Signifyin(g) connotes a variety of ways of speaking and interacting characterized by irony, parody, needling, and trickery. It is not a particular subject matter but rather a group of related rhetorical practices that might be employed across many subjects. Similarly, the Signifying Monkey, the archetypal Signifier in African-American oral tradition, is not "engaged in the game of information-giving," as Gates says, so much as he is involved in the manipulation and mediation of others' information. Thus "one is signified upon by the signifier"; or again, "one does not signify something; rather, one signifies in *some way*" (pp. 52–54).

Gates's emphasis on Signifyin(g) as a mediating strategy for discourse implies its interaction with things signified, its position between or among texts. This in turn leads him to employ it generally as a trope of repetition and revision. Signifyin(g) represents, then, an engagement with preceding texts so as to "create a space" for one's own. This clearing of new space takes place by means of "riffing upon [the] tropes" of the received tradition, that is, by a restating and altering of the tropes of earlier texts that reshapes, in the very act of enabling a text, our conception of the tradition in which these texts occur (p. 124). In Gates's own case, the trope that he riffs on is Signifyin(g) itself, as it is embodied thematically and rhetorically in various earlier manifestations of black expressive culture. He dramatically enlarges on this trope, expanding it into a trope-of-tropes that is rooted in pan-African discursive mythologies, arches over the whole of African-American discourse, and, in some loose sense, guides the unfolding interrelations and transformations of this discourse. So Gates's theory of African-American criticism is, first of all, a *tropological* one, to borrow Hayden White's term.

By singling out and analyzing his trope-of-tropes Gates aims to uncover the guiding principles beneath the visible surface of the African-American literary tradition. Signifyin(g) is for him "the black rhetorical difference that negotiates the language user through several orders of meaning" (p. 79). It represents, in other words, a set of (mainly preconscious) rules of formation that have shaped African-American discourse. The terms I use here are, not accidentally, Foucault's; for in its search for the formative premises of black discourse Gates's theory is not only tropological but *archaeological* as well.

My own riffing on Gates's trope of Signification will stress a third essential aspect of his theory, one somewhat underemphasized, I think, in *The Signifying Monkey:* its *dialogical* aspect. As a figure of intertextuality and repetition-with-difference, Signifyin(g) is necessarily also a figure of dialogue. It is a trope of mediation between or among texts or languages. Or, more precisely, it is a figure representing the strategies by which a text or voice finds its place between (among) differing discourses. Thus we may affirm with Gates that Signification is a double- or multi-voiced figure and that its archetypal master in African-American folklore, the Signifying Monkey, inhabits the space between linguistic domains. But language itself is also betwixt and between; "it lies between oneself and the other," in famous words of Mikhail Bakhtin that Gates quotes as an epigraph for his book. So Signification comes to represent the linguistic process by which we traverse the space between self and other or, better, by which we locate meaning in that space. Signifyin(g) aims to subdue momentarily Bakhtin's heteroglossia, the unruly tugging at our words by the multiple forces and contexts surrounding them, in order temporarily to fix meaning. Signifyin(g) is an African-American mode of what Bakhtin called "dialogism."

This dialogical essence is signaled in the concept of vernacular theory. Vernacular thought emphasizes its own boundaries, its own range of authority and territorial claims, in counterpoint with other theoretical domains. Because of this, vernacularism is a mode of thought that attempts, in contrast to transcendentalism, universalism, and essentialism, *to theorize the space between itself and others*—to keep sight, so to speak, of the other modes of thought around it by keeping them above its horizon. In the case of Gates's theory of black expressive culture, Signification represents on the most general plane the linguistic mediation between black vernacular(s) and the discourse(s) of white hegemonic culture. It constitutes a compelling theoretical formulation of the means by which blacks mediated between themselves and dominant others. But the struggle toward this mediation is common to all communication (even if it is often found in less abusive structures of power than those that have typically existed between American blacks and whites); so Signification illumines from Gates's particular perspective the heteroglot situation in which all utterance seeks its meaning. All theories, whether or not they own up to the fact, are formulated in the midst of this dialogical predicament. All theories are vernacular theories.

Tropology and Archaeology

Tropological thought is a discursive mode that employs unfamiliar (or exotic) figures to qualify what is deemed "traditional" in a given discourse. To extrapolate from [Hayden] White, one might assert that attempts to signify the force of meaning of the economics of slavery by invoking . . . *blues* . . . constitute an analytical move designed to incorporate into reality phenomena to which traditional historiography generally denies the status "real." The end of a tropological enterprise is the alteration of reality itself.

Models, or tropes, are continually invoked to constitute and explain phenomena inaccessible to the senses. Any single model, or any complementary set of inventive tropes, . . . will offer a selective account of experience—a partial reading, as it were, of the world. While the single account temporarily reduces chaos to ordered plan, all such accounts are eternally troubled by "remainders."

(Baker 1984:28, 9–10)

Naming the black tradition's own theory of itself is to echo and rename other theories of literary criticism. Our task is not to reinvent our traditions as if they bore no relation to that tradition created and borne, in the main, by white men. . . . To name our tradition is to rename each of its antecedents, no matter how pale they might seem. To rename is to revise, and to revise is to Signify.

(Gates 1988:xxiii)

The source of the merger evident in Gates's *Signifying Monkey* of White's tropology, Foucault's archaeology, and African-American theories of expressive culture is Houston A. Baker's *Blues, Ideology, and Afro-American Literature: A Vernacular Theory.* Gates is frank about his indebtedness to Baker. From an advocate of the view that Western, white criticism had to be mastered by African-American critics and then applied to their own traditions, Gates has been converted, mainly by Baker's reasoning, into a most eloquent spokesperson for indigenous black theory; he has refashioned himself from a universal into a vernacular theorist (see Gates 1985:13; also Gates 1988:x). Baker, for his part, traces his intellectual roots to the Black Aesthetic movement of the 1960s and 1970s (see Baker 1984: chap. 2). His revision of the philosophies of that movement into a distinctive theory of vernacular theorizing, which he accomplished in the early 1980s, depended most importantly on his assimilation of the metatheoretical strategies of tropology and archaeology.

Tropological knowledge functions for Baker as a way of remaking reality by juxtaposing the familiar with the unfamiliar. By joining, through imaginative intellectual play, ostensibly well-mapped traditions with unanticipated images or figures—tropes—it "effectively disrupt[s] familiar conceptual determinations" (1984:110), bringing about a sort of global defamiliarization of what-we-know. It functions, we might say, as metaphor writ large, blown up to the dimensions of an epistemological challenge. The new conceptual landscape it creates incorporates previously unreal things into our cognitive reality (and perhaps dismisses previously real things from it); it reconfigures the exclusionary boundaries of our perceptions. In the process it brings home to us the contingent, impermanent nature of those boundaries and, as Baker says, introduces an essential uncertainty into cultural explanation (pp. 9–10).

Both Gates's Signifyin(g) and Baker's blues function in this way. Signifyin(g) alters our view of African-American expressive traditions, bringing into sharp focus the brilliant and original riffing of one text on another that characterizes those traditions and diverting our attention from "the mimetic representation of novel content," an evaluative category often overemphasized by conventional theory (Gates 1988:79). For Baker the blues is a matrix through which African-Americans transmute the "obdurate 'economics of slavery'" into moments of "resonant, improvisational, expressive dignity" (1984:13). Each of these tropes is an overarching figure that brings into the realm of theory manifestations of African-American expressive culture that are usually excluded by Eurocentric theorizing: the blues themselves, rap, the dozens, Signifying Monkey stories, the play of chains of signifiers, and so on.

By incorporating such cultural acts into a theoretical reality, these tropes also restructure everything else in that reality; this is, perhaps, the most resonant effect of tropology. Gates conceives of this effect as a meta-example of Signifyin(g): by naming the black tradition from within itself we revise and rename all the other traditions with which it (and its vernacular theory) interacts. From Baker's point of view we might state the matter somewhat differently: by truly perceiving the selectivity of our tropological models of the world we become not only more comprehending of the things embraced by our tropes but more cognizant of the things excluded from them. Tropology provides new models of reality. But at the same time it asserts the partiality of those models and refuses to let us ignore the cultural "remainders" standing outside them. In this it functions much like the shifting organizations of knowledge unearthed by Foucauldian archaeology.

> The goal of the archaeology of knowledge as project is to advance the human sciences beyond a traditional humanism, focusing scholarly attention on the discursive constitution and arbitrary figurations of bodies of knowledge rather than on the constitution and situation of human subjects (traditional concerns of humanism).
>
> Epistemological cataclysms in historical discourse bring to view dimensions of experience excluded from extant accounts. And in the reordering effected by such ruptures (i.e., their constitution of revised models), one discovers not only new historical terms but also the variant historicity of the statements and terms of a traditional discourse.
>
> (Baker 1984:17, 60–61)

> Identity and alterity are always . . . expressed or silenced according to personal desires vis-à-vis an *episteme*.
>
> Foucault seems to be an unhappy "historian of the Same." . . . [A]s an unbelieving historian, he "rewrites" the ambiguous passion of knowledge. All his books provide good examples of this exercise, which brings to light the long, difficult, and permanent struggle of the Same and the Other. By promoting a critical archaeology of knowledge, not only does he separate himself from a history but also from its classical presuppositions, which lead to and serve the arrogance of the Same. . . . Foucault's horizon is, one might say, a relativization of the truth of the Same in the dispersion of history; in other words "a decentralizing that leaves no privilege to any center."
>
> In effect, the invention of an African history coincides with a critical evaluation of the history of the Same.
>
> (Mudimbe 1988:xi, 34, 177)

Archaeology yields knowledge of the laws that govern the formation of discourses. It isolates, as Foucault put it in *The Order of Things*, "rules of formation, which were never formulated in their own right, but are to be found only in widely differing theories, concepts, and objects of study" (1973:xi). Archaeology diverts our attention from the what-was-said of particular thinking and speaking subjects in specific historical situations to the preconceptions that enabled such things to be spoken or thought in such situations in the first place. It exposes the ideological preconditions that have guided conceptualizations and expressions of the world and reveals the contingent and arbitrary nature of both those preconditions and the bodies of knowledge founded on them.

The radical force of Foucauldian archaeology resides in this revelation. For in revealing how the ordering of knowledge depends on deeper rules, archaeology simultaneously discovers the partiality of that knowledge. This is the "decentralizing that leaves no privilege to any center" that V. Y. Mudimbe cites in his subtle analysis of African and Western conceptions of Africa, *The Invention of Africa: Gnosis, Philosophy, and the Order of Knowledge* (see Foucault 1972:205). In the archaeological region of knowledge, to return to *The Order of Things*, "a culture, imperceptibly deviating from the empirical orders prescribed for it by its primary codes, instituting an initial separation from them, causes them to lose their original transparency, relinquishes its immediate and invisible powers, frees itself sufficiently to discover that these orders are perhaps not the only possible ones or the best ones" (1973:xx). The visibility of the orders prescribed by primary codes, their loss of transparency, reveals their partial and contingent natures.

Because of this contingency, the archaeology of knowledge broaches at the deepest level the problem of otherness. The ruptures between Foucault's *epistemes*, what Baker calls "epistemological cataclysms," call into question the stability of all *epistemes*; they point up the multiplicity of *epistemes* and thus bring to light the otherness of differing models of reality, the "variant historicity" that others (or even we ourselves in another situation) have created. They destabilize truth and reveal its contingency by dispersing knowledge across the history of discourse, as Mudimbe might say.

Foucault saw this and was as a result "an unhappy historian of the Same." The history of ideas that he took pains to differentiate from his archaeological analysis was for him tautological in its inability to move behind the writers and *oeuvres* that constituted its object to their (or its own) governing discursive formations. In focusing on these works and authors, Foucault wrote in *The Archaeology of Knowledge*, the conventional history of ideas "set out to recapture that elusive nucleus . . . in which thought still remains nearest to oneself, in the as yet unaltered form of the same, and in which language . . . has not yet been deployed in the spatial, successive dispersion of discourse" (1972:139). Nonarchaeological historical analysis tends not to distance itself from its object or from the hegemony of the knowing subject that makes that object. It sees only dimly beneath its own customary ways of thinking and speaking and hence is hard pressed to bear witness to their selectivity and contingency.

Tropology appears, then, on the surface of the archaeological project as a source of leverage, a powerful tool for prying away layers of thought and action to reveal the discursive structures underneath. "The effective trope," Baker writes, "is merely the lever long enough for the purpose" (1984:110). Tropology is a tool and archaeology a method for building contingent, local histories that include an awareness of the alternative histories on their horizons. Thus, to paraphrase Mudimbe, the appearance of a truly African history has had to await the archaeological and tropological critique of the Euro-American history of the same. In more general terms, vernacular theories of culture themselves have had to await this critique. And, in Baker's echoing words, "the magnificent appearance of America's blues people" has had to await "the relinquishing of a self-certainty that strives to annul 'otherness' and to masterfully fix its own place" (p. 202).

In the African and African-American discourses of writers like Mudimbe and Baker, conventional histories that have posed as histories of the same are shown to be histories of the other. Baker even speaks of "a Foucaultian 'rupture' . . . between traditional American history and literary theory and an alternative Afro-American discourse" (p. 57), though this may be saying too much: it seems to me that the new discourse of African-American theory does not so much reflect an epistemic shift away from other theory as it performs, alongside other alternative theoretical discourses offered in recent years, an archaeological exposé of conventional academic critical theory in general. African-American theory is one major variety of recent theorizing, in other words, that has urged us to recognize the vernacular selectivity of all theory in the human sciences. (We might say, to be whimsical, that theory's vernacularism is its only universal aspect.) This recognition of theory's vernacular partiality brings with it an awareness of the multiplicity of individual theories, of the existence of other modes of conceiving the world. And this leads us to scrutinize the dialogical situation between alternative theories, histories, and even discourses in which knowledge is born. "What one gets," Mudimbe says, "is . . . a decisive critique of traditional methods of correlating the Same to the Other" (1988:199).

Difference and Dialogue

Afro-American intellectual history is characterized by engagement in the senses of being committed *and* interlocutory. . . . A negotiation between two traditions—the hegemonic and the non-hegemonic— that results in a change for both . . . constitutes an emerging consensus in poststructuralist Afro-American criticism. We can no longer regard either Afro-American literature or criticism as separate and disengaged from other literary-critical discourses. Nor, I might add, can other literary-critical discourses any longer be considered in isolation from Afro-American discourse.

Part of the commitment of the black feminist project . . . is the privileging of difference. It is, after all, the rhetoric of universality that has excluded gender, race, and class perspectives from the dominant literary-critical discourse as well as the socio-political centers of power. It is the reduction of multiplicity to undifferentiated sameness that has empowered white feminists to speak for all women, black men to speak for all blacks, and white males to speak for everyone. What I propose is a multiplicity of "interested readings" which resists the totalizing character of much theory and criticism—readings that can enter into dialogic relationship with other "interested readings"—past and present.

Our literary history speaks to dialogue and debate among various and competing critical camps.

(Henderson 1989:156, 162–63)

Just as the self is fluid, dynamic, and formed in relation, so is identification a process involving a dialogue between the self and the "otherness" of writers, texts, literary characters, and interpretive communities.

(McDowell 1989:69–70)

It has no doubt always been true, but is particularly pressingly so in today's postmodern "global village," that discourses are created and evolve in dialogue with other discourses. But a discourse (or theory, or model, or way of speaking and writing the world) that will retain the memory of its own partiality, one that will not soon stake the customary illegitimate claims to universality, must maintain its dialogue with the others at its horizon. So if it is true, as Derrida suggests, that we must learn "to speak the other's language without renouncing [our] own" (1985:294), it is likewise imperative that we learn our own language without in the process renouncing others. Dialogical knowledge consists in this precarious maneuver of clearing space and building in it a discourse that never pushes other ways of knowing beyond its own horizon.

As Mae G. Henderson argues, this is the ambivalent situation in which African-American literary theory finds itself, and its predicament again brightly mirrors the too-little-avowed situation of all theorizing. African-American theory has needed to enunciate clearly this situation in part because it has been a discourse shouldering for space among hegemonic, mainly white discourses. It is especially significant that the African-American voices calling loudest for this dialogical view—for what Henderson describes as a "dialogic engagement with the various and multiple discourses of the other(s)" (1989:157)—seem to be women's voices, for they have been doubly marginalized, by ethnic origin and by gender. Thus the black feminist project has been especially intent upon privileging difference, diversity, and otherness.

This privileging movement brings with it a compulsion to dialogue. But there is a danger in the dialogical stance—a danger feminists are well aware of. Its resolute differentiation of self and other can be distorted into a precisely nondialogical cult of otherness that can serve to reinstate the subjugation of others. The attempted dialogue can become illusory; it can collapse into a monologue of empowered speakers speaking with themselves about marginalized and excluded others. Monologue can wear the mask of dialogue.

A way of easing this danger has been sketched by Deborah E. McDowell in her essay "Boundaries: Or Distant Relations and Close Kin." McDowell suggests that a truly "dialogical critical practice" will need to start from a deconstruction of the absolute, clearly bounded self of Western metaphysics and its unblurred distinction from others. In this project the self will be seen to be "formed in relation to and dialogue with others" (1989:56), to be "multiple, fluid, relational, and in a perpetual state of becoming" (p. 61). With the boundaries between self and other weakened, we will discover that otherness is a dialogical component within as well as outside us, "that we are always one and the other at the same time" (p. 60).

The echo of post-Heideggerian hermeneutics, especially the theory of Paul Ricoeur, resounds here. Indeed, already in 1955 Ricoeur issued a challenge to the Western self to remake itself in relation to others. Ricoeur's words, quoted by Mudimbe (1988:20–21), are worth repeating: "When we discover that there are several cultures instead of just one and . . . when we acknowledge the end of a sort of cultural monopoly, be it illusory or real, we are threatened with destruction by our own discovery. Suddenly it becomes possible that there are just *others*, that we ourselves are an 'other' among others." This free-floating, unsettling awareness of being an other among others seems to me to be the most rewarding aim of archaeology, tropology, and vernacularism. It is brought about by a profound engagement in dialogue.

And, experienced in its fullness, this unsettling awareness might undermine any lingering confidence in transcendentalism and universalism. In the place of these epistemological models it offers a new conception of coming-to-know, which I might express, indulging in my own tropology, as a *parallactic* conception. Parallax is a metaphor for the decentered, dialogical construction of knowledge. It represents a way of knowing in which all vantage points yield a real knowledge, partial and different from that offered by any other vantage point, but in which no point yields insight more privileged than that gained from any other. It represents, in other words, a knowing in which none of our vantage points grants us a claim to any more singular status than that of being an other among others. It suggests that our knowledge is fundamentally indirect, not a knowledge of things-in-themselves but a knowledge of the negotiations by which we make things what they are. Parallax also configures the most effective means to gain knowledge in a decentered cosmos: the deepest knowledge will result from the dialogue that involves the largest number of differing vantage points. Knowledge is a product of the differing displacements of reality perceived from different viewpoints, not a product of a singular, authoritative perception.

Monologue, Canons, and the Case of Jazz

What . . . happened [in anti-bebop criticism of the 1940s] was that even though the white middle-brow critic had known about Negro music for only about three decades, he was already trying to formalize and finally institutionalize it. It is a hideous idea. The music was already in danger of being forced into that junk pile of admirable objects and data the West knows as *culture*.

Recently [ca. 1963], the same attitudes have become more apparent in the face of a fresh redefinition of the form and content of Negro music. Such phrases as "anti-jazz" have been used to describe the most exciting music produced in this country. But as critic A. B. Spellman asked, "What does anti-jazz mean and who are these ofays who've appointed themselves guardians of last year's blues?" It is that simple, really. What does anti-jazz mean? And who coined the phrase? What is the definition of jazz? And who was authorized to make one?

Negro music is essentially the expression of an attitude, or a collection of attitudes, about the world, and only secondarily about the way music is made. . . .

Usually the critic's commitment was first to his *appreciation* of the music rather than to his understanding of the attitude which produced it.

(Baraka 1967:18, 13)

If knowledge results from a parallactic negotiation of differing viewpoints, so also, clearly, does value. Archaeological, tropological, and vernacular views of knowledge challenge the universality and permanence not only of the meanings we construct but also of our evaluations and of the structures that most overtly reflect them—I mean, of course, our canons. This point returns us once more to the current concerns of African-American studies, for there is among them a strong movement afoot to institute a canon of black literature. The leaders of this movement—Henry Louis Gates is one—proceed in the face of a risk that is no doubt obvious to them: in instituting a black canon they are in danger of reinscribing the same monological, hegemonic premises that have for so long supported the white, male, European canon to which they would offer an alternative.

These premises constitute, in their most basic forms, three closely related strategies that function to distance the value and significance of canonic works from cultural constraints and situational determination. They are aestheticism, the view that the meaning and expression found in artworks are of a different, higher order than those found in other cultural acts; transcendentalism, the view that artistic value and significance can somehow travel with an artwork outside of the specific contexts that determine or redetermine them; and formalism, the view, closely related to transcendentalism, that meaning and value inhere in the internal formal arrangements of artworks themselves, independent of their contexts of creation or recreation. Such values will all too easily be reaffirmed in Gates's and others' pragmatic zeal to crystallize the canon of African-American literature.

Indeed these values have already conspired in the making of the canon of jazz, and in this jazz provides a cautionary tale for those who would crystallize black literary canons. Notwithstanding Amiri Baraka's warnings, now a quarter-century old, we have institutionalized jazz, evaluated its works, and enshrined those judged to be best in a glass case of cultural *admirabilia*. The jazz canon has been forged and maintained according to old strategies— Eurocentric, hierarchical notions behind which the rules of aestheticism, transcendentalism, and formalism are apparent. The canon operates, in the hands of most writers on jazz, with little serious regard for the contexts in which cherished works were created and even less for those in which their meaning and value are continually discovered and revised. The jazz canon is a canon of the same serving a history of the same, and we have already all but lost sight of the partiality and impermanence of its structures of value.

Like the canon of European music, the jazz canon is a strategy for exclusion, a closed and elite collection of "classic" works that together define what is and isn't jazz. The definition sets up walls, largely unbreachable, between "true" or "pure" jazz and varieties of music-making outside it. These walls close out as "non-jazz" whole realms of music that have resulted from the intersections of the critics' "true" jazz with other idioms—popular balladry, crooners' song-styles, rhythm-and-blues styles and the related Motown and funk, rock 'n' roll of various sorts, World Beat syncretisms, New Age minimalism, and so on. But, we might ask with Baraka, who *are* the self-appointed guardians of the borderlines setting off jazz from such musics? Certainly not most jazz musicians themselves, who from Louis Armstrong on have more often than not been remarkably open to interaction with the varied musical environment around them. Indeed, if, as Gates has suggested, the jazz tradition is essentially a Signifyin(g) tradition (see 1988:63), it is also true that much of the jazz musician's Signification has played on musical works and styles from outside the jazz critics' mainstream. Jazz Signification is largely extracanonic.

The values behind the institutionalization of jazz are revealed particularly clearly in the jazz textbooks for college and university courses that have appeared in the last two decades. This is not surprising; textbooks and the survey courses they abet have an awkward habit of revealing our tacit structures of evaluation. A glance at four typical texts—Frank Tirro's *Jazz: A History* (1977), Mark C. Gridley's *Jazz Styles: History and Analysis* (1985), Donald D. Megill and Richard S. Demory's *Introduction to Jazz History* (1989), and James McCalla's *Jazz: A Listener's Guide* (1982)—demonstrates some recurring patterns.

First of all, all four books rely on Martin Williams's *Smithsonian Collection of Classic Jazz* for many of their examples. The reliance is one of convenience, of course; recordings need to be easily available for students. But its effect is to monumentalize Williams's choices, to magnify into a statement of transcendent artistic worth the personal canon of one insightful (but conservative) critic, constructed itself in a given time and place according to particular formative rules and limiting contingencies. In jazz courses around the country, Williams's "classics" have come to function in precisely the same way as the classics of the European musical canons taught in the classrooms across the hall. They have come to stand as exemplars of timeless aesthetic value instead of being understood—as the European works next door should also be understood but too rarely are—as human utterances valued according to the dialogical situations in which they were created and are continually re-created. In this way the jazz canon embodies the aestheticism that continues to circumscribe our teaching of European canons and that short-circuits our understanding of the conditions in which they are made and remade.

In the service of this aestheticism, the makers of the jazz canon employ a resounding formalism. All four of the texts named above insist in their prefaces and their presentations on the priority of listening to and analyzing musical styles; their approach ranks musical above other kinds of understanding. This listening orientation might at first glance seem unexceptionable. But Baraka's remarks on narrowly musical appreciation should sensitize us to its ideological basis. Behind it hides the view that meaning (and hence value, which only arises alongside meaning) inheres somehow in the notes themselves. Behind it lurks the absurd proposition that music alone, independent of the cultural matrices that individuals build around it, can *mean*—that a recording or transcription of a Charlie Parker solo, for example, or the score or performance of a Beethoven symphony, can convey *something* even in the hypothetical absence of the complex negotiations we each pursue with them. This is the internalist ideology that has led most writers on jazz at least since André Hodeir to seek its "essence" mostly or exclusively in its musical features.

Instead of repeating such Western myths of the non-contingency of artworks, why not search for jazz meanings *behind* the music, in the life-shapes that gave rise to it and that continue to sustain it? Why not, in other words, scrutinize the interactions between our own rules of formation and those we impute to the makers of jazz as the source of our evaluations of it? Why not create a jazz pedagogy in which our construction of the varieties of black life-experience takes priority, saving the music—intricately bound up with those experiences, after all—for last, construing it in light of them, and resisting the aestheticizing tendency to exaggerate its differences from other manifestations of expressive culture? At least one writer, Amiri Baraka, long ago attempted a history along such lines. His *Blues People* of 1963 is a resonant example of vernacularism *avant la lettre*, but to judge by the textbooks named above it has had little influence on the developing pedagogy of jazz studies. (Baraka's vernacularism is not, however, without its own internal inconsistencies; I will return to them below.)

Placing the music first will always distance it from the complex and largely extramusical negotiations that made it and that sustain it. It will always privilege European bourgeois myths of aesthetic transcendency, artistic purity untouched by function and context, and the elite status of artistic expression. (Such myths concerning the composers of the European canon badly need to be exploded, so it is all the more troubling to see them neatly transferred to African-American composers and performers.) Foregrounding the musical appreciation of jazz only transfers to the study of African-American music the formalist view that remains debilitatingly dominant in Eurocentric musicology, with its continuing emphasis on internalist music analysis.

In their internalism, then, the jazz textbooks cited above reinscribe rules that inform the European musical canon. Thus the worst results to be feared in Gates's structuring of a canon of black literature have been anticipated in the making of the canon of black music. The laudable impulses, similar to Gates's, behind the formation of the jazz canon—jazz historians have worked hard to loosen the stranglehold of European "art music" on college and university curricula—have certainly not protected it from retracing the limited trajectory of earlier European canons, musical or otherwise. The jazz canon now shares all the misguided pretensions to transcendent value and meaning that characterize those other canons.

Another way of putting this is to say that the musicological makers of the jazz canon have not Signified on the earlier European musical canon. To have done so would have necessitated a questioning, ironic distance from that canon. It would have called for the staking out of a rhetorical stance vis-à-vis that canon; and this stance would have provided a tropological lever, Signification itself, that jazz historians could have used to uncover the impermanent, selective rules of formation of the earlier canon and thus to discover also their own partiality and impermanence. Signifyin(g) on the European canon would have led to an archaeology of it and of the jazz canon as well. Instead, by not scrutinizing the postulates of earlier canons, jazz historians have engaged in a wholesale restatement of them. In the place of dialogical Signification they have offered monological Imitation.

The result is a brand of narrowly based value judgment that cannot do justice to the complex dialogues of self and other in which culture is created. Such judgment is ill-equipped in the face of all expressive culture; but it is perhaps especially feeble in dealing with nondominant cultural strains, such as African-American traditions, that have developed in multivalent interaction with hegemonic cultures around them. The dialogical drama of such nondominant cultures is intensified by the marginalizing ploys of dominant cultures; white attempts to silence black voices highlight the negotiations from which those voices arise in the first place. Thus the monological judgments that have appeared repeatedly in the brief history of jazz—the early, negative critiques of bebop, for example, or the cries of "anti-jazz" Baraka noted that greeted the innovations of Coltrane, Coleman, Dolphy, and others around 1960—have often taken the form of white critics' attempts to silence or at least "whiten" innovative black expression.

But this forfeiture of dialogue can cut both ways. Just as white writers have sometimes been intent on ignoring or minimizing the blackness of jazz innovations and of individual jazz voices, so black writers have sometimes proved just as intent on impoverishing the interethnic dialogues that inform jazz styles. Both positions fail to grasp the Signifyin(g) richness of the jazz tradition; both start from premises that drastically reduce the dialogics itself of cultural production. A case in point of these monological positions is the critical response to one of the richest stylistic amalgams in jazz history: the jazz-rock fusion brought about by Miles Davis in works from the late 1960s and early 70s.

Miles Davis, Musical Dialogician

And then came the fall. *In a Silent Way,* in 1969, long, maudlin, boasting, Davis's sound mostly lost among electronic instruments, was no more than droning wallpaper music. A year later, with *Bitches Brew,* Davis was firmly on the path of the sellout. It sold more than any other Davis album, and fully launched jazz rock with its multiple keyboards, electronic guitars, static beats, and clutter. Davis's music became progressively trendy and dismal. . . . His albums of recent years . . . prove beyond any doubt that he has lost all interest in music of quality.

(Crouch 1990:35)

[On *In a Silent Way*] the solos are dissipated; the understated rock ostinato of the title piece turns at times into an enervated Chicago blues line. "Shh/Peaceful" is even more precious, with electric pianos tinkling in and out. The impersonality of the guitarist is the finishing touch on a performance with all the enduring, debilitated stimulation of a three-day drunk on white port wine: sickly sweet and effective.

The music [of "soul" jazz] was thoroughly blues-drenched; it emphasized the beat; people danced to it. The next kind of pop-jazz,

the fusion music that grew out of the decadence of the modes, sub-
dued and eventually eliminated these features.

As Miles Davis's music declined in the late 1960s, the sales of his
records declined, too, and this was during the period when the new
management of Columbia Records was raising sales quotas. Davis's
bosses ordered him to make a hit record or else; *Bitches Brew* was his
response.

In general, what fusion music fused was the atmospheric tendencies
of modal jazz with the rhythm patterns of rock. The gravitational
pull of the modern rock beat upon soloists' accenting discourages
any but the simplest kinds of linear development; as a result, other
features—atmosphere, color, small variation of subsidiary detail—
become primary among the values of a music in which decoration is
raised to the essential . . . . Creating a coherent musical line even
becomes dispensable.

(Litweiler 1984:126–27, 222–23, 227)

Strictly on the face of it, there is no reason why fusions might not
have worked. Jazz has always been able to meet, absorb, and put to
its own purposes almost everything in popular prospect. . . .

Nevertheless, I don't think jazz fusion worked very well. . . : the
beat in jazz moves forward; it is played so as to contribute to the all-
but-irresistible momentum of the music: jazz *goes* somewhere. The
beat in most rock bobs and bounces away in one place—like the
kids on the dance floor these days. Rock *stays* somewhere. And to be
a bit more technical about it, "jazz eights," the implied "triplet feel"
of jazz, is rarely heard in fusion, and can seem strangely out of place
when it is. . . .

About Miles Davis and fusion, maybe I can be as blunt and out-
spoken as he usually is about everything and everybody. When I last
heard Miles Davis he was stalking around a stage in what looked
like a left-over Halloween fright-suit, emitting a scant handful of
plaintive notes. . . .

Davis has always been one of those musicians who could come
up with something so fresh, even on familiar material, as to make
one forget, temporarily, all of his beautiful past. That evening everything I heard made me remember that beautiful past with pain.

(Williams 1989:47–49)

We could credit Miles Davis for the mainstream creation of Fusion as
a jazzlike trend. His Bitches Brew bands and Post-Bitches Brew
bands read like a who's who of Fusion. . . .

But so trendy and faddish was the Fusion mini-epoch that it was
possible to trace its ebb very clearly. . . .

> There was by the downturn of the Fusion trend a reawakening, it
> would seem, of a neo-BeBop voice. . . . To me this was a healthy
> sign, concrete evidence that fusion, for all its great sweeping trendi-
> ness which saw a few of our greatest musicians turn out a couple of
> new-style mood-music albums and bands, could not erase the
> deeper mainstream traditions of the music.
>
> (Baraka 1987c:178)

What's eating these people? The coercive power of the institutionalized jazz canon is repeatedly evident in their rejections of the innovations
Miles Davis introduced on *In a Silent Way, Bitches Brew,* and the albums that
followed. The four authors represent the best writing from a wide spectrum
of approaches to jazz: Litweiler tending toward the academic and musicological, Crouch and Williams journalistic from both black and white perspectives, and Baraka—we are surprised to find him in this company, after
his earlier calls for vernacularism—probing and poetically allusive, perhaps
the most insightful and original voice on African-American music over the
last three decades. But however different their approaches, all four writers
reveal the same stark inability to hear Davis's fusion music except against the
background of what jazz was before it (and what it has since become in the
hands of some neo-bop jazz technicians). The rich dialogue of musical voices
from outside as well as inside the walls of "pure" jazz that went into the
making of Davis's new styles around 1970 seems to carry no musical/
cultural excitement for these writers. Far from it. Instead they hear only a
departure from the canonized jazz tradition of their own making. And this
departure, the occasional vehemence of their tone makes clear, sounds to
them like a betrayal.

It is worth pausing to analyze the rhetoric of these condemnations (and of
many others, for the passages quoted are not unique among writings on fusion music). It is, first, a rhetoric of *absence*—absence, of course, conceived in
tandem with the characteristic presence of earlier jazz. This rhetoric usually
appears in descriptions of the musical features of fusion styles. Litweiler,
for example, finds the solos on *In a Silent Way* dissipated (compared to
what?); in general, fusion music lacks "linear development" and melodic
"coherence" (whose development? what coherence?). Williams, mean-
while, finds fusion music lacking in "jazz eights," the unequal and syncopated eighth notes prominent in most earlier varieties of jazz—and for
Williams, apparently, a *sine qua non* of all possible music that would deserve
the name. (We may leave aside Williams's specious distinction between a
beat "going somewhere" and one "staying somewhere," with its offhanded

dismissal of rock music.) The strategy operating here of chastising one music because it lacks the features of another, even though the two were conceived in different cultural circumstances, is a familiar one in musicology—compare, for example, the continuing undervaluation of Verdi's operas in comparison to Wagner's. But the strategy is no more legitimate for its familiarity. And it does not gain in legitimacy, but only in teleological illogic, when the favored style precedes and even influences the rejected one.

The condemnations of Davis's fusion styles also invoke a complex rhetoric of *transgression,* one that cuts rather deeper than the rhetoric of absence. The transgressions involved take different forms in the hands of different writers. Some are matters of personal behavior: the hinted distaste in Williams's words above at Davis's recent concert persona swells to self-righteous disgust in the similar description that opens Crouch's essay. Crouch is also particularly harsh on Davis's personal foibles, though, strangely, he seems to voice this criticism only to reinforce the case against the later music of Davis that he despises. The criticism of lifestyle is muted or disappears entirely in his reverential treatment of works like Davis's sessions with Thelonious Monk and Milt Jackson of 1954—as if Davis treated women better or used drugs less in the 1950s than he did in 1970 or 1985.

By far the most often mentioned transgression of Davis's fusion music is its commercialism. With *Bitches Brew* and with later albums, the writers above and many others claim, Davis sold out, breached the rampart between the artistic integrity of jazz and the pimped values of pop. Fusion, Baraka writes and other writers agree, was mostly "dollar-sign music" (1987c:177); indeed the very fact of *Bitches Brew*'s large sales seems for some writers to convict it without trial, discounting the artistic efforts that went into its production. This view, first of all, manifests a psychological naiveté that reaches a nadir in Litweiler's recounting of Davis's acquiescence to his bossman's orders. Even a rough gauge of Davis's ambivalent psyche, we shall see, leads to stories of much greater complexity than this.

Second, the condemnation of fusion for its commercial success drastically underestimates the vitality, subtlety, and expressiveness of the pop traditions that influenced Davis. It is nothing more than an antipopulist chauvinism that turns from the unacceptable view that "what sells is good" to the opposite and likewise unacceptable view that "what sells must be bad."

And finally, the contrast of commercial fusion with noncommercial earlier jazz amounts to elitism pure and simple, to a snobbish distortion of history by jazz purists attempting to insulate their cherished classics from the messy marketplace in which culture has always been negotiated. Those who advocate such a view should reread Ralph Ellison's review of *Blues People,* where he reminded Baraka that even Bird and the other early boppers, the *ne plus ultra* for many critics of esoteric jazz intellectualism, "were seeking . . . a fresh form of entertainment which would allow them their fair share of the entertainment market" (1978:59). Or, in a different connection, they should read recent nonhagiographical music histories that have Beethoven hawking the same opus to three different publishers, or Mozart conniving, with a sad lack of savvy, at one music-business killing or another. Music created with an eye to eternal genius and blind to the marketplace is a myth of European Romanticism sustained by its chief offspring, modernism.

One final transgression of fusion music offends Baraka and particularly Crouch: the transgression of the boundaries of pure ethnic expression. Baraka does not accuse Davis of this in his early fusion albums, at least not in so many words. But he does regard later fusion from the late 1970s and early 1980s as an aspect of a *"desouling* process" by which corporate powers whitened previously genuine black expression (see 1987b:274); and at times, as in the quotation above, he portrays all fusion music as an unfortunate departure from the "mainstream" black traditions of jazz.

Crouch goes much farther. He attempts to evaluate all jazz according to its purity of blackness. Such a view could only inspire deep reservations about Davis's musical achievement, which always derived vitality from its disquieting perch in the middle of interethnic musical dialogues. Crouch, to give him his due, is at least consistent in his rejection of Davis's most overtly dialogical styles. He regards the famous *Birth of the Cool* sessions of 1948–50 as "little more than primers for television writing" that "disavowed the Afro-American approach to sound and rhythm" (1990:31). He sees the later collaborations with Gil Evans as a sign of Davis's seduction "by pastel versions of European colors"; for him "they are given what value they have . . . by the Afro-American dimensions that were never far from Davis's embouchure, breath, fingering" (p. 34). And, of course, he regards Davis's fusion music as the ultimate sellout to (white) corporate America, a mining of "the fool's gold of rock 'n' roll" (p. 30). This tendency to forsake the blackness of his ethnic origins, combined with his other personal foibles, led Davis in Crouch's narrative to a moral failure that is biblical in dimension: Crouch talks of Davis's "fall from grace" and the "shriveling" of his "soul" (p. 30).

Another interpretation of Davis's fusion music is more plausible than these. It recognizes in Davis's musical efforts from 1969–1974 a compelling expressive force created by his unflinching facing of the dialogical extremes of his background and environment. It recognizes, in other words, the Signi-fyin(g) power of Davis's music in this period. This interpretation gains credence from Davis's own remarks about his fusion and other music. It has been adumbrated in recent years by two prominent African-American critics, Greg Tate and—we return to him, surprisingly, once more—Amiri Baraka. Tate's position, in a two-part article on "The Electric Miles" in *Down Beat*, is doubly significant, first for his sensitivity to Davis's new styles and the pop elements in them and second because he has elsewhere emerged as a nonacademic advocate of a black vernacular critical theory (see his remarks in Gates 1989:21, 27–28). Baraka's position signals a deepening of his earlier views of fusion, a coming to grips with tendencies in Davis's music that have long gone against his own Black Aesthetic grain; in this it reveals a healthy complexity and deep self-questioning in his thought. It emerged first in a moving profile of Davis he wrote for the *New York Times* in 1985 and was further unfolded in the expanded version of this essay he published in 1987. This latter version ranks among the most psychologically astute writings on Davis.

> White musicians are overtrained and black musicians are undertrained. You got to mix the two. A black musician has his own sound, but if you want it played straight, mix in a white musician and the piece will still be straight, only you'll get feeling and texture—up, down, around, silly, wrong, slow, fast—you got more to work with. There's funky white musicians. But after classical training you have to learn to play social music.
>
> (Miles Davis quoted by Amiri Baraka in Baraka 1987a:295)

> Miles Davis's music, like African-American culture generally, originates as a specific reflection of African-American life and perception in the still mostly segregated black communities of the society, but it, like Miles, reaches in all directions within the whole of that society and transforms them.
>
> Interracial bands are nothing new to Miles. So talk of Miles's eye to the buck as being the principal reason for using white musicians doesn't really wash. Though it is my own feeling that Miles knows always almost exactly what he is doing around the music—form and content, image and substance.
>
> There is something in the mix Miles *wants* us to hear. It might be commercial, to some extent, but it is also social and aesthetic.
>
> Miles's special capacity and ability is to hold up and balance two musical (social) conceptions and express them as (two parts of) a single aes-

thetic. . . . [B]y *Miles Ahead,* Miles understood enough about the entire
American aesthetic so that he could make the *cool* statements on a level
that was truly *popular* and which had the accents of African-America included not as contrasting anxiety or tension but as an equal sensuous-
ness!

(Baraka 1987a:289–90, 294, 304)

Behind Miles Davis's frequent stereotyping of white and black musicians, behind all the ethnic generalizations he voiced over the years that led
many to accuse him of racism, stood an acute fascination with *difference.*
The refutation of the charge of overt racism has always been easy: Davis's
bands, since his first collaboration with Gil Evans in 1948, featured white
musicians more often than not. The issue is not simple racism. Instead,
Davis's insistent matching of musical to ethnic differences over the years bespeaks the collaborative musical variety that he felt compelled to seek by
merging various approaches. There is, indeed, something in the *mix* he
wanted us—all of us, whites as well as blacks—to hear. More, perhaps, than
any other contemporary musician, Davis made this stylistic, cultural, and
ethnic mix the stuff of his music.

It is hard not to see in Davis's musical expression of difference a reflection
of his own ambivalent background, situated between the marginal status
white America accorded him because of his skin color on the one hand and
the middle- or upper-middle-class affluence in which he was raised on the
other. His values were shaped by two contradictory statuses, a disen-
franchised ethnic one and an empowered economic one; this was the first
mix Miles Davis learned. He grew up with the contradictory messages that
come with such mixed status. His situation was from the first a situation
between—between mainstream bourgeois aspirations historically identified
in America as white aspirations and the deep tributary of the proud and angry selfhood of a marginalized ethnos.

By virtue of his relatively secure and even privileged economic status, his
background was unlike those of most earlier jazz greats. What must the boppers at Minton's, Parker and Gillespie and the others, have made of him
when he first arrived in New York in 1944? He, a precocious eighteen-year-
old with an enrollment at Juilliard and a generous allowance from his father? (Parker, at any rate, was not one to overscrutinize a gift horse: he soon
moved into Davis's digs.) More generally, how did his affluence set him apart
from the very musicians he idolized? And, later, how did the many of Davis's
close associates who like him struggled with drug addiction view his good

fortune of having a supportive father and a three-hundred-acre farm to retreat to while he kicked his habit? Few of them were so lucky. The affluence
of Davis's family was simply not a typical background for black jazz
musicians—or perhaps any jazz musicians—in the 1940s and 1950s.

Davis's recent memoir, *Miles: The Autobiography* (1989), provides little insight into the difference and distance that must have conditioned his relations with the great boppers and many of his later black collaborators. Davis
portrays his acceptance among them as a matter of competitive artistic respect growing in some cases into friendship. But the disparity in backgrounds suggests that the emotional bonds between Davis and a musician
like Parker must have been tinged with ambivalence on both sides. And for
Davis, I think, this kind of ambivalence quickly grew to be a defining trait of
his musical personality. It was an uneasiness at sitting on the fence, between
worlds, that impelled him always to seek out distinctive middle voices, stylistic mediations and compromises between differing idioms. This is the
source of his special capacity, so well expressed by Baraka, to meld two mu-
sical/social conceptions into a single way of making music. And the capacity
revealed itself early on: by late 1948, a scant three years after his first recording sessions with Parker, Davis was already following his ambivalent star,
leading an ethnically mixed nonet in a new, cool style that was in important
respects an anti-bop reaction. "The mix" was on; it was already beginning to
saturate Davis's musical thought.

Almost from the beginning, then, Davis's musical achievement was an
acutely dialogical one, reveling in the merging of contrasting approaches
and sounds, highlighting the cognizance of difference that seems so crucial a
part of Davis's own personality. This does not deny, of course, the blackness
of Davis's music, its origins, in Baraka's words, "as a specific reflection of
African-American life and perception"; rather, it affirms the wide-ranging
variety of African-American perceptions themselves. As Baraka sums up,
"Miles went to Juilliard. Miles's father was a medium-sized landowner and
dentist. All that is in his life and to a certain general extent is in his art"
(1987a:306). ("But Miles is still tied to the blues," Baraka continues; I'll return to this point below.) Davis's perceptions of African-American life differed from Parker's just as surely as they differed from Armstrong's, Jelly Roll
Morton's, or Leadbelly's. His perceptions were, especially, a product of the
particular matrix of ethnic marginalization and economic assimilation that
characterized his youth. From this cultural ambivalence, refracted through
the unique lens of Davis's psyche, arose a powerfully synthetic Signifyin(g)

voice. From ambivalence—or, better, from multivalence—arose musical dialogue.

Davis's fusion music from 1969–1974 represents the culmination of this dialogue, a logical outgrowth of his earlier musical development and the mediating concerns expressed in it—whether in the cool style, in his later orchestral collaborations with Gil Evans, or in the laid-back blues of his extraordinary work with Bill Evans, John Coltrane, and Cannonball Adderley in the late 1950s. Taken as a whole, Davis's fusion music is a melting pot into which he stirred an ever-changing melange of ingredients from his (our) fragmented and dizzyingly varied musical environment. Each new recording session from those of *In a Silent Way* (February 1969) on—or even from those of *Filles de Kilimanjaro* (June and September 1968) on—seems to add ingredients to the mix with increasing relish, greater abandon (I take session dates, here and below, from Chambers 1983–85). Sometimes the new ingredients float on top of the earlier mix like oil on water, seemingly incapable of successful blending with it. But more often Davis succeeds in dissolving the new elements in the old to create a novel and effective brew. The old ingredients are hardly ever discarded. They may be chemically altered by the new, perhaps now almost unrecognizable, but they remain to make their contribution.

The fusion mix as a whole challenges, with an aggressiveness matched only by some of the free jazz of the early and mid-1960s, the "verities" of earlier jazz. The famous—notorious among jazz purists—expanded rhythm section, or "bottom," which on *Bitches Brew* involves as many as ten players (three drummers, a percussionist, three electric pianists, an electric guitarist, an electric bass player, and an acoustic bass player), no longer functions straightforwardly either in the traditional supporting manner of post-bop ensemble jazz or in the soloistic manner of some free jazz. Instead, it usually fulfills versions of both functions at once. It is a thick web of simultaneous solos, radically loosed from subjugation by the treble soloists, at the same time as it lays down, in the form of insistent ostinatos suggesting static or repetitive harmonies, an uncompromising metric framework borrowed from such sources as African and Brazilian polyrhythms and James-Brown-style rhythm and blues.

At times this functional balance of the bottom swings to one extreme or the other. In Davis's fusion style that remains closest to the formal procedures of earlier jazz, evident for example on most of *On the Corner* (1972), the bottom simply provides intricate rhythmic support for a succession of treble solos. It is characterized usually—and in this, of course, it departs from jazz precedent—by funky rhythm-guitar riffs and percussive poly-rhythms governed by an insistent backbeat. At other times the bottom beat dissolves into nonmetrical collective soloing, as in the recurring echo-trumpet passages of the title track of *Bitches Brew.*

Most intriguing are the moments, especially prominent on *Bitches Brew* and a number of works recorded soon after it (for instance, those later collected on *Big Fun*), when the traditional functions of treble soloists and rhythmic bottom seem almost to be reversed. In these passages Davis, perhaps along with Wayne Shorter on soprano sax or Bennie Maupin on bass clarinet, states a melodic fragment over and over, with minimal variation, which serves paradoxically as a sort of *cantus firmus* "bottom" for the collective improvisations below. In nonmetrical or irregularly metrical contexts—for example the opening section of "Lonely Fire" on *Big Fun*—this *cantus-firmus*-like riff not only serves as a structural anchor but simultaneously directs attention away from itself to the intricate web of collective soloing around and beneath it (in "Lonely Fire" the web consists of electric bass guitar, electric pianos, sitar, and a variety of percussion). Something of a functional reversal of top and bottom results. When the *cantus firmus* technique appears in a metrical context, on the other hand, both bottom and top share in traditional rhythm-section functions; but the anchor of Davis's repeated riff allows individual instruments from the bottom to depart from supportive roles and take off at will on soloistic flights.

In general, this functional freedom of the rhythm section is what Greg Tate hears when he describes Herbie Hancock as "break[ing] down on electric keyboards like solo and rhythm parts were one and the same" on the album *Jack Johnson,* or when, on "Calypso Frelimo" from *Get Up with It,* he characterizes Peter Cosey's guitar as "a second set of congas to Mtume's, a second rush of cymbals to Al Foster's, a second steel drum simulacrum to Miles' Gnostic organ, a second rhythm guitar to Lucas', and . . . one of three solo voices" (1983:22–23). Other earlier examples of this multivalent effect are "Spanish Key" from *Bitches Brew* and "Great Expectations" on *Big Fun;* listen especially to John McLaughlin's electric guitar.

Indeed, McLaughlin's role in Davis's ensembles from *Bitches Brew* on is emblematic not only of the functional flexibility of the fusion bottom as a whole; its breadth of expression suggests also some of the varied influences Davis gradually incorporated into his fusion music. Departing from his more traditional and lyrical jazz guitar style evident on *In a Silent Way,* a style that harkens back all the way to Charlie Christian, McLaughlin moved in two directions in his later work with Davis. The first of them to emerge was a syncopated, offbeat, sometimes wah-wah rhythm-guitar comping indebted more to the funky rhythms of James Brown and Sly and the Family Stone than to any jazz predecessors. The second was a psychedelic, fuzz-toned, bad-axe virtuosity taken over especially from Jimi Hendrix. This style begins to take shape on *Bitches Brew* and the earliest cuts of *Big Fun,* all recorded late in 1969; it explodes into the works recorded in the first sessions of 1970: "Gemini/Double Image," later released on *Live Evil,* "Go Ahead John" on *Big Fun* (where McLaughlin's funky comping is also prominent), and others. It is carried on by the later guitarists Davis used after McLaughlin left the band (especially by Cosey; on his role see Tate 1983:23–24). And, most intriguingly, Davis himself adopted the style by the end of 1970, playing his muted trumpet through an amplifier with a wah-wah pedal on works like "Sivad" and "Funky Tonk" (both on *Live Evil*) to achieve an acid-rock solo style combining the Hendrix/McLaughlin sound with his characteristic articulation, phrasing, and melodic figures.

Davis's adoption of the electrified sounds of psychedelic rock and the complex rhythm-guitar offbeats of funk is one of the developments in his fusion music most sorely lamented by jazz purists. A more comprehending view would regard it as another of the dialogical moves to achieve an interethnic sound that have recurred across his career. Both Sly and Hendrix, the most important influences on these aspects of Davis's fusion, were musicians mediating between two worlds much in the manner of Davis himself. Sly's achievement in his early music with the Family Stone (roughly 1967–69) was to merge black funk and white counterculture in an unprecedented and peculiarly Bay Area amalgam. Hendrix's acid-singed virtuosity moved along a parallel path. His merger of authentic blues with psychedelia spoke mainly to middle-class, white audiences of the late 1960s—audiences who had moved through *Sgt. Pepper's* and *Magical Mystery Tour* and the Stones, through the early head-rock of Jefferson Airplane and the folk-acid of the Grateful Dead, and were looking for higher thrills. Hendrix answered the needs of the mainly white listeners at Monterey and Woodstock for a mediated, "whitened" rock-blues.

Baraka, though he mentions Sly only in passing, captures eloquently the significance of Davis's affinity for "the white or 'integrated' media-ubiquitous rebellion Hendrix represented." It reflected Davis's position "at the other side of the social and musical equation" from musicians like John Coltrane and Pharaoh Sanders, his partaking of the "coalition politics of the Panthers rather than the isolating nationalism of the cultural nationalists"

(1978a:309). Baraka's reading is on the money. Davis's thoroughgoing elec-
trification of jazz allowed it to incorporate rock 'n' roll styles that were in
themselves coalitions reaching across ethnic lines. The fusion music of
Bitches Brew captured a huge audience—by jazz standards, at any rate—
made up in large part of venturesome white rockers willing to try something
new. (I was one of them, I should acknowledge, a fledgling jazz-rock trum-
peter who turned on to *Bitches Brew* and its predecessor *In a Silent Way* when
they emerged during my first year of college; my own commitment to engage with Davis's fusion music stems from this formative musical/cultural
experience.)

But it does not follow from all this interethnic dialogue and coalition politics that in *Bitches Brew* and his later albums Davis renounced or sold out his
black artistic self, any more than Crouch's accusation follows from Davis's
cool jazz or his collaborations with Gil Evans. It is simply that Davis's blues-
saturated ethnic self is a more complex affair than Crouch wants to recognize. In all the styles Crouch censures—in *Bitches Brew* just as surely as in
Birth of the Cool—Davis's distinctive, blue plangency remains at the heart of
his achievement. He is still tied to the blues, as Baraka says. His trumpet contributions to his fusion works vary from minimalist utterances—which he
tended toward especially in the early fusion works in order, I think, to purge
his style of the post-bop phrasing that lingers, sometimes incongruously, on
Filles de Kilimanjaro—to amplified, virtuosic assaults. But all his fusion work
sings the blues, its melodies pivoting again and again on ♭VII or playing
subtly on ♭III/♮III exchanges. Indeed, Davis speaks the blues rather more
plainly here than in many of his earlier styles; Tate is right to say that Davis
turned from "post-bop modernism" to funky fusion "because he was bored
fiddling with quantum mechanics and just wanted to play the blues again"
(1983:18).

And Davis's bluesy fusion lines *swing* in his inimitable manner: fuzzy,
arch, suspicious of the listener's motives, sometimes almost offhanded,
sometimes angrily spat out, always from the heart. Listen to how he plays
the straightforward modal ruminations of "SHHH/Peaceful" on *In a Silent
Way* or the repeated (and sometimes transposed) I–to–♭VII scalar riff that
makes up much of his role in "Spanish Key." Even such simple material exhibits Davis's personal vision of the freedoms of pitch, timbre, and articulation that have marked the great jazz trumpeters from Armstrong on. It is
these freedoms that constitute Crouch's "Afro-American dimensions" of
embouchure, breath, and fingering. They represent the technical revolution
brought to the trumpet by black Americans, a revolution that toppled the

prim Arban methods and military precision of Victorian cornet virtuosos and broke wide open the expressive range of the instrument. As for Davis himself, the power of his vision was such that it could embrace as a convincing expressive aspect even his famous cracked and fluffed notes.

The dialogical dimensions of Davis's fusion music, then, are numerous. This music opened lines of communication between traditional jazz, with its blues background and improvisational impetus, on the one hand and rhythm and blues, funk, and white acid rock on the other; these communicative channels are enriched all the more since the non-jazz musics involved in them were ultimately blues-based as well. The dialogics of fusion music involved also an extraordinary freedom of colloquy within the ensemble, a freedom of exchange wherein the complex bottom and any of its constituents could function as top and vice versa. This far-reaching democratization of the ensemble has an obvious antecedent in various versions of free jazz; but it came to Davis's music also from pop sources—specifically Sly and the Family Stone, whose vocal and instrumental arrangements featured all the musicians with an equality rarely heard in earlier rhythm-and-blues styles. And the democratic multiple improvisations of much of Davis's fusion music took encouragement also from European avant-garde trends— specifically the structural indeterminacy sometimes explored by Karlheinz Stockhausen, whose music and thought Davis came to know around 1970.

The fusion dialogue reached in other directions as well. Davis's self-conscious incorporation of extra-American sounds in his fusion albums looks back to various precedents: to the Spanish accents of his earlier efforts (especially *Sketches of Spain* with Gil Evans) and to bossa-nova influences on him and other jazz musicians. But his transmutation of these borrowed sounds in the new mix moves farther than those precedents and qualifies his fusion music as a legitimate ancestor of some recent international pop idioms. The Brazilian and African percussionists and the Indian musicians of his ensembles contribute not so much full-fledged styles as raw sound-materials. More flavors for the mix.

And even when a full-fledged style is borrowed, it is transformed in arresting ways. The haunting, nonmetric "Selim" on *Live Evil*, arranged by Brazilian musician Hermeto Pascoal, takes over melodic and harmonic inflections from the samba or bossa nova but leaves behind their most salient features, their rhythms. "Maiysha," on both *Get Up with It* and *Agharta*, juxtaposes its primary theme, a well-behaved samba, with a hard-driven, guitar-dominated blues; the grinding gearshift that results is repeated over and over on the (superior) *Agharta* version. And in "Calypso Frelimo" the calypso is sublimated, reduced to Davis's recurring theme-fragment on organ, stated usually against Mtume's furious conga-drumming. This constructive technique, involving repeated, wispy allusions to tamer styles, is a frequent one in Davis's fusion works. It looks back to cuts like "Mademoiselle Mabry" from *Filles de Kilimanjaro,* whose long, free-formed theme is punctuated by two cadential figures, a modal/chromatic one borrowed from Hendrix's "The Wind Cries Mary"—even Crouch likes this "elevation" of "pop material"—and a keyboard interjection in the proto-funk style of Joe Zawinul's "Mercy, Mercy, Mercy."

It may not be too farfetched to suggest that the opening of one more dialogue is signaled in the title of *Bitches Brew.* This is the dialogue of equality between woman and man, which—to judge from his autobiography—Davis always found extremely difficult to sustain. The title *Bitches Brew* at first seems no more than a tired play on Davis's demeaning and obsessive epithet for women, all women. Then we look more closely and discover that there is no apostrophe in it: *Bitches Brew,* not *Bitches' Brew.* "Brew" is a verb, not a noun, and the title does not describe the music on the album so much as the musicians and their activity in making it. The musicians themselves are the bitches; the separate linguistic realms of "bitch" as demeaning epithet and "bitch" as admiring title, akin to "motherfucker" in Signifyin(g) talk, are joined. It is as if the title hints at Davis's hesitant coming to grips with the bitch in himself, his recognition of his own otherness and his desire to enter into a meaningful, nondemeaning colloquy with it. On the deepest level, this desire might even subsume all the other dialogical axes of his fusion music: black and white, American and non-American, top and bottom, pop, jazz, and avant-garde.

♪

The four condemnations of fusion I quoted at the beginning of this section demonstrate the fundamental difficulties the dialogics of culture poses for us. They are a microcosmic expression of the abiding threat that the recognition of difference carries with it. Their intolerance of fusion music reflects the discomfort of both black and white critics with the *mix* that Davis created. It amounts to a dismissal of Davis's eloquent Signifyin(g) on the many musical idioms around him.

On a more general level, their intolerance stems from Davis's breaching of too many walls of the kind we habitually set up to order and make sense of the world. So I have not cited the views of Crouch, Litweiler, Williams, and Baraka to condemn them for an atypical narrowness and intolerance, but rather to exemplify in a particular musical situation an aversion that we all share to the dialogical complexity of our construal of the world around us. Without struggling against this aversion, we will construct, as they constructed in their accounts of fusion music, solipsistic, monological values and meanings.

Henry Louis Gates wrote, in words I quoted at the beginning of this essay, "Anyone who analyzes black literature must do so as a comparativist." I have tried to extend the reference of this maxim beyond black literature to embrace African-American music and expressive culture in general, and beyond that to embrace all culture of any variety. African-American texts may well have a particularly salient dichotomy of antecedents on which they Signify. But this does not set them qualitatively apart from all other texts and indeed all other products of culture, for all these arise from multivalent colloquy with earlier cultural acts. The condition of African-American culture and its theory, once again, provides a compelling instance of the dialogical condition of all culture and cultural theory.

Dialogical knowledge, as I said above, is the building of a precarious discourse that never fully displaces the other discourses around it. It is unsettling precisely because it works against our natural impulse to be settled in the complacency of our own rules and terms. It threatens because it relinquishes the comforting idea of mastering a fully cleared space with open horizons in order instead to scrutinize uneasily the mysterious others crowding in on it. Mastery is no doubt the easy route to follow. But the path of mystery, if steeper, will surely lead to more humane rewards.

WORKS CITED

Baker, Houston A., Jr. 1984. *Blues, Ideology, and Afro-American Literature: A Vernacular Theory.* Chicago: University of Chicago Press.

Baraka, Amiri [LeRoi Jones]. 1963. *Blues People: The Negro Experience in White America and the Music That Developed from It.* New York: William Morrow.

———. 1967. "Jazz and the White Critic." In Amiri Baraka, *Black Music,* 11–20. New York: William Morrow.

———. 1987a. "Miles Davis: 'One of the Great Mother Fuckers': P. J. Jones in Conversation." With Amina Baraka. In *The Music: Reflections on Jazz and Blues,* 286–316. New York: William Morrow. Revised version of "Miles Davis," *New York Times,* 16 June 1985.

———. 1987b. "The Phenomenon of *Soul* in African-American Music." With Amina Baraka. In *The Music: Reflections on Jazz and Blues,* 268–76. New York: William Morrow.

———. 1987c. "Where's the Music Going and Why?" With Amina Baraka. In *The Music: Reflections on Jazz and Blues,* 177–80. New York: William Morrow.

Chambers, Jack. 1983–85. *Milestones: The Music and Times of Miles Davis.* 2 vols. New York: William Morrow.

Crouch, Stanley. 1990. "Play the Right Thing." *New Republic,* 12 February, pp. 30–37.

Davis, Miles. 1989. *Miles: The Autobiography.* With Quincy Troupe. New York: Simon and Schuster.

Derrida, Jacques. 1985. "Racism's Last Word." *Critical Inquiry* 12:290–99.

Ellison, Ralph. 1978. "Blues People." In Kimberly W. Benston, ed., *Imamu Amiri Baraka (LeRoi Jones): A Collection of Critical Essays,* 55–63. Englewood Cliffs, N. J.: Prentice-Hall.

Foucault, Michel. 1972. *The Archaeology of Knowledge and The Discourse on Language.* Trans. A. M. Sheridan Smith. New York: Pantheon.

———. 1973. *The Order of Things: An Archaeology of the Human Sciences.* New York: Vintage Books.

Gates, Henry Louis, Jr. 1985. "Writing 'Race' and the Difference It Makes." *Critical Inquiry* 12: 1–20.

———. 1988. *The Signifying Monkey: A Theory of African-American Literary Criticism.* New York: Oxford University Press.

———. 1989. "Canon-Formation, Literary History, and the Afro-American Tradition: From the Seen to the Told." In Houston A. Baker, Jr., and Patricia Redmond, eds., *Afro-American Literary Study in the 1990s,* 14–39. Chicago: University of Chicago Press.

Gridley, Mark C. 1985. *Jazz Styles: History and Analysis.* 2d ed. Englewood Cliffs, N. J.: Prentice-Hall.

Henderson, Mae G. 1989. Response to Houston A. Baker, Jr. In Houston A. Baker, Jr., and Patricia Redmond, eds., *Afro-American Literary Study in the 1990s,* 155–63. Chicago: University of Chicago Press.

Jones, LeRoi. *See* Baraka, Amiri.

Litweiler, John. 1984. *The Freedom Principle: Jazz after 1958.* New York: Da Capo.

McCalla, James. 1982. *Jazz: A Listener's Guide.* Englewood Cliffs, N. J.: Prentice Hall.

McDowell, Deborah E. 1989. "Boundaries: Or Distant Relations and Close Kin." In Houston A. Baker, Jr., and Patricia Redmond, eds. *Afro-American Literary Study in the 1990s,* 51–70. Chicago: University of Chicago Press.

Megill, Donald D., and Richard S. Demory. 1989. *Introduction to Jazz History.* 2d ed. Englewood Cliffs, N. J.: Prentice-Hall.

Mudimbe, V. Y. 1988. *The Invention of Africa: Gnosis, Philosophy, and the Order of Knowledge.* Bloomington: Indiana University Press.

Tate, Greg. 1983. "The Electric Miles," Parts 1, 2. *Down Beat* 50, no. 7:16–18, 62; and no. 8:22–24, 54.

Tirro, Frank. 1977. *Jazz: A History.* New York: W. W. Norton.

Williams, Martin. 1989. *Jazz in Its Time.* New York: Oxford University Press.

SIX

History and Works That Have No History: Reviving Rossini's Neapolitan Operas
Philip Gossett

When in his *Foundations of Music History* Carl Dahlhaus asks "What is a fact of music history?", he addresses a problem well known to twentieth-century historiography. According to Max Weber, the sociologist from whom Dahlhaus derived many concepts, "the quality of an event as a 'social-economic' event is not something which it possesses 'objectively.' It is rather conditioned by the orientation of our cognitive interest, as it arises from the specific cultural significance which we attribute to the particular event in a given case" (Weber 1949:64). Dahlhaus writes: "While it is facts, not fancies, that confront the honest historian, these facts have nevertheless been selected on the basis of particular interests, and have risen from the status of mere source material to that of historical fact solely by virtue of a conceptual system of the historian's own making" (Dahlhaus 1983:42). Though Weber refers to "events" of social and economic history while Dahlhaus is concerned with "facts" of music history, the communality of their formulations is apparent.

What differentiates music, art, or literary history from other historical enterprises is the historian's relationship to the primary "facts" of these disciplines, the works of art themselves. This is not to say that a novel cannot be read as a historical document or that a historical document cannot be read as a novel. One can analyze a Victorian parliamentary bill in order to penetrate its underlying structures of thought just as one can analyze a paragraph from a novel by Dickens as a political tract. One can study the rhythm of poems by Ezra Pound and of computer-generated greeting-card verse. One can employ Leonard Meyer's theory of "gap-filled" melodies to analyze the melodic structure of a theme in a Mozart piano sonata, a political chanson arranged by Béranger, or a chorus in Auber's *La muette de Portici*. One can ponder the reception history of Beethoven's *Grosse Fuge*, the sentimental ballad "Meet Me by Moonlight Alone," or Tchaikovsky's *Marche Slav*. The value to the historian of any particular approach depends on the nature of the questions asked and the results obtained, not on an abstract sense of propriety between methodology chosen and "fact" under consideration.

In the spectrum of approaches to individual musical works, it is useful to imagine a continuum. At one extreme, the work is viewed in isolation, a "fact" to be measured against a theory of internal structure, whether one based on linear analysis, harmonic patterning, or thematic transformation; at the other extreme, the work is meaningful not in itself but only in its social and cultural interactions with historical events or, indeed, with other works. In practice, most activities by historians or theorists place the individual work somewhere between these extremes, although the fringes are actually present in scholarly discourse. One can store the pitches and rhythms of a composition in a computer data base and run a program that sorts simultaneous sonorities into variously defined sets. One can study the reception history of a "work" without being concerned about its contents. Indeed, in its more extreme forms, reception history denies precedence to any particular manifestation of a "work": a Bach fugue from the *Well-Tempered Clavier* is the same whether played from a critical edition or from a nineteenth-century text that corrects its harmonic barbarities; whether performed on the harpsichord or rendered in an arrangement for string trio, concert band, or electronic synthesizer.

The questions we ask about a work, which determine its position in our continuum of approaches, often reflect aesthetic biases. For most musicologists, string quartets and barbershop quartets flow naturally to opposite extremes, but it is possible to invert this apparently natural order. We do not distrust analyses of Brahms's symphonies or reception histories of Paganini's tours, although we might be less comfortable with Schenkerian reductions of a rag by a follower of Scott Joplin or a history of Renaissance music that gave equal weight to versions of motets performed in the sixteenth century and those performed in the nineteenth century by the Cecilian movement. The issue is not whether one approach is "correct" or not, but rather the nature of the insights that can be drawn from a particular approach.

On what basis do we make such judgments? What criteria determine the repertories we choose to examine and enshrine (the "canons" we study), and what criteria determine the ways in which those canons are brought into our professional discourse (i.e., disciplined)? Disciplining supports canon formation and vice versa: for Schenker, not only is great music susceptible to a particular form of analysis, but it is defined by it. Hence the elaborate exercises that have been carried out in the pages of *The Music Forum*, and elsewhere, to demonstrate that musics other than those of the central European tradition from Bach to Brahms should be admitted to the hallowed circle.

Those concerned with musics, not to mention literatures or art objects, standing outside the central canon find themselves in an unenviable position. Applying traditional disciplinary methodologies (where these seem appropriate and useful), they risk the opprobrium of being perceived as merely wishing to gain entry into the canon for works or repertories that have been previously excluded; inventing new modes of analysis, whether historical, sociological, or theoretical (where these promise to provide new perspectives on particular repertories), they appear to accept tacitly the tyranny of the central canon. These are issues that affect every aspect of our work as teachers and scholars at a moment in which debates about preserving or redefining the "canon" are raging throughout the intellectual community.

≀

Considerations of this kind, which color every historical enterprise, have particular resonance for Italian opera in the early nineteenth century. With this repertory, a complex interaction of reception history, text-critical considerations, changing attitudes toward the notion of a standard repertory, or "canon," as well as ethnographic biases, has created a unique social and intellectual environment; it is against this complex background that we must understand and measure the increased presence of Rossini's serious operas in opera houses throughout the world over the past two decades.

By the mid-nineteenth century, even before his death in 1868, most of Rossini's operas had fallen out of the repertory in a way that seemed definitive. Some hagiographic biographers, such as Azevedo in Paris and Silvestri in Milan, sought to keep the variety of the composer's achievement before the public; but with rare exceptions, the works considered representative were on the one hand *Il barbiere di Siviglia* and *L'Italiana in Algeri,* and the little-performed and much-lauded *Guillaume Tell* on the other (see Azevedo 1864 and Silvestri 1874). Profound changes in vocal style had put the melodic lines of Rossini's *opera seria* beyond the capabilities of contemporary singers; the powerful impact of the Romantic drama on the content and form of the Italian opera libretto had made Rossini's more controlled dramas seem abstract and cold; and the classicistic formal perfection for which Rossini appeared to strive, even in his passionate moments, was out of touch with the varied musical dramaturgy that a composer such as Verdi, operating in the shadow of French Grand Opera, appeared to instill in Italian musical theater.

That Rossini had been primarily a composer of *opera seria* had disappeared as a "fact" of music history, a victim of the subsequent reception of these works. His historical role was defined as the last great composer of eighteenth-century *opera buffa*, an artist who miraculously produced one serious but hardly performable Gargantuan masterwork in *Tell*, before retiring in 1829.

Although he lived almost forty years more, he never wrote another opera. Instead, he watched most of his works gradually fall from favor. By the 1860s he could himself adopt the reigning view of the period, writing in the dedication to God of his *Petite messe solennelle:* "I was born for *opera buffa*, you know it well. Little science, a little heart, that's all. Be blessed then, and grant me a place in Paradise."[1] To take this statement as Rossini's measured assessment of his own worth would be absurd, a denial of the psychological conditions imposed on an artist by thirty-five years of self-enforced semi-idleness in a world that had canonically enshrined only a few of his comic operas.

In any discussion of Rossini that addresses individual works as aesthetic objects as well as historical "facts," the operas he wrote for Naples between 1815 and 1822 play a central yet ambiguous role. Since the Venetian premieres of *Tancredi* and *L'Italiana in Algeri* in 1813, the young Rossini was acclaimed as a composer of both serious and comic opera; practically every work written between 1813 and 1817, even some barely known today (*Aureliano in Palmira, Torvaldo e Dorliska*), immediately entered the contemporary operatic repertory, to be reproduced throughout the Italian peninsula and usually in other European centers. These were mature works with a measurable reception history.

Already in 1815, however, Rossini signed the first of a series of contracts with the Neapolitan impresario Domenico Barbaja through which he became musical director of the Neapolitan theaters, composing new works and overseeing other activities. Rossini retained this post until 1822, while occasionally preparing operas for theaters in other cities. A few of his Neapolitan operas were widely performed, including *Otello* (1816), *Mosè in Egitto* (1818), and *La donna del lago* (1819); others were failures in Naples itself and were unknown beyond its borders. In Stendhal's *Vie de Rossini* (1824), which served as the primary source for biographical and critical writing about Rossini for well over a century, many were grouped summarily in a composite chapter, "De huit opéras de Rossini." Of these eight, five are Neapolitan; they represented, for Stendhal, the refuse of a composer who betrayed his natural talent by adopting a style that left him in danger of becoming "more *German* than Beethoven himself."[2] They are operas with little or no history and critical tradition before the past fifteen years.

As a result of this view, sanctioned by history (functioning largely as reception history), most of Rossini's serious operas were treated contextually until the 1960s. None was subjected to analytic or critical scrutiny. Several additional reasons for this attitude are worth considering.

1. *Rossini's operas were largely unavailable in accurate editions.* Beneath this true statement lurks a subtext: does it make sense to talk about "accurate" (let alone critical) editions of Italian opera? If we, as historians, stress the flexible nature of performances in the early nineteenth century, with a revival offering what amounts to a new "version" of an opera, the concept "accurate editions" seems to contradict the social and contextual meaning of the repertory. It is one thing to state that Italian composers altered their operatic texts to suit the needs of individual singers or instrumentalists, or particular theaters, or national usages; it is quite another to presume that any manipulation, no matter how extreme, is (or was) acceptable. The latter position implies that an Italian opera has no existence apart from its multiple and equally valid performance incarnations. That Rossini occasionally made extreme adaptations of his works for extreme social conditions (the happy ending grafted onto *Otello* to suit Roman censors is a prime example) does not imply he was indifferent about the performance of his operas. That local music directors regularly reworked operas for particular performances does not mean that their composers would give equal preference to these pastiches and their own scores (in one of their authentic manifestations, as conceived by or performed under the auspices of their authors).

The apparent lack of extensive documentary evidence pertaining to Rossini's years as an active operatic composer, as opposed to his years in retirement (for which documentation is abundant), makes it difficult to assess his views from external evidence. Yet nothing in the published correspondence of Donizetti or Bellini, not to mention Verdi, gives any reason to believe that Italian composers were indifferent to excesses in contemporary performance practice. Their correspondence with the Ricordi publishing houses of Milan, in fact, returns obsessively to the issue of unauthorized adaptations. Although economic considerations played a role in these composers' desire to maintain control over performances of their operas, only an unbridled cynic could consider this their primary goal.

Thus, the absence of accurate editions manifested both a failure to know the works of Rossini as the composer conceived or revised them and an implicit denial that such editions made sense for this repertory.

2. *Rossini was believed to have been cynical about his art.* Facetious anecdotes are legion, mostly generated after his withdrawal from operatic

composition. Who doesn't know that Rossini composed in bed, and that, when the wind blew a sheet of paper away, the lazy composer, rather than pick it up, started again? Who doesn't know that Rossini wrote at breakneck speed (witness the six weeks between the choice of the subject of *Il barbiere di Siviglia* and its first performance) and, when time ran short, employed other composers to write recitatives and even musical numbers? Who doesn't know that Rossini copied from himself relentlessly, reusing the same pieces again and again?

While some of these anecdotes have a basis in reality, to take them as emblematic distorts the situation. Rossini's autograph manuscripts attest to the care and clarity of his work: despite some approximation in rhythmic notation, his precision and accuracy even in complex ensembles is breathtaking. He was capable of working quickly, and some of his more popular operas were written in restricted time frames; but there is no evidence that he preferred to work in this manner.

Several recently discovered documents attest to a more deliberate approach.[3] In the spring of 1815 Rossini wrote to Angelo Anelli (the librettist of *L'Italiana in Algeri*), asking him on behalf of the Teatro Valle of Rome to prepare a new libretto based on a story the composer describes in detail. Athough Anelli refused the commission, the subject ultimately became *Torvaldo e Dorliska,* first performed, to a libretto by Cesare Sterbini, on 26 December 1815. In other words, the subject was chosen more than six months before the premiere.

The situation is analogous for *Bianca e Falliero,* Rossini's 1819 opera for the Teatro alla Scala of Milan. It was first performed on the night of St. Stephen, 26 December; Rossini had approved the subject in an August letter to Felice Romani. In the case of *Semiramide,* Rossini's librettist Gaetano Rossi describes the progress of the opera in a series of letters to Meyerbeer. It is early October 1822; Rossi is a guest in the composer's villa outside Bologna. As he supplies verses, Rossini sets them to music, a full four months before *Semiramide*'s February premiere. Verdi employed considerably less time composing *Rigoletto.*

The pressure of time did cause Rossini occasionally to employ collaborators for recitative or even musical numbers; but often, as in the cases of *L'Italiana in Algeri, La Cenerentola, Mosè in Egitto,* and *Matilde di Shabran,* Rossini later eliminated these numbers or replaced them with new compositions of his own. Likewise, he sometimes borrowed from himself, but rarely were his motives cynical. When during the 1850s the proximate publication of his complete works in arrangements for piano and voice threatened to demonstrate the extent of his "self-borrowing," he said: "I thought I had the right to remove from my fiascos those pieces which seemed best, to rescue them from shipwreck by placing them in new works. A fiasco seemed good and dead, and now look—they've resuscitated them all!"[4] These self-borrowings, furthermore, are often elaborately revised settings rather than simple copying.

These considerations of artistic "intent" and "seriousness" lead to a final group of aesthetic issues.

3. *Rossini's operas were assumed to be mired in conventional procedures, with only occasional moments of originality.* As Janet Levy has pointed out, the idea that the presence of conventional procedures in a work of art is sufficient reason to denigrate its value is part of our heritage from the later nineteenth century (Levy 1987). It leads some critics into contorted justifications for works with "conventional" bases, while it forces others to exaggerate what is simply "original" into the "bizarre" when they withhold a judgment of positive aesthetic value from a composition. The extent to which we speak of a work's conventional aspects, as opposed to its particularities, is not simply a matter of its "content." The more closely we examine an individual work, the more we recognize what differentiates it from apparently similar works; the more we treat the individual work as part of a class, the more we focus on its similarities to other works. This is as true for Beethoven's symphonies as for Henri Herz's piano concertos.

I am not suggesting an unthinking relativism in which we fail to differentiate between, on the one hand, works whose individual qualities are less striking than the qualities that make them part of a group and, on the other hand, works whose individuality overshadows their compositional or social context. Too many voices, however, have proclaimed Italian opera of the first half of the nineteenth century an ideal site for contextual studies, analyzing conventional procedures in aria or duet design, insisting on the primacy of performance, or presuming that artistic content is a function of social history.[5] This is unfortunate not only because we fail to focus critical attention on individual works, but also because in treating these works largely contextually we duplicate the error of some of Rossini's contemporaries, an error which, I believe, hardened his resolve to retire from the operatic stage.

Italian opera of the early nineteenth century worked within a finely tuned system of musical and dramatic conventions, many of which were developed and codified in Rossini's earlier operas. What history has failed to record, because many of the most relevant works have no history, is that

TABLE 1. Rossini's Neapolitan Operas, 1815–1822

Title	First Performance
Elisabetta, Regina d'Inghilterra	→Naples, Teatro San Carlo, 4 October 1815
Torvaldo e Dorliska	Rome, Teatro Valle, 26 December 1815
Il barbiere di Siviglia	Rome, Teatro Argentina, 20 February 1816
La gazzetta	→Naples, Teatro Fiorentini, 26 September 1816
Otello	→Naples, Teatro del Fondo, 4 December 1816
La Cenerentola	Rome, Teatro Valle, 25 January 1817
La gazza ladra	Milan, Teatro alla Scala, 31 May 1817
Armida	→Naples, Teatro San Carlo, 11 November 1817
Adelaide di Borgogna	Rome, Teatro Argentina, 27 December 1817
Mosè in Egitto	→Naples, Teatro San Carlo, 5 March 1818
Ricciardo e Zoraide	→Naples, Teatro San Carlo, 3 December 1818
Ermione	→Naples, Teatro San Carlo, 27 March 1819
Eduardo e Cristina	Venice, Teatro San Benedetto, 24 April 1819
La donna del lago	→Naples, Teatro San Carlo, 24 October 1819
Bianca e Falliero	Milan, Teatro alla Scala, 26 December 1819
Maometto II	→Naples, Teatro San Carlo, 3 December 1820
Matilde di Shabran	Rome, Teatro Apollo, 24 February 1821
Zelmira	→Naples, Teatro San Carlo, 16 February 1822

Rossini, in his Neapolitan years, endeavored to write a series of individual and original operas, as different from one another in tone and content as *Le nozze di Figaro, Don Giovanni,* and *Così fan tutte*

Table 1 provides a list of Rossini's operas from *Elisabetta, Regina d'Inghilterra* of 1815 through the final Neapolitan opera, *Zelmira* of 1822. From 1815 through the middle of 1817, Rossini divided his attention between Naples and the northern cities of Rome and Milan. His first two Neapolitan operas, *Elisabetta* and *La gazzetta*, were "trial" works: a great deal of their music is crafted from pieces in earlier operas, pieces unknown to the Neapolitan public and unlikely candidates for revival. These years marked the pinnacle of Rossini's success as a composer of *opera buffa* and *opera semiseria*. Beginning with *Armida* in November 1817, the picture changes radically. If we recognize that *Adelaide di Borgogna* is a minor work (on which Rossini expended little effort) and *Eduardo e Cristina* is a pastiche, we find that during this period (1818–1822) Rossini averaged essentially two operas a year. It was not unusual for him to allow from six months to a full year between major works.[6]

Thus, in Naples, Rossini had ample time to concentrate his creative energies on individual works, and he chose to write exclusively *opera seria*. Many of these works were completely unknown until very recently. Three crucial Neapolitan operas, *Armida, Ermione,* and *Maometto II,* were failures in their original performances. *Armida* was occasionally revived elsewhere without Rossini's presence, then disappeared until the mid-twentieth century; *Ermione* was performed during one season in Naples, then vanished from the stage until the Rossini Opera Festival of Pesaro revived it in 1987. Rossini himself recast *Maometto II* for Venice in 1822, then adapted it as *Le siège de Corinthe* for Paris in 1826; but its original version, unquestionably the most individual and complex, was not performed again until 1985 at Pesaro.

I want to consider two issues pertaining to Rossini's Neapolitan operas: the nature of their librettos and their approach to large-scale musical planning. These remarks are intended to suggest directions in which studies of Italian opera from this period could be fruitfully pursued, contrasting what we learn from generic and contextual approaches with critical insights dependent on the close study of individual works.

Librettos

In his *Abitare la battaglia,* the Italian critic Gabriele Baldini tells the story of Verdi's *Ernani* in musical terms: "A youthful, passionate female voice is besieged by three male voices, each of which establishes a specific relationship with her" (Baldini 1980:74). Although Baldini here focuses attention on ways in which the dramatic structure "could exist purely and simply within musical means" (ibid.:89), the observation touches a more general nerve: the existence of formulaic relationships between vocal and dramatic types in Italian opera.[7]

In the case of Rossini's operas, certain patterns recur again and again. In figure 1, I have presented some representative examples from the operas listed in table 1, mostly from the Neapolitan works. Typically there are four elements in the design: a father who favors a marriage of his daughter against her will, the heroine herself, and two suitors for her hand. The reciprocated love relationship is usually between the soprano and a tenor or mezzo-soprano; when the relationship is with a tenor/baritone or a bass, trouble almost inevitably follows. (In *Otello* the bass kills the soprano out of jealousy over the tenor; in *Maometto II,* knowing that she should wed the mezzo-soprano but hopelessly in love with the bass, the soprano kills herself rather than be united with an enemy of her people.) The situation in *La donna del lago* is further confused because there are *three* rivals for the soprano's hand, but the pattern remains the same.

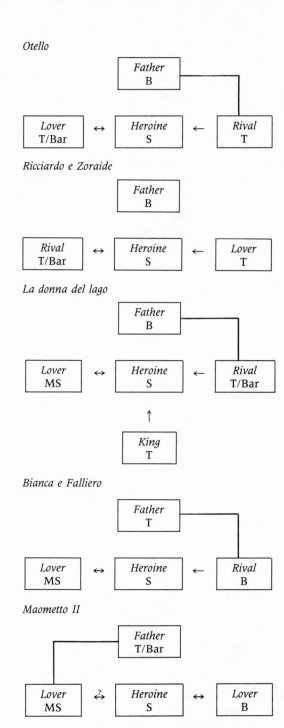

FIGURE 1. Structural Models for the Libretto

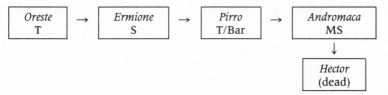

FIGURE 2. Structural Model for the Libretto of *Erminoe*

These structures are not abstract models. They are directly related to the configurations of voices available in Naples during Rossini's tenure. In a Metastasian-Pirandellian *Five Singers in Search of a Plot,* a soprano (Isabella Colbran), a tenor (Giovanni David), a tenor/baritone (Andrea Nozzari), a mezzo-soprano (Rosmunda Pesaroni), and a bass (Michele Benedetti) interact in various, but largely similar configurations.

For comparison, examine the model for *Ermione,* given in figure 2. The pattern is substantially different: its dramaturgical construction (derived from the Greeks via Racine) enmeshes four of our standard types in a hopeless series of relationships. Ultimately, Pirro compels Andromaca to wed him, but at the altar is killed by Oreste, in return for which act Ermione promises herself to Oreste. When Oreste presents her with the bloody dagger, Ermione berates him for having killed the man she loved.

These structural models are useful not only for comparative purposes; they also provide a means for understanding the reasons behind major modifications of a literary source. The transformation of Shakespeare's play brings *Otello* into the general pattern. Notice particularly how Rodrigo (the tenor) becomes an active suitor for Desdemona's hand, blessed by her father (the bass). In *La donna del lago,* Elena's father (the bass) supports the claim of Roderick Dhu (the tenor/baritone), not of Malcolm (the mezzo-soprano), as he does in Sir Walter Scott's poem.

However useful these structural analyses may be, we must not let them obscure the remarkable diversity of sources (see table 2) that Rossini and his librettists used in constructing these Neapolitan operas. These sources run the gamut from an Italian Renaissance verse epic, through two major dramatic traditions of the seventeenth century (English Renaissance drama and French classical tragedy), into the characteristic mock-epics and neoclassical styles of the eighteenth century in France and Italy, and finally reach the most up-to-date literary forces of the early nineteenth century (the Gothic novel, English Romantic poetry, and early Italian Romantic drama). Had Rossini laid down a formal program for the absorption of the major Euro-

TABLE 2. Literary Sources for the Neapolitan Librettos

Opera	Source	Genre
Elisabetta, Regina d'Inghilterra	Sophie Lee, *The Recess*	English Gothic novel, late 18th century
Otello	Shakespeare, *Othello*	English Renaissance drama
Armida	Tasso, *Gerusalemme liberata*	Italian Renaissance verse epic
Mosè in Egitto	Biblical narrative; Ringhieri, *L'Osiride*	Bible; Italian neoclassical sacred drama, 18th century.
Ricciardo e Zoraide	Forteguerri, *Riciardetto*	Italian verse mock-epic, 18th century
Ermione	Racine, *Andromaque*	French classical drama, 17th century
La donna del lago	Scott, *The Lady of the Lake*	English Romantic poetry
Maometto II	Della Valle, *Anna Erizo*	Italian early Romantic drama, 19th century
Zelmira	De Belloy, *Zelmire*	French neoclassical drama, late 18th century

pean literary genres onto the Italian operatic stage, he and his librettists could not have produced a more impressive and varied list of sources.

A structuralist analysis might insist on the ways in which all these genres simply became transformed into Italian opera. A critical analysis, while not denying the truth of that claim, would focus on what is uniquely determined in each work. The tone, language, and poetic style of the libretto of *La donna del lago,* for example, betray throughout an effort to enter the cultural phenomenon of the Scotland celebrated in the poetry of Sir Walter Scott and given a mythic history in the so-called Ossian epics, actually written by James Macpherson. As Stefano Castelvecchi has demonstrated, Rossini's librettist, Andrea Leone Tottola, drew not only on Scott but on the translation of the Ossian epics prepared by the important Italian poet, Melchiorre Cesarotti. This translation sought to render into Italian verse both the spirit and the unusual technical qualities of Macpherson's poetry (Castelvecchi 1991).

Otello's third act (with its willow song and prayer for Desdemona, before the catastrophe), *Armida*'s second act (the timeless "regno di piacer"), *Mosè*'s biblical protagonist (who, in a manner analogous to that of his Schoenbergian descendant, communicates almost exclusively in recitative), *Er-mione's* unique dramaturgical construction, *Maometto II's* coherent patterns of imagery and reference—all these phenomena reflect the efforts of Rossini and his librettists to transfer to the operatic stage what is unique in their literary sources. We need to concentrate our efforts on exploring the delicate balance (not always perfectly maintained) between the structuralist principles by which literary sources are transformed into Italian librettos and the poetic or dramaturgical features of these sources that individualize those librettos.

Large-Scale Musical Planning

Musical equivalents of these structuralist analyses have occupied scholars of Italian opera for the past twenty years, and although we still have no comprehensive *Formenlehre* for Italian opera, significant progress has been made in uncovering the forces at work in early Ottocento opera. Archetypical patterns for the construction of overtures, arias, duets, ensembles, and finales have been identified; their changes over time, and rates of change have been established in a kind of calculus of forms (for some representative examples see Gossett 1979, 1974–75; Powers 1987; and Balthazar 1988).

These scholarly activities inevitably highlight the interchangeability of elements in the design. If it can be determined, for example, that the construction of an aria is governed by laws changing only slowly during the course of a twenty-year period (laws that determine the aria's formal structure, instrumentation, melodic design, and harmonic language), there can be little aesthetic objection to the substitution of one aria by another to suit the preferences of a singer. Social structures in which Italian opera was produced favored the accommodation of these preferences.[8] Singers were the highest-paid participants in performances, adored by both audiences and patrons (including royal patrons). Opera houses were places of social interaction, and successful works were repeated night after night. Many attended simply to hear their favorite performers singing favorite arias, ignored the remainder, and were anything but scandalized when the *prima donna* produced an *aria di baule* (a so-called trunk aria) to enliven the evening's proceedings.

The structuralist tendency in scholarly investigations of early Ottocento opera and the social/contextual treatment of the entire repertory are, then, natural allies. Rossini's compositional and directorial activities during the Neapolitan period provided numerous examples in support of this alliance. He snatched the rondò finale from *La donna del lago* and inserted it (though with important changes) into *Bianca e Falliero* just two months later. He gave the second soprano in *Mosè in Egitto* a thoroughly inappropriate aria lifted from his 1812 opera *Ciro in Babilonia* (though he had the good sense to drop the piece when reviving *Mosè in Egitto* at the San Carlo in 1819). He allowed—or perhaps even encouraged—the young Gian Battista Rubini to insert a magnificent but irrelevant aria from the popularly despised *Ermione* into the final scene of *La donna del lago* for its second run of performances in Naples during the summer of 1820. And he transformed the tragic finales of both *Otello* and *Maometto II* for particular later performances. In the case of *Otello*, the reconciliation of Desdemona and Otello (with the insertion of a duet from *Armida*) avoided the potential for offended morals in a city (Rome) whose theaters were under strict religious censorship; for the Venetian performance of *Maometto II* in 1822, the public was treated to the theatrical fantasy that their ancestors had actually defeated the Turks at Negroponte in 1470, and Anna concluded the evening with the by-now-obligatory rendition of the rondò from *La donna del lago*.

There is a curious emergent dialogue concerning musicology and Italian opera, a dialogue in which both scholarly imperialism and nationalism (or even racism) figure prominently, if not always explicitly. During the course of the past twenty years, musicological study of Italian Ottocento opera has been welcomed as one of our discipline's "canonical" activities, but there have been pockets of marked resistance to the "canonic" enshrinement of the individual work of art. Don Randel, in his essay in the present volume, comments on "musicology's traditional imperialism," noting that musicology "has typically added repertories to its domain by a process of colonization that imposes traditional methods on new territories. After years of regarding Italian opera as peripheral if not frivolous, we discovered that it too had sources and even sketches to study and edit and that it too could be investigated in terms of large-scale formal coherence." In short, scholarship appropriated Italian opera without inventing "new methods appropriate for its study." Randel implicitly suggests (and he is not alone) that such investigations are inappropriate for a repertory whose meaning is so dependent on cultural or social/contextual issues. In this formulation, the activities of editing such "peripheral, if not frivolous" music, studying its sources, and analyzing it with techniques derived from "central, and serious" (that is, German) music fail to address what is "most interesting or characteristic about it." This, in *poche parole*, can be translated as meaning that Italian composers, absorbed in their *dolce far niente*, should be allowed to soak in the warm Mediterranean sun and leave canonical matters to their northern brethren. The same "methodology" isolates Russian, English, American,

French, and Czech music on the "peripheries" of a central Austro-German tradition and both defines and evaluates them in terms of that tradition.[9]

Most of us, even those who investigate, respect, and love early Ottocento Italian opera, have been so infected by these cultural prejudices that we have neglected to subject individual works to the kind of analytic scrutiny we take for granted when the composer's name is Mozart, Weber, or Wagner. Verdi, particularly *late* Verdi, is only slowly and grudgingly being admitted to the hallowed circle. Even when we do undertake such studies, we are burdened by doubts concerning the significance of our findings. Despite the complex issues involved in defining an opera as being in a "key," for example, the claim that *Così fan tutte* is in C major, *Die Zauberflöte* in E♭ major, and both *Le nozze di Figaro* and *Don Giovanni* in D major is widely accepted. Has anyone understood, though, that *Mosè in Egitto* is in C minor/major, *Ermione* in F minor/major, and *La donna del lago* in E♭ major?

Such a claim goes beyond the simple statement that an opera begins and ends in the same key. *Mosè in Egitto*, for example, opens with three sustained C's, played by the entire orchestra. The curtain rises immediately, revealing the stage bathed in darkness. The Egyptians lament the veil that has covered the sun and beg Faraone to call for Mosè. Their words are sustained by an orchestral figure that moves throughout the orchestra and through a series of keys, but this opening is centered in C minor. In a strong, declamatory "invocazione," Mosè subsequently implores God to show his power again, and as "the most luminous day returns" the music shifts from C minor to C major. The first-act finale begins with a joyous chorus in C major for the Hebrews, who are about to leave Egypt. Political machinations and unresolved sentimental attachments convince Faraone to prevent their departure. In another show of strength, Mosè causes the rain of fire to fall on the Egyptians, and it is on their terror (with which the finale turns to C minor) that the curtain falls.

C major is also the key of the central composition of the second act, at least from the moment that its opening duet becomes a quartet. In the closing moments of the opera, the pattern is finally resolved, as the Hebrews (after the famous Prayer) begin their traversal of the Red Sea in C major. The Egyptians arrive and determine to follow them, but as they do the waters close and the mode changes to minor. They struggle and are consumed by the sea, after which the audience "sees the Red Sea tranquil, and on the opposite shore the Hebrew people, kneeling in thanks to God," as the music settles for the last time into C major.

Did Rossini know Beethoven's similar use of these tonalities in *Christus am*

Ölberge (not to mention the Fifth Symphony)? We have no direct evidence. But one can hardly pretend that an analysis of their presence in *Mosè in Egitto* is a sample of musicological imperialism, particularly when similar processes return in other works. *La donna del lago* is dominated by E♭ major, particularly associated with the Scottish clan in revolt and the forests in which the action of the opera unfolds. E♭ major is the key of the opera's extensive introduction, the aria of Douglas, the first-act finale (where it is used not only for the external sections, but also for Malcolm's entrance and the Chorus of the Bards), and finally the chorus and Elena's rondò finale that conclude the opera.

Rossini begins *Ermione* with an unusual overture that incorporates laments from the chorus of Trojan prisoners behind the closed curtain. A descending F-minor scale (divided into two tetrachords) is heard, first played in unison by the entire orchestra, then delicately harmonized in the winds. The music continues until the chorus intervenes with its lament: "Troja! qual fosti un dì! / Di te che resta ancor?" (Troy! how proud you used to be! What remains of you now?) After the F-minor/major overture, the curtain rises to reveal the prison where the Trojan slaves are being held; the opening bars of the introduction are melodically akin to the first measures of the overture. As the opening chorus concludes, the initial tetrachord is used as the basis of the cadences. The remainder of the introduction, which will conclude in F major, features the arrival of Andromaca and her tender scene with the son she bore Hector, Astianatte.

The concluding scene of the opera—an extended accompanied recitative for Ermione solo, her duet with Oreste, and the latter's abrupt departure—is perhaps the most dramatically intense monologue and confrontation in Italian opera from the first half of the nineteenth century (a statement I do not make lightly). The *scena* features prominently the tetrachords and scales of the opening measures of the opera, and the latter also provide the accompaniment for the initial melody of the duet (at "Vendicata! e di quel sangue . . ."). When the Greeks come rushing in to remove Oreste from the fury of Pirro's people, the music moves to F major for the brief last movement. After a final reappearance of the opening F-minor tetrachord (in the bass at "Vieni . . . Ti arrendi . . . Che osate, oh barbari!"), a repeated tetrachordal cadence (now chromatic) concludes the opera.

Maometto II is particularly interesting for the way in which Rossini sought various musical means to unify a work and give it a particular character. It is a tragic opera that sets the fate of four characters against a background of historical events—the wars between the Turks and the Venetians, culminating in the fall of Negroponte. Paolo Erisso is in charge of the Venetian forces; Maometto II leads the assault of the Turks. It is a fourfold tragedy: of Anna, Erisso's daughter, who is in love with Maometto but cannot permit herself to surrender to feelings that betray her people; of the conqueror Maometto, who cannot have the only joy he truly desires; and of Erisso, who loves his daughter above all else but feels honor-bound to supply her with the dagger she will ultimately use to take her own life; of Calbo, the young Venetian warrior, who wishes to wed Anna but will not impose his affections on a woman who loves another.

On several layers, Rossini sought to provide thematic unity within the opera, and some of these elements convey a subtle yet perfectly audible series of tonal/thematic references throughout the work. The opera opens with a chorus, in which the Venetian warriors gather to plan their course of action. Faced with the prospect of a long siege by the Turks, they nonetheless vow at the conclusion of the introduction to fight until death. Though the two choruses are separated by a lengthy ensemble, Rossini transforms the opening, hesitant, triple-time movement into a strong final section in 4/4, giving the entire introduction a sense of dramatic and musical unity. It is not far-fetched to hear the cabaletta of Calbo's Aria toward the end of the second act, where he assures Erisso of Anna's moral strength to face death rather than dishonor her people, as another transformation of this same motive.

The introduction, with which the opera begins (there is no overture), is in E♭ major; Calbo's aria is in E major, the key in which the entire opera will conclude with the suicide of Anna. A casual glance at the score might suggest that Rossini was indifferent to tonal structure, since he ends the opera a semitone higher than its point of departure; but there is strong evidence that this is not the case. A central image of the opera is the tomb in which the ashes of Anna's mother lie. When Erisso asks his daughter to wed Calbo, he invokes his wife's tomb:

> Or vieni al tempio,
> Là dove il sacro cenere riposa
> Della spent tua madre.
>
> [Now come to the temple, where the sacred ashes of your dead mother repose.]

Accompanied by tremolo strings alone, the phrase begins in E♭ major, then modulates upward a semitone to E major.

The last scene of the opera takes place in the church, amid the tombs. It begins with a strong ritornello, invoking the desperate situation of the be-sieged Venetians. Soon after, Erisso pauses before the tomb of his wife and, within the course of a recitative passage, breaks into a lyrical phrase, accom-panied by strings alone. The phrase begins not in E♭ major, but in the closely related A♭ major. As Erisso invokes the heaven, where his wife now resides ("Tenera sposa! / In ciel riposi or tu" [Beloved wife! You now rest in heaven]), the music sits on the dominant and then tortuously modulates up a semitone to the familiar E major. After Calbo's E-major aria (whose cabaletta theme invokes the introduction of the opera), Anna enters. Before her mother's tomb, she vows to follow her father's wishes and accept the hand of Calbo ("Madre . . . dal cielo in questo cor tu leggi" [Mother . . . from heaven you see into my heart]). Her music is identical to the phrase Erisso sings earlier in the scene.

Ultimately, her vow of fidelity before the tomb of her mother and her vow to kill herself rather than be captured by the Turks are musically integrated by their similar settings and tonality. During the course of the first-act *terzet-tone* (a "big fat trio" that lasts almost twenty-five minutes), Erisso hands her a dagger, her "inheritance" on this fatal day: she is to use it rather than fall captive to the Turks. It is a phrase declaimed first over a tremolando accom-paniment on the pitch E. At the very end of the opera, faced with the defeat of her people, Anna turns on Maometto and tells him that, in front of her mother's tomb, she has sworn her faith to Calbo; then she stabs herself, singing:

> Sul cenere materno
> Il porsi a lui la mano;
> Il cenere materno
> Coglie il mio sangue ancor.

> [Over my mother's ashes I gave him my hand; let my mother's ashes now receive my blood.]

In a passage that refers explicitly to the earlier phrase, the first two lines are declaimed on the pitch E over a tremolando accompaniment in E major.

Hence, the E♭-major-to-E-major progression heard in Erisso's very first invocation of his wife's tomb takes on a wider musical and dramatic mean-ing throughout the opera and duplicates on a small scale the large-scale E♭-to-E-major tonality of the entire work. Rossini apparently has used a se-ries of melodic and harmonic similarities to join music and drama in a tight web of meaning.

⁙

We have practically no written documents pertaining to Rossini's artistic views during the period in which he was actively composing operas. We cannot reconstruct his psychological states from surviving letters, nor are the meager newspaper reports of the epoch helpful. Study of the Neapolitan operas themselves, however, reveals a composer poised in a highly creative fashion between the social, cultural, and musical context in which he is operating and the artistic desire to create mature, independent works, each with a definite character, each coming to grips in a different way with the problem of convention and originality. Is it too much to presume that Rossini's disillusionment with the Italian theater of his time can be read in these stillborn compositions, these non-facts of music history, whose rejection by the Neapolitans—one of the most cultivated operatic publics of Europe—was a rejection of Rossini as a creative artist? He responded first by leaving Italy, then (after the *succès d'estime* of *Guillaume Tell*) by retiring from the stage, a cynically detached observer, conscious of what he had had to offer but psychologically unable to press his claim.

In a certain sense, these Neapolitan operas are being heard today for the first time. As we learn more about them, they play an ever-larger role in our conceptual systems. We can no longer see other, more familiar works in quite the same light. Certain aspects of *Le siège de Corinthe* (Rossini's first French opera) seem a trivialization of his earlier art. *Semiramide* becomes not the pinnacle of Rossini's career as a composer of Italian *opera seria*, but rather a measured retreat from the ambitions of his Neapolitan works. Acknowledgment of the variety of these compositions makes it more difficult to generalize about Rossini's art and leads us instead to investigate more attentively the individual qualities of his operas. Indeed, the efforts to understand the nature of the canon inevitably lead us to reexamine the discourses our discipline employs to study and evaluate the "facts" it enshrines. Each new "fact" of music history forces us to reinterpret what we thought we knew, and works that had no history become instrumental in leading us to rewrite the history in which they played no part.

NOTES

1. The inscription is found on the last page of the original version of the *Petite messe solonnelle* (1863): "J'étais né pour l'Opéra Buffa, tu le sais bien! Peu de science, un peu de coeur, tout est là. Sois donc Béni, et accorde-moi le Paradis."

2. The remark arises in the context of a comparison between Rossini and Mozart: "Ces deux hommes de génie ont marché en sens inverse. Mozart aurait fini par s'ita-

lianiser tout à fait. Rossini finira peut-être par être plus allemand que Beethoven (Stendhal [1824] 1960:430; and Coe 1970:394).

3. These documents and letters appear in the first volume of the Rossini correspondence, edited by Bruno Cagli and Sergio Ragni (scheduled for publication by the Fondazione Rossini, Pesaro, in 1992).

4. The remark comes from a conversation held in Florence in 1854 and published in the *Revue de Paris* on 1 March 1856 (quoted in Azevedo 1864:98–99). Rossini expressed similar feelings in a letter to Tito di Giovanni Ricordi of 14 December 1864 (see G. and F. Mazzatinti and Manis 1902:284–85).

5. The six-volume *Storia dell'opera italiana*, edited by Lorenzo Bianconi and Giorgio Pestelli (of which three volumes have been published), is a prime example. The planners proclaim their conceptual position in their choice of titles and subtitles, where not a single composer's name is mentioned. Specific works are invoked as part of a historical or theoretical narrative, never for their individual qualities.

6. The history of Rossini's Neapolitan years is recounted in Cagli and Ziino 1987:133–68. This study is based largely on newly discovered documents that will be published in the first volume of the Rossini correspondence, mentioned in note 3.

7. Many structuralist literary critics, such as Mario Lavagetto, have vigorously pursued research in this direction (see Lavagetto 1979).

8. For an excellent introduction to the social context of nineteenth-century Italian opera, see Rosselli 1984.

9. Carl Dahlhaus undertakes a similar operation with the concept of "realism" in his *Realism in Nineteenth-Century Music:* the book focuses on works that do not participate in "the dominant style in music at any point in the nineteenth century" (Dahlhaus 1985:120). It comes as no surprise that these works are largely by composers with names such as Berlioz, Verdi, Bizet, Mussorgsky, Janáček, and Mascagni.

WORKS CITED

Azevedo, A. 1864. *G. Rossini: Sa vie et ses oeuvres.* Paris: Heugel.

Baldini, Gabriele. 1980. *The Story of Giuseppe Verdi: Oberto to Un Ballo in Maschera.* Trans. Roger Parker. Cambridge: Cambridge University Press. Originally published as *Abitare la battaglia* (1970).

Balthazar, Scott L. 1988. "Rossini and the Development of the Mid-Century Lyric Form." *Journal of the American Musicological Society* 41:102–25.

Cagli, Bruno and Augostino Ziino, eds. 1987. "Al gran sole di Rossini." In *Il Teatro di San Carlo: 1737–1987*, 3 vols. Vol. 2, *L'opera, il ballo.* Naples: Electa.

Castelvecchi, Stefano. 1991. "Walter Scott, Rossini, and the *Couleur ossianique:* The Cultural Context of *La donna del lago.*" Unpublished.

Coe, Richard. 1970. *Life of Rossini.* New and rev. ed. London: Calder & Boyars.

Dahlhaus, Carl. 1983. *Foundations of Music History.* Trans. J. B. Robinson. Cambridge: Cambridge University Press.

———. 1985. *Realism in Nineteenth-Century Music.* Trans. Mary Whittal. Cambridge: Cambridge University Press.

Gossett, Philip. 1974–75. "Verdi, Ghislanzoni, and *Aida:* The Uses of Convention." *Critical Inquiry* 1:291–334.

————. 1979. "Le sinfonie di Rossini." *Bollettino del centro rossiniano di studi,* pp. 5–123.

Lavagetto, Mario. 1979. *Quei più modesti romanzi: Il libretto nel melodramma di Verdi.* Milan: Garzanti.

Levy, Janet M. 1987. "Covert and Casual Values in Recent Writings about Music." *Journal of Musicology* 5:3–27.

Mazzatinti, G. and F., and G. Manis, eds. 1902. *Lettere de G. Rossini.* Florence: G. Barbèra.

Powers, Harold S. 1987. "'La solita forma' and 'The Uses of Convention'." *Acta Musicologica* 59:65–90.

Rosselli, John. 1984. *The Opera Industry in Italy from Cimarosa to Verdi: The Role of the Impresario.* Cambridge: Cambridge University Press.

Silvestri, Lodovico Settimo. 1874. *Della vita e delle opere di Gioachino Rossini.* Milan: A spese dell'autore.

Stendhal, Marie-Henri Beyle. 1960. *Vie de Rossini.* Ed. V. del Litto. Lausanne. Originally published 1824.

Weber, Max. 1949. "'Objectivity' in Social Science and Social Policy." In Edward A. Shils and Henry A. Finch, trans. and eds., *The Methodology of the Social Sciences.* Glencoe, Ill.: Free Press.

SEVEN

Ethnomusicology's Challenge to the Canon; the Canon's Challenge to Ethnomusicology
Philip V. Bohlman

During the 1950s the Dutch ethnomusicologist, Jaap Kunst, published three editions of a work he called *Musicologica* in the first edition, but simply *Ethnomusicology* in the subsequent editions. As an epigraph for this detailed bibliography and study of the concepts, literature, scholars, and teaching and research programs in ethnomusicology, Kunst used the following eight lines from Goethe (Kunst 1959:x):

> Wer sich selbst und andre kennt
> Wird auch hier erkennen:
> Orient und Okzident
> Sind nicht mehr zu trennen.
>
> Sinnig zwischen beiden Welten
> Sich zu wiegen laß ich gelten:
> Also zwischen Ost- und Westen
> Sich bewegen sei zum Besten!
>
> [One who knows oneself and others
> Will also recognize that
> Orient and Occident
> Can no longer be separated.
>
> I admit consciously to living
> In both worlds;
> Indeed one is best enjoined to travel
> Between the two worlds of East and West!]

Both literally and metaphorically a marginal text in the intellectual history of ethnomusicology, these lines, cited by Kunst with the title "Epigrammatisch," stand at the threshold of the field's modern era. Probably written by Goethe in 1826, these two quatrains, the second and third of a poem intended for an expanded version of "Moganni Nameh, Buch des Sängers," the first section of *West-östlicher Divan* (1819), Goethe's poetic representation of non-Western culture, specifically Muslim and Sufi mysticism, never appeared in print during Goethe's lifetime. They acquired, instead, a life of their own that came to symbolize nineteenth-century Europe's attempt to ponder itself in the mirrors of Middle Eastern and Asian culture. Standing alone, innocently and innocuously in small print at the bottom of the page facing the opening page of *Ethnomusicology*, these lines, in effect, announce the beginning of both the first book that deliberately employed the word *ethnomusicology* in its title and the scholarly discipline that deliberately distinguished itself from others by the same designation.

That the epigraph proclaims a message that has in many ways been axiomatic for the field is obvious from the rapid growth of ethnomusicology among the musical disciplines in the 1950s. Just as Goethe wrote at a time of increasing European intellectual engagement with cultures other than its own and sought increasingly to transform the classical canon of German *Lyrik* with the form and sensibility that he discovered when engaging himself with non-Western poetry and thinking, so too did ethnomusicology seek the transforming potential that the study of non-Western music and culture afforded. Goethe also recognized that engagement meant direct encounter—indeed, living in both worlds—and he underscored this with his closing call to travel between the two worlds, a reflexive process that Goethe framed with a simple reflexive verb, *bewegen sich*.

During the 1950s ethnomusicologists had themselves engaged with the worlds of East and West in ways previous generations had not imagined possible. Not only could one pursue field research in virtually any area of the world, but the increased ease with which one could record, retrieve, and represent music in its cultural context transformed the "travel between the two worlds" into a disciplinary imperative empowering one to know both "oneself and others." The ethnomusicologists of the 1950s had brought about a radical new way of disciplining music, of determining even what music might be. Music could no longer be understood simply as an expressive phenomenon only of the self, for it ineffably reflected the presence of the Other in a world that both self and Other cohabited.

The epigraph also conveys its message in a manner that became remarkably paradigmatic during the decades witnessing the emergence of modern ethnomusicology. Just as the epigraph is distinctive because of the reflexivity of its syntax—"Wer sich selbst und andre kennt"—so too did the formation of ethnomusicology in the 1950s and 1960s become an increasingly reflexive process of self-examination, self-criticism, and self-reflection. We witness this reflexivity in the field's major texts, which are inevitably replete with what must seem to scholars from other disciplines like inordinate fussing over methods, goals, self-identity, and the sheer burden of the expansive field ethnomusicology has chosen for itself (see, for example, A. Seeger 1985).

The canons that I examine in this essay lie within these reflexive texts and, it almost goes without saying, assume the reflexive quality of those texts. I cannot quite forgo saying this because I do not believe that it has been obvious to all that these paradigmatic canons in ethnomusicology are not the musics studied by the field's scholars, but the texts created by those scholars. In this sense, I interpret modern ethnomusicology not as a field devoted to non-Western and folk music, but as a field devoted to the *study* of these musics and others. The field's canons form within this notion of "study" and become the texts that symbolize this study. Here, I follow the distinction offered by Roland Barthes between "work" and "text," the former being a "fragment of substance" and the latter being "a methodological field" that exists because it is constantly "restored to language" (1977:156, 159; see Boon 1986:239–41). Restoring music to language, the formulation of poesis through praxis, has been fundamental to the ways modern ethnomusicology disciplines musics (see Bohlman 1991b and A. Seeger 1991, both of which explore the diverse ways in which ethnomusicological texts represent music).

Canonic reflexivity—challenging a canon while being challenged by it— has been a distinctive trait of ethnomusicology's development since the 1950s and is coeval with the modern coming-of-age of the field. The full articulation of this reflexivity began with the decision to break with other fields in the early 1950s and to chart an independent disciplinary course. Although it has been commonplace to view this break with the past as a revolt against historical musicology—that is as a final flurry of frustration over historical musicology's unwillingness to listen to most of the musics in the world—I offer a rather different historiographic explanation in this essay. Indeed, there was dissatisfaction with historical musicology's canons, but that was nothing new. The schism of the 1950s was, I believe, less a confrontation with historical musicology and its claims to canonic authority than a challenge to the lineage extending from the direct predecessors of ethnomusicology—its patrilineal ancestors, one might say. Ethnomusicology did not, in fact, go about challenging historical musicology to trash its canons. Rather, it engaged in the extensive reassessment of its own canons and effected this reassessment by shifting those canons from the "works" with which it was concerned, that is, with musical "pieces," to the "text" it was rapidly producing, namely the writing about music, which we now call musical ethnography (see Etzkorn 1988).

Ethnomusicology's challenge, then, was self-imposed; it came from within, from a recognition of the desire and impulse to reformulate its own canons. Accordingly, ethnomusicology internalized a process of canon formation that reflexively embraced canons not as a means of fixing the field, but as a means of constantly endowing itself with the potential to change in response to its own self-reflective discourse.

Ethnomusicology's Critical Moment in the 1950s

The emergence of modern ethnomusicology in the 1950s has spawned an abundance of origin myths. Many of the most basic myths attempt to recount the origins of the external markers of the field: its name, for example, or the symbol of the Society for Ethnomusicology. Did Jaap Kunst simply coin the word, *ethno-musicology,* and then did Richard Waterman insist upon dropping the hyphen between *ethno* and *musicology* in order to appease those disgruntled by a terminologically schizophrenic field? And who was it that took such a liking to the gold Panamanian flute player in the Art Institute of Chicago that it should bedeck the official publications of the SEM ever since? Other origin myths are more theoretical in import, pertaining more directly to the subject matter and early literature of modern ethnomusicology. One myth holds that the new ethnomusicologists, fed up with comparative musicology, scattered about the world to engage in fieldwork, collecting exactly the data that the comparativists had failed to take into account. Other myths recount the various battles waged against historical musicology, which had reputedly and repeatedly snubbed ethnomusicology.

These myths create a picture that makes the origin appear both more radical and more conservative than it really was. But these same myths emanate from a time of intellectual foment in the two-century history of ethnomusicology that was unlike any moment of change before (see Bohlman 1988a). It was a moment of change in which the field of ethnomusicology turned toward itself in self-criticism, using radical change—scientific revolution in the Kuhnian sense of the concept (see Kuhn 1970)—as a protest against its own ancestors. The discursive struggle was, therefore, internecine, not externally directed against some presumed hegemony of historical musicology. Significant in the waging of this intellectual struggle is that it set the tone for modern ethnomusicology's insistence on self-reflection as essential to the proper course of the field.

The ancestors against whom the new ethnomusicologists of the 1950s turned were clearly identifiable because of the disciplinary rubric *vergleichende Musikwissenschaft*, comparative musicology. The problem posed by comparative musicology that so plagued ethnomusicologists in the 1950s was one of distance, namely, the gap between our music and the music of the Other. Comparative musicology, by its very nature, took that gap as a given, as a fixed element in a skewed cultural equation in which the canonic presence of Western art music was also a given. In essence, the study of another's music began only after its hypothetical relation to Western art music had been established. Probably the classic concern in such cases of comparison was the question of whether a music did or did not have harmony (see Blum 1991 and Waterman 1991 for two critiques of this concern and others in early Africanist musical scholarship).

Comparative musicologists believed much of the value in studying non-Western or folk musics lay in the potential influences of these on their own art music. Their definitions of comparative musicology stressed this value and these influences, and the praxis of research was often designed so that the musical capital produced through investment in non-Western musics transferred directly to the store of European musical thought. Erich M. von Hornbostel and others associated with the Berlin Phonogrammarchiv, for example, toured the musical world from their armchairs and *Lehrstühle*, methodically defining one *Tonsystem* after another, creating a paradigm for comparability and a potentially endless series of articles in the standard German musicological literature about the *Tonsystem* of yet another people.

Rather than pondering still more ways that studying the musics of other cultures could reveal more about their own, scholars forging the new discipline in the 1950s sought to create a discourse that would embody a major reformulation and reversal of the fundamental relation between our music and that of the Other. Ethnomusicology, it was believed, should halt the appropriation of non-Western musics, a process that had purposefully bolstered the authority of European canons. Jaap Kunst stated early in *Ethnomusicology* that the power embedded in the privileging of the Western canon had to be avoided in the new discipline. "The original term 'comparative musicology' (vergleichende Musikwissenschaft) fell into disuse, because it promised more—for instance, the study of mutual influences in Western art music—than it intended to comprise" (1959:1).

The disciplinary ancestors—the comparative musicologists—had earlier treated the music they studied as belonging to other cultures. They therefore enforced a distance between other musical repertories and one that was clearly their own. The new ethnomusicologists, in contrast, sought to draw themselves closer to the music of the Other, in essence negating the implicit distancing mechanism altogether. The music they would study, then, was *all* music, the musics of all cultures; and clearly they understood that these other musics were not necessarily Western music. To understand what made other musics different—to move difference itself to the center of the new discipline—the field distanced itself from Western art music.

> The study-object of ethnomusicology, or, as it originally was called: comparative musicology, is the *traditional* music and musical instruments of all cultural strata of mankind, from the so-called primitive peoples to the civilized nations. Our science, therefore, investigates all tribal and folk music and every kind of non-Western art music. Besides, it studies as well the sociological aspects of music, as the phenomena of musical acculturation, i.e. the hybridizing influence of alien musical elements. Western art- and popular (entertainment-) music do not belong to its field. (Ibid.)

The new ethnomusicologists insisted that the hermeneutic potential of a music must lie in that music's uniqueness, in its bearing no relation whatsoever to any other music, least of all to Western music. Moreover, they discovered as a means of further reducing the distance between musics the enchanting proposition of embracing some of these musics as their own. A canonic reversal therefore occurred, in which the true music of the Other was Western art music. Thus, it was not a revolt against Western art music that stripped that music of its privilege, but a shift of reflexive perspective that resituated the distance between the musics studied by the ethnomusicologist. This was less a matter of rebelling against *the* canon of Western art music than of turning to the rather more numerous and more enticing canons of non-Western music.

Anthropology's role in this realignment of disciplinary kinship structures was complex, yet catalytic, for it was responsible in several essential ways for rendering ethnomusicology's canons reflexive. At one level, anthropologists turned to ethnomusicology in larger numbers. Encouraged, perhaps, by Alan Merriam's seminal role as editor of ethnomusicology's first newsletter of its own, anthropologists participated in the institutionalizing of the Society for Ethnomusicology. Anthropologists reported their fieldwork regularly in the *Ethno-Musicology Newsletter*. Ethnomusicological panels and papers frequently appeared in reports of anthropology conferences, in the early newsletters far more often than at music conferences, and it was in conjunction with the meeting of the American Anthropological Association in 1955 that the SEM officially constituted itself (*Ethno-Musicology Newsletter* 5 [September 1955]:1).

At another level, this new interest from anthropology brought with it a sweeping new methodology. Fieldwork was not simply a matter of serving up a body of tunes in a representative anthology, but of specifying precisely the recording techniques and contexts of fieldwork. Early newsletter reports consistently addressed questions of tape speed or microphone placement. Anthropology also relied on a different system for disseminating information, which, in turn, redefined recordings, movies, and photographs—in fact, cutting-edge technologies of all kinds—as the most effective ethnographic texts. On their surfaces, the prosaic field accounts of the 1950s seem today deliberately dry and factual, but the forceful message they conveyed was that the new study of music was concerned with a different concept of music, a concept determined by differences. In the first *Ethno-Musicology Newsletter* we read, for instance:

> In September 1952, *Alan P. Merriam* returned from a year's ethno-musicological research in the Belgian Congo and Ruanda Urundi with a total of thirty-eight hours of music, recorded at 7$\frac{1}{2}$ ips with a three-input Magnecorder. Of the 932 songs recorded, 121 were of the music of the Bashi, 179 of the Bahutu, 68 of the Batwa, 154 of the Abatutsi, 115 of the Barundi, 25 of the Bambuti, 31 of the Bahima, and 151 of the Bakwale clan of the Ekonda people. In addition, extensive photographic work concerned for the most part with subjects of ethno-musicological interest, was carried out by *Barbara W. Merriam* in both black and white, and color stills as well as color movies. (1953:3)

At still another level, anthropology was an essential player in the internecine realignment symbolized by the controversies over words and their messages in ethnomusicology. Whether or not Jaap Kunst actually coined the term *ethnomusicology,* those with an anthropological background found it particularly appropriate for their acceptance of and in the field. It is hardly coincidental, in fact, that the term recalled a movement within anthropology during the 1950s, namely, the so-called New Ethnography, which promised to lend greater precision to the explanation of cultural phenomena by drawing to a large extent on linguistics for models (see Sturtevant 1964 and Harris 1968). Signaling the "New Ethnography" was the proliferation of subdisciplines such as "ethnolinguistics," "ethnohistory," and, of course, "ethnomusicology." This being the case, we might wish to rethink the origin myths that insist anthropologists created the Society for Ethnomusicology to protest their exclusion from the institutions of historical musicology. Again, I think it fairer to say that the new ethnomusicologists were far more concerned with reformulating the approaches of their own field than debunking those of another.

At a final level, the anthropological impetuses motivating the new ethnomusicologists led them to the discovery of new musics. Here, we witness the direct convergence of canons and musics, ways of thinking about and studying music that blew open what music could be. Nothing could have been more distinct from the comparativist's charts detailing *Tonsysteme* than the anthropologist's sensitivity to representing music in the terms of another culture. These terms (or the lack thereof) may bear no relation to Western musical vocabularies, and hence they must be formulated into texts unlike those of Western musicology. David McAllester's fieldwork among the Navaho led him to pose some of the most trenchant and self-reflective of these anthropological questions in the 1950s.

> Perhaps the most basic question, and one of the hardest to approach, *is what music is conceived to be.* A striking example of my own cultural bias in this respect became apparent when I had the first section of my questionnaire translated into Navaho: there was no general word for "musical instrument" or even for "music." . . . A "fact" in the Navaho universe is that music is not a general category of activity but has to be divided into specific aspects or kinds of music. I learned, moreover, that beating a drum to accompany oneself in song was not a matter of esthetic choice but a rigid requirement for a particular ceremony, and a discussion of musical instruments was not an esthetic discussion for the Navahos but was, by definition, a discussion of ceremonial esoterica. (1954:4; emphasis in the original)

Navaho music did not lend itself to direct comparison with Western music. And for that matter, neither does music in the Muslim Middle East or circumpolar Europe. Music means different things in different societies, and those different things found their ways into ethnographic texts not as "music" in general, that is, as an abstract, universal phenomenon, but as "a music" or as "musics" with specific and distinctive qualities. These abundant musics, in turn, revealed the presence of vastly different canons, which challenged ethnomusicology to find a new language, a new discourse for the representation of musics and their defiant differences.

Canonic Implications of Dubbing
the Field "Ethnomusicology"

Rarely does a field take up a new name quite so abruptly as ethnomusicology did in the 1950s. The dramatic redubbing of the field was
symbolic of ethnomusicology's response to a number of canonic challenges.
This response was often voiced at the level of terminology, in the words with
which ethnomusicologists sought to understand their field and in the texts
with which they created that field. Terminology came to represent, for example, one of the primary quarrels with *vergleichende Musikwissenschaft.* Did
this field really compare more than any other? Did it really compare at all?
Was there even enough available data to permit fair comparison?

One might suppose that such questions established a new imperative for
fieldwork; and to some extent that is true. Because the inefficacy of the comparative approach had so vividly pointed out how little we knew about certain musics, it was necessary to go into the field to collect and collect, thereby
filling in the gaps. The ethnomusicological literature of the ensuing period,
then, should have been filled with ethnographic lacuna-stuffing. Studies of
individual music cultures or particular genres did proliferate, but they did
not become the predominant genre of the period. Instead, it was the monographic study of the field and its methods that dominated the literature
(A. Seeger 1991). Jaap Kunst, Alan Merriam, Bruno Nettl, David McAllester,
and others used the large-scale study to search for definitions, terminologies,
and new words to give the field its meanings and its texts: Nettl's *Music in
Primitive Culture* (1956) and *Theory and Method in Ethnomusicology* (1964),
Kunst's *Ethnomusicology* (1950, 1955, and 1959), and Merriam's *The Anthropology of Music* (1964)—these are the texts that mark the 1950s and
1960s. And the canonic debate, particularly, took on an international
character in the writings of Fritz Bose (e.g., 1953), Marius Schneider (e.g.,
1957), Kurt Reinhard (e.g., 1968), and others seeking to define meanings
and refine texts.

Even those who failed to produce monographs engaged in this war of
words within ethnomusicology. Charles Seeger is, no doubt, the best example of an ethnomusicologist who never tired of wrestling with every possible nuance of terminological meaning. His textual wrestling matches
appeared as his most significant articles, with terminological implications
clear from their very titles: "On the Moods of a Musical Logic" (1960) or
"Speech, Music, and Speech about Music" (1977). Seeger often seems the
most curmudgeonly in these texts, arguing that the term *ethnomusicology* was
a misnomer. For Seeger, the discipline in which ethnomusicologists engaged

themselves was really studying all musics (precisely Kunst's call); hence that discipline was the "real" musicology, rather than the one that limited itself to the historical study of Western art music (see C. Seeger 1970). Critics from outside the field, for example, Joseph Kerman (1985) and Gilbert Chase (1972), seem to take a certain comfort in Seeger's challenge and apparent unwillingness to abandon the privilege embedded in musicology as a term. Ethnomusicologists themselves have variously agreed or disagreed with Seeger, although in the end the name of the field has stuck because of the insistence of the prefix *ethno-* (from the Greek for "race," "culture," or "people"), signaling that it is not just "all musics" but the differences engendering these that are essential. "All music" is by no means equatable with all musical phenomena or concepts of music; hence Seeger's call for a "unitary field theory for musicology" is a canonic non sequitur (C. Seeger 1970).

Ethnomusicology's emergence as a distinctive discipline therefore took on the quality of a struggle of words against words, in fact against the words of the Western-art-music canon and their use to restrict music to a Western discursive framework. Four textual areas emerged as the arenas for this linguistic struggle. The first was, of course, the very name of the field. In some ways, renaming the field was the main impetus precipitating the changes of the early 1950s. The new name symbolized most visibly a direct break with the past, especially with that generation which had benefited from designation as comparative musicologists. In more ways than one, the new name paved an entry into the field for anthropologists. It signaled a new system of intellectual exchange, in which musical and anthropological ethnomusicologists learned from each other, disciplining themselves outside the area in which they conducted Ph.D. studies or found academic positions. This was particularly important for anthropologists, who were often nervous about the inflexible and hard-to-master artifacts of musical notation. The ethnomusicologists therefore wrote as if to seduce their anthropological colleagues into a field that was not as daunting as they had imagined and in which, for that matter, they had been participating all along. David McAllester could still write in 1954 that

> of all the arts, perhaps music has seemed the hardest to study as
> social behavior. Aside from the accompanying poetry in the song
> texts, the actual substance of music appears forbiddingly abstract.
> Melodic line and phrasing, meter, pitch, and scale have been re-
> served for highly trained musicologists, few of whom have been
> interested in cultural applications. The unfortunate result of this
> specialization and the feeling that one must have "talent" to
> study music has been a general abdication from this field by so-

cial scientists, even to the extent that the most elementary questions about attitudes toward music have often remained unasked. In the realm of cultural values this rich source of insight still awaits systematic exploration. (1954:3)

This form of cajoling was, in fact, particularly effective in the 1950s, and early publications of the SEM record the active interest of many anthropologists (e.g., Sol Tax and Raymond Firth) who do not appear to have taken an active interest in subsequent decades (Bettigole 1990). With the implementation of the new name, not only did anthropologists recognize a language borrowed from their own kinship system, but they understood by that name that music was not the *only* object of study in ethnomusicology.

The second arena of linguistic struggle was, in fact, the object of study. Whereas some argued that "music" was the obvious object of study for ethnomusicology (e.g., Hood 1971:3), others rejoined that we must also take into consideration cultures where music meant nothing whatsoever (e.g., Merriam 1977:189–90). Thus, to know what music was meant understanding first how words came to define and describe it. The words, in this sense, meant those of the cultures in which a particular music was practiced. There were cultures in which vocabularies for the description of music were so rich that it seemed plausible to conclude that music was extraordinarily important in everyday activities (e.g., the Hausa of Nigeria; see Ames and King 1971). There were Muslim societies of the Middle East in which loan words such as *mūsīqī* and *mūsīqā* were used to identify questionable behavior but nevertheless took their place in the constellation of words that surrounded music-making and other expressive acts—for example, the performance of sacred texts or the enactment of ritual in religion.

Methodology was the third arena. Methodology was not simply a matter of following certain procedures in the field, but of debating them. The "field report" became standard practice as a type of ethnographic text in which the ethnomusicologist described what she was doing to come to certain conclusions, rather than offering those conclusions themselves as isolated facts. The field report also located the ethnomusicologist in the society where she was working, thereby identifying her not just as an observer but as a participant-observer. The concern over words forced the ethnomusicologist to fret about methodology and to document painfully the methodology that framed each monograph. The individual's preoccupation with methodology inevitably becomes reified in the central concerns of the field, for example, the long-standing debate over whether methodology must address "music in culture" or "music as culture" (for a discussion of this debate, see Nettl

1983:131–46). In more recent years, methodology itself has played so central a role as to act as a disciplinary metaphor for ethnomusicology, the "musical anthropology" posited by Anthony Seeger. When this becomes so, the ethnomusicologist's text—for example, Anthony Seeger's *Why Suyá Sing* (1987) or Steven Feld's *Sound and Sentiment* (1990)—takes its shape from the musical thought and praxis of the culture it represents.

Methodological debates and experimentation notwithstanding, there have been areas of significant accord, for example, in assertions that any methodology must collapse the differences between our music and the Other's. The final arena of linguistic tussling, it follows, concerned ownership of the canon. To what extent was any canon someone else's or only one's own? Virtually every major theorist argued at some point that ethnomusicology concerned itself exclusively with non-Western music. Surely this bolstered the notion of the canon's belonging to the Other. A second thrust broadened the concept of the Other, subsuming under it folk and tribal music and specifying geographically delimited genres such as "Asian art music." Finally, there was the urge to envelop all musics, thereby admitting no difference between ours and the Other's. Ownership indeed became a fuzzier issue when the field purported to concern "traditional," "orally transmitted," or "ethnic" musics.

The Confrontation of/with Canons

The discursive debates clearly signaled ethnomusicology's concern for the stance of its canons within Western scholarship. Did these canons, did self-reflection and self-criticism, free ethnomusicology from its own Westernness? Could one in any substantive and real way change one's stance simply by dismissing anything that smacked of Westernness? What if one were unwittingly to inherit some of the canons from comparative musicology? Would that further taint one with Westernness?

Beyond the presence or residue of specific canons, ethnomusicology was particularly concerned with not being canonical and with not formulating an intractably canonic subject matter. I base this assertion on my reading of writings from the 1950s, in which one does not, in fact, find Western art music frequently identified as an anti-canon. By implication Western art music might be understood in this sense, simply because it falls within the purview of historical musicology, but I fail to see it accorded any special status. Western art music quietly exists in these writings, dismissed as it were because it no longer was of particular interest to ethnomusicologists or because the long-awaited cross-influences just were not happening.

There were, moreover, other musics that, even more surprisingly, failed to occupy a salient position in ethnomusicology's attempts to reformulate its field in the 1950s. For example, the early appeals of young ethnomusicologists to attract colleagues to the field included little direct contact with folk-music scholars and scholarship. Communications in the early newsletters of the Society for Ethnomusicology only occasionally touched on folk music, and the International Folk Music Council, especially its major figures involved with the study of European folk music, is noticeably absent from discussions about the development of the field.

Surely folk music more explicitly fitted the subject categories established by the new ethnomusicologists, but I believe that it was also suspect as a result of its overly and overtly canonic nature. Folk-music scholarship, especially in Great Britain, had insisted on a privilege for folk music. For these scholars, every culture had a folk music. Every folk song, it followed, had its particular integrity, which one determined by finding the Urtext from which all variants ensued. Differences, therefore, were valuable only insofar as they provided clues for the identification of the authentic; in effect, folk-music scholars built a canon that regarded differences as aberration and disintegration. The early volumes of the *Journal of the International Folk Music Council* bear witness to this insistence on privilege, with articles on folk music in Pakistan, Ceylon, Turkey, or wherever, even though ethnomusicology was showing such nationalist classification of folk music to be increasingly less tenable. Even the term *folk music* became problematic to the extent that it was thrown out as an official designation when the International Folk Music Council regrouped as the International Council for Traditional Music in 1981 and moved its administrative offices to the United States, soon after the defenders of its value-laden canon, particularly Maud Karpeles, had passed on (further discussion of the implications of the institutional abandonment of the term *folk music* by the IFMC/ICTM appears in Bohlman 1988b: xii–xx).

The failure to espouse the canons of folk-music scholarship, the increasing role of anthropologists, the institutionalization of ethnomusicology in the academy—all these factors reveal also that the moment during which modern ethnomusicology emerged depended on the historical conditions obtaining in a particular place, namely, the United States. Many of the comparativists—Curt Sachs, Béla Bartók, and even, briefly, Hornbostel—had moved to North America before and during World War II, and many of the younger scholars of the 1950s were also immigrants (e.g., Bruno Nettl). American ethnomusicology, then, benefited from the same flood of intellectuals that had proved so important to historical musicology in the 1940s and 1950s.

Also important, certainly more so in the creation of a new form of discourse, was the central role of anthropology in the United States. In Central Europe, primary home to *vergleichende Musikwissenschaft*, anthropology and ethnology recovered only slowly from their prewar nationalist associations, and accordingly they remained less influential on musical studies. Only in recent years have European ethnomusicologists drawn more deeply from anthropological theory, and at that most frequently from American cultural anthropology. Rooting themselves more in folk music meant for Europeans that, at least at some level, they remained committed to studying their own music, and it was therefore most common for folk-music scholars to institutionalize their field in academies of science or national and regional archives, which necessarily canonized practices such as fieldwork and folk-song classification in completely different ways. Ethnomusicology in the United States, in contrast, found support for its activities primarily in the institution of the university. The collegial atmosphere and daily fare of the university, of course, demanded a recognition of differences, especially as the American university embarked on several decades of building international programs. Otherness therefore entered the curriculum of ethnomusicological study, where it was sanctioned by the institution and crafted by the many disciplinary languages of the academy.

Ethnomusicology's Musics

Where did music fit in ethnomusicology's reflexive canons? Did ethnomusicology, with its increasing interest in the role of words in the disciplining of music, in effect abandon music itself? Through the egalitarian gesture of placing sound phenomena in the midst of many other aspects of culture, did ethnomusicology abdicate its responsibility to the object of historical musicology's study? On its surface, the evidence would seem to provide rather unequivocal justification for the presumption that ethnomusicology was swerving into research directions that would eventually lead it away from music. The history of the field has, however, proved that presumption to be false. If indeed music is different and embodies differences in ethnomusicological study, it nevertheless remains the central focus for that study. Far from becoming less important, music has arguably become more important for ethnomusicology—and precisely because the discipline's canons are so very different.

The importance of music turned into a datum that spurred ethnomusicologists on and forced them to direct questions toward music itself. The ethnographic monographs and field reports of the 1950s almost inevitably note that music is extremely important to a given society. The observation of the importance of music makes it clear that what is taken to be music is vastly different from Western-art-music canons, which indeed seem not to exhibit widespread importance in Western society. Bruno Nettl, in the first monographic essay in English on the field of study constituting modern ethnomusicology, states straightforwardly that music is important because it is a part of so many domains of cultural activity:

> In primitive societies, music frequently plays a far more important role than in Western civilization. The stylistically simple music of a primitive tribe often has great prominence within its culture because of its prevailing functionality: most primitive music (despite some notable exceptions) serves a particular purpose other than providing pure entertainment or aesthetic enjoyment. (1956:6)

The importance of music compelled ethnomusicologists to stick with it and to increase their enticement of anthropological colleagues. Music was so important that it just might provide the key for unraveling the complexities of an entire culture—indeed, of some fairly universal cultural practices, such as religion.

During the 1950s ethnomusicological texts turned to several distinct music cultures in search of explanations for the importance of music. No music was more paradigmatic in this search than that of Native Americans. Native American music was the primary field of study for many scholars participating in ethnomusicology's coming-of-age during the decade, and even those who would devote the bulk of their studies to musics outside North America (e.g., Alan Merriam) worked extensively also with Native American music. The study of Native American music quickly led to the codification of a disciplinary lingua franca, an arena in which to stage the debates over words and their meanings.

Why Native American music? No single reason explains why this paradigm should have become so sweeping and powerful. Obviously, there is the reality that one could conduct fieldwork close to home, especially as the field found such succor in North America in the 1950s. A host of other pragmatic explanations also comes into play. Both anthropologists and musical scholars had long been interested in Native American music. Disciplinary canons had already formed by the end of the nineteenth century. Library shelves were filled with monographic studies sponsored by natural-history museums (e.g., Harvard's Peabody Museum or the Field Museum in Chicago), studies in which the expressive components of individual ceremonies were detailed. As her methodological modus operandi, Frances Densmore had compiled anthologies for the Smithsonian Institution of musical traits and repertories for as many tribes as she could humanly survey in her long life.

The texts of Native American music—transcribed repertories, sound recordings, summary treatments of the entire field (e.g., Curtis 1907)—were accessible to scholar and layperson alike. The nestors of American anthropology (for example, Franz Boas) had studied Native American music and impressed its importance upon their students; and their students (for example, Helen Roberts and George Herzog, both Boas students) came to play seminal roles in the formation of ethnomusicological practices in the 1950s. Native American musical studies had even been for decades a disciplinary domain in which women scholars were extraordinarily active (see Frisbie 1991 for a detailed description of women ethnomusicologists and their roles in the institutionalization of the SEM during the 1950s).

Geographic and ancestral propinquity are just a bit too facile as explanations for canon formation. Native American music also posed some specific problems that lay close to the central debates within ethnomusicology in the 1950s. A panoply of moral issues also coalesced around Native American music, making it paradigmatic for critical questions of value and ideology. Native Americans were, after all, the most glaring victims of colonialism in North America, and the crisis of colonialism facing Europe after World War II was felt no less among North American scholars (see Bettigole 1990 and Asad 1973).

The crisis in representation felt by anthropologists in the 1950s also challenged those studying Native American music. Representing Native American music, which existed in oral traditions and did not precipitate out from other cultural activities, was particularly thorny. Native American music had not lent itself well to the representational techniques of the comparativists. It had been too difficult to pin down *Tonsysteme*. Differences were so prevalent—from performance to performance, from society to society—that questions of musical style and form appeared hopelessly complicated. Native American music was too different for the comparativists to appropriate it conveniently. As a music, it may have been close to home, but conceptually it inhabited another realm completely.

The demand for new modes of representing Native American music was, therefore, nonnegotiable. In the new ethnomusicological texts, there emerged in response an increasing tendency to represent everything "about" the music, in effect overdetermining the music itself. The ethnomusicology of the 1950s was not, in fact, the first case of overdetermining the texts of musics in oral traditions. Bartók is a notable example of a folk-music scholar who transformed every aural nuance to a symbol and left nothing to chance for the readers of his texts. Native American music was overdetermined in a different way: it was presented as a parallax text of many layers. Any description of "a song" required extensive commentary concerning performer and performance, form and function, technique and technology. To understand the music, one had to read all these texts and acquire a new vocabulary. David McAllester's *Peyote Music* (1949), which is about no more nor less than its concise title claims, was one of the first books to employ multiple textual layers to overdetermine the music itself. Preceding the 84 transcriptions of individual songs are 104 pages that painstakingly prepare one for reading the notes that eventually appear on the printed page.

Musical ethnography should represent the musical moment, the creator of that moment, and the indigenous meaning of that moment (see Friedrich 1986). We might understand the nature of this parallax language even from a postmodern linguistic perspective, in which the ethnographer seeks to employ as many signifiers as possible to represent a single signified, admitting in the process that true representation will ultimately elude us. If such processes of juxtaposition overdetermined the music, they also insisted on the moral imperative confronting the ethnomusicologists. *How* one created and limited one's texts could reflect one's position vis-à-vis another culture; in other words, writing musical ethnography could either enforce or narrow the gap imposed by colonialism. Overdetermining the music of the Other in the texts of musical ethnography revealed the inadequacy of the Western representational system: it tried harder and harder to represent as many differences as possible, insisting that these differences were essential and that therefore the music must be important.

Again, it was the nature of the texts about music that brought ethnomusicologists closer to the music itself. The enjoinder to study "all musics" gradually came to mean something else by taking on the reflexivity that the representation of music afforded. There is perhaps no better evidence of this impact of writing on practices of representation than the return of ethnomusicology's texts to Western art music. Taking the form of a disciplinary parallax, Western art music is distributed in numerous layers in the new texts, embodying myth (see Nettl in this volume), ritual (Bohlman 1991a), and entire cultural systems (Kingsbury 1988). Here, too, one witnesses the subtle confession that, of course, Western art music has been our music all along, and it therefore refracts the language with which we describe another music. But the point of this new interest in Western art music is distinctively different from the ways historical musicology views the music. Rather than turning up some new evidence about style in Mozart, voice-leading in nineteenth-century string quartets, or authentic versions for modern performance, the new ethnomusicological studies have revealed just how complex the readings of Western art music in the past and present really are. These studies have, in fact, moved closer to the music. In their different ways, they have confirmed just how important music really can be in our own culture.

The Challenge of Reforming Canons

Modern ethnomusicology has, then, challenged the very processes of canonization, which it believed hammered a wedge between our music and the Other's. These were the processes of canonization that permitted scholars to be comfortable simply with "non-Western" music as an object of study. These were the processes of canonization that underscored a methodology that rendered musics in other cultures as normative Western texts. These were the processes of canonization that relied on an analysis that might yield a misreading of other musics and that too often ignored those meanings that were extrinsic to the Western canon. And finally, it was precisely these processes of canonization that emphasized a system of values that had grown from the canon formed by Western cultural history (see Kerman 1984:190–93).

Modern ethnomusicology has taken the challenge posed by the canon no less seriously. The field has by no means abandoned canons as a means of disciplining itself, and, arguably, it is in the sheer surfeit of canons that ethnomusicology is most distinctive as a domain of musical discourse. The surfeit of canons that confronts the ethnomusicologist—the overwhelming body of knowledge that one must lay claims to—is daunting. At times, it is the penchant for disciplining music gone amok; it offers the clearest evidence that to know "all musics" is one of the most flagrant assaults on the right of individuals and music cultures to retain their own integrity and authority. Ethnomusicologists, therefore, dare not believe that they are immune to the challenges of the canon. Those challenges become metonymic for the new modes of ethnography and musical-text production with which ethnomusicology reformulated its own use of language to study and represent music. Those challenges form the discomfiting motivation that insists on self-criticism and reflexivity. Those challenges provide the discipline with a mirror in which to see itself.

It was not only a single canon of Western musicology itself, but the ways whereby canons were constructed that so troubled and challenged ethnomusicologists in the 1950s. With its attention to the function of words in the definition of the field and the creation of its texts, ethnomusicology sought to respond to this challenge, not by abandoning a single canon but by seeking ways that would allow for the formation of many canons. Ethnomusicology was able to effect this formation through its constant reexamination of the use of words, the representation of music, and the persistence of the reflexivity that resulted from the field's own self-criticism and the examination of its own values. It would be historically uncharacteristic—even impossible—for this reflexivity to settle upon any single canon. Instead, the field embraces what must be regarded as the anti-canonic notion that many canons are not only possible but desirable, and that engaging in the persistent process of forming these many canons will only enhance their desirability. To conclude, then, as Goethe, Jaap Kunst, and one of the canonic texts of modern ethnomusicology began: "Also zwischen Ost- und Westen sich bewegen sei zum Besten!"

Works Cited

Ames, David W., and Anthony King. 1971. *Glossary of Hausa Music and Its Social Context.* Evanston: Northwestern University Press.

Asad, Talal, ed. 1973. *Anthropology and the Colonial Encounter.* Atlantic Highlands, N.J.: Humanities Press.

Barthes, Roland. 1977. *Image, Music, Text.* Trans. Steven Heath. New York: Hill and Wang.

Bettigole, Cheryl. 1990. "Before the Deluge and after the Fall: On Defining the Relationship between Anthropology and Ethnomusicology." M.A. thesis, Department of Anthropology, University of Chicago.

Blum, Stephen. 1991. "European Musical Terminology and the Music of Africa." In Nettl and Bohlman, 1991, 3–36.

Bohlman, Philip V. 1988a. "Traditional Music and Cultural Identity: Persistent Paradigm in the History of Ethnomusicology." *Yearbook for Traditional Music* 20:26–42.

———.1988b. *The Study of Folk Music in the Modern World.* Bloomington: Indiana University Press.

———.1991a. "Of *Yekkes* and Chamber Music in Israel: The Ethnomusicological Dimensions of Modern Music History." In Stephen Blum, Philip V. Bohlman, and Daniel M. Neuman, eds., *Ethnomusicology and Modern Music History,* 254–67. Urbana: University of Illinois Press.

————. 1991b. "Representation and Cultural Critique in the History of Eth-nomusicology." In Nettl and Bohlman 1991, 131–51.

Boon, James A. 1986. "Symbols, Sylphs, and Siwa: Allegorical Machineries in the Text of Balinese Culture." In Victor W. Turner and Edward M. Bruner, eds., *The Anthropology of Experience*, 239–60. Urbana: University of Illinois Press.

Bose, Fritz. 1953. *Musikalische Völkerkunde*. Freiburg im Breisgau: Atlantis.

Chase, Gilbert. 1972. "American Musicology and the Social Sciences." In Barry S. Brook, Edward O. D. Downes, and Sherman van Solkema, eds., *Perspectives in Musicology*, 202–26. New York: W. W. Norton.

Curtis, Natalie. 1907. *The Indians' Book: An Offering by the American Indians of Indian Lore, Musical and Narrative, to Form a Record of the Songs and Legends of Their Race.* New York: Harper and Brothers.

Etzkorn, K. Peter. 1988. "Publications and Their Influence on the Development of Ethnomusicology." *Yearbook for Traditional Music* 20:43–50.

Feld, Steven. 1990. *Sound and Sentiment: Birds, Weeping, Poetics, and Song in Kaluli Expression.* 2d ed. Philadelphia: University of Pennsylvania Press.

Friedrich, Paul. 1986. *The Language Parallax: Linguistic Relativism and Poetic Creativity.* Austin: University of Texas Press.

Frisbie, Charlotte. 1991. "Women and the Society for Ethnomusicology: Roles and Contributions from Formation through Incorporation." In Nettl and Bohlman 1991, 244–63.

Goethe, Johann Wolfgang. 1988. *West-östlicher Divan*. 8th ed., enlarged. Frankfurt am Main: Insel. Originally published 1819.

Harris, Marvin. 1968. *The Rise of Anthropological Theory: A History of Theories of Culture.* New York: Thomas Y. Crowell.

Hood, Mantle. 1971. *The Ethnomusicologist*. New York: McGraw-Hill.

Kerman, Joseph. 1984. "A Few Canonic Variations." In Robert von Hallberg, ed., *Canons*, 177–95. Chicago: University of Chicago Press.

————. 1985. *Contemplating Music: Challenges to Musicology.* Cambridge: Harvard University Press.

Kingsbury, Henry. 1988. *Music, Talent, and Performance: A Conservatory Cultural System.* Philadelphia: Temple University Press.

Kuhn, Thomas S. 1970. *The Structure of Scientific Revolutions.* 2d ed., enlarged. Chicago: University of Chicago Press.

Kunst, Jaap. 1959. *Ethnomusicology: A Study of Its Nature, Its Problems, Methods and Representative Personalities to Which Is Added a Bibliography.* The Hague: Martinus Nijhoff. 1st ed., 1950; 2d ed., 1955.

McAllester, David P. 1949. *Peyote Music.* Viking Fund Publications in Anthropology, no. 13, New York.

————. 1954. *Enemy Way Music: A Study of Social and Esthetic Values As Seen in Navaho Music.* Cambridge, Mass.: Peabody Museum, Harvard University.

Merriam, Alan P. 1964. *The Anthropology of Music.* Evanston: Northwestern University Press.

————. 1977. "Definitions of 'Comparative Musicology' and 'Ethnomusicology': An Historical-Theoretical Perspective." *Ethnomusicology* 21, no. 2:189–204.

Nettl, Bruno. 1956. *Music in Primitive Culture.* Cambridge: Harvard University Press.

————. 1964. *Theory and Method in Ethnomusicology.* New York: Free Press.

————. 1983. *The Study of Ethnomusicology: Twenty-nine Issues and Concepts.* Urbana: University of Illinois Press.

Nettl, Bruno, and Philip V. Bohlman, eds. 1991. *Comparative Musicology and Anthropology of Music: Essays on the History of Ethnomusicology.* Chicago: University of Chicago Press.

Reinhard, Kurt. 1968. *Einführung in die Musikethnologie.* Wolfenbüttel: Möseler.

Schneider, Marius. 1957. "Primitive Music." In Egon Wellesz, ed., *Ancient and Oriental Music,* 1–82. London: Oxford University Press.

Seeger, Anthony. 1985. [Review of] "General Articles on Ethnomusicology and Related Disciplines" [in the *New Grove*]. *Ethnomusicology* 29, no. 2: 345–51.

————. 1987. *Why Suyá Sing: The Musical Anthropology of an Amazonian People.* Cambridge: Cambridge University Press.

————. 1991. "Styles of Musical Ethnography." In Nettl and Bohlman 1991, 342–55.

Seeger, Charles. 1960. "On the Moods of a Musical Logic." *Journal of the American Anthropological Society* 13:224–61.

————. 1970. "Toward a Unitary Field Theory for Musicology." *Selected Reports* [in Ethnomusicology] 1, no. 3:171–210.

————. 1977. "Speech, Music, and Speech about Music." In C. Seeger, *Studies in Musicology, 1935–1975,* 16–30. Berkeley and Los Angeles: University of California Press.

Sturtevant, William. 1964. "Studies in Ethnoscience." *American Anthropologist* 66: 99–131.

Waterman, Christopher A. 1991. "The Uneven Development of Africanist Ethnomusicology: Three Issues and a Critique." In Nettl and Bohlman 1991, 169–87.

Mozart and the Ethnomusicological Study of Western Culture: An Essay in Four Movements
Bruno Nettl

In works such as this, it is common to begin by defining ethnomusicology. I shall give three definitions and use them all: the comparative study of musical systems and cultures; the study of music in or as culture; the study of a musical culture from an outsider's perspective. None of these excludes the art-music culture of Western society, but few ethnomusicological studies have actually been devoted to it. I would like to deal with this topic, speaking at times as an American ethnomusicologist, at other times pretending to be an outsider, and sometimes acting as the native informant of this study. For comparative perspective I shall turn to one or two other societies with whose musical cultures I have become acquainted. I doubt that this essay states anything new. It is intended to provide food for thought, but it is also—by implication, at least—a critique of ethnomusicological approaches.

I. Adagio: We Begin in Montana
Guiding Principles

As this paper is also presented in homage to Mozart, the most special of composers, it follows, in its attempt to establish interplay of ideas and cultures, the form of an eighteenth-century symphony. And as the first movement may begin with an introduction quite removed, at least on the surface, from the main subject matter of the movement, I take the liberty of

This essay is presented as a token of gratitude to my father, Paul Nettl (1889–1972), author of *Mozart und die königliche Kunst* (Berlin: F. Wunder, 1932), *Mozart in Böhmen* (Prague: Neumann, 1938), and *Mozart and Masonry* (New York: Philosophical Library, 1957); and as homage to Anthony Burgess, author of *Napoleon Symphony* (New York: Knopf, 1974), and to Claude Lévi-Strauss, author of "The 'Good Manners' Sonata," "Fugue of the Five Senses," and "The Opossum's Cantata" in his famous book *The Raw and the Cooked* (English translation, New York: Harper and Row, 1969). An earlier version of this essay appeared in *Yearbook for Traditional Music* 21 (1989):1–16.

beginning an essay about Mozart with an excursion to the Blackfoot people of Montana.

After working with them for a time, I came to believe—influenced by a series of recent musical ethnographies published in the wake of significant works by Alan Merriam (1964, 1967)—that the system of ideas about music held in each society, however small, is complex but coherent and that it informs importantly about both music and culture. It became clear to me, for example, that the principal unit of musical thought in Blackfoot culture is the song, an indivisible unit which is thought by Blackfoot people not to undergo change or variation and which is identified by use and secondarily by persons and events with which it is associated. The musical universe of the Blackfoot is capable of infinite expansion, as new songs can always come into existence although their style may not be new. One melody dreamed separately by two seekers of visions is in certain respects considered to be two songs. The concepts of composition and learning are closely related, as new songs are seen as extant musical units learned from an outside source. Most important, songs are significant mediators among groups of beings— between groups of humans and between humans and supernatural forces.

It became clear also that in Blackfoot culture, certain things about music and not others are evaluated. A person may say that he likes or dislikes genres of song, such as gambling songs or Grass Dance songs, and a singer or a singing group may be praised for the totality of their performance. But most individual songs, and individual performances, are not verbally evaluated. People say, "I like hand-game songs," "That's a good singing group," and "He's a good singer," but not "That is a fine song" or "I like the way they sang that particular song." And they do not say things like "That group is good because they work so hard" or "I like this group of songs because it must have taken a long time to make them." (For explanations in more detail, see Nettl 1989.)

Allegro Assai: Ethnography of the Music Building
First Theme: A Visitor from Mars

This summary may be a guide to the kinds of things that a perfect stranger in Western art music culture might note and investigate. When I teach courses in the anthropology of music, one of my favorite figures is an "ethnomusicologist from Mars" who has the task of discerning the basics of Western art music culture as manifested by the community of denizens of a fictitious (well, maybe not so fictitious) Music Building. Would the visitor's experiences be a bit like mine in a Blackfoot community? We can imagine him or her (or it?) on arrival looking in the windows of the little practice rooms, seeing people playing on various instruments to themselves, and being told by a bystander, "He's a very talented young man, practicing Mozart, but until recently he used to play only bluegrass." A woman turns on the radio, there is music, and she says, "Aha, it's Mozart" (or Brahms, maybe; but not, for instance, "Aha, it's piano music" or "It's Heifetz," or "Thank heavens, a rondo!"). The Martian is told that he simply *must* hear the symphony orchestra that evening, or the opera—but he is confused when he is told that he shouldn't bother with the day's soap operas or the evening TV's "Grand Ole Opry." He is urged to go to a concert of student compositions, told that what he may hear will surely be wonderfully new and experimental, even though it actually might sound quite awful.

Walking around the Music Building, he sees names engraved in stone around the top: Bach, Beethoven, Haydn, Palestrina (on Smith Memorial Hall in Urbana); or a more hierarchical, much longer list clearly featuring Beethoven, Mozart, Bach, Haydn, and Wagner (in Bloomington). No names are found on the English Building, and no Franz Boas or Claude Lévi-Strauss or Margaret Mead at Social Sciences. And he hears of no music buildings with "Concerto," "Symphony," "Oratorio." Seeking a score at the library, he must look under "Mozart." "Symphony," "long pieces," "loud pieces," "sad" or "meditative," "C minor" and "Dorian" won't do.

There is no need to belabor the impact that the initial experiences may have on any newcomer to a culture. Confronting the Music Building, one is quickly exposed to a number of guiding principles of Western art music. (For anthropological studies of schools of music, see Cameron 1982 and Kingsbury 1988.) Importantly, they include the concept of hierarchy—among musical systems and repertories and, within art music, among types of ensembles and composers. There is a pyramid, at the top one of two or three composers. There is the preeminence of large ensembles and grand performances, and their metaphorical extensions to other grand, dramatic events in life. Talent and practicing go together in a way, but they are also opposing forces, the one both practically and philosophically a possible complement for the other. There is the great value placed on innovation, but it is the old and trusted, the music of the great masters of the past, that is most respected. In particular, our visitor is struck by the enormous significance of the concept of the master composer, a concept of which the figure of W. A. Mozart is paradigmatic.

Second Theme: Amadeus

In his stay, our Martian friend runs into the concept of Mozart in many guises; and having read Merriam, Steven Feld (1983), Lorraine Sakata (1983), and others, he realizes that one way to do good fieldwork is to pursue a concept wherever it leads you. What he pursues, of course, is the Mozart of today; and so he is doing—and I want to do—something quite different from what is done by the many scholars (prominent among whom was my father) who have studied the Mozart who lived in the eighteenth century. The two are closely related and depend on each other, but they are not identical. In suggesting that the study of today's Mozart may be a task for ethnomusicology, I must add that what I say here is at best suggestive, that I have not really done much research and have little hard data. My claim to authority is really that I am speaking as the Martian's native informant in the culture.

So far he has been confronted by Mozart as a composer or, perhaps more properly, Mozart as a group of pieces. A second, perhaps relatively minor form of Mozart is the composer as a person. Denizens of the Music Building think of a composer in these two forms, forms that are partly congruent but that sometimes also conflict. It is in this context that the ethnomusicologist encounters the play *Amadeus* (Shaffer 1980).

Let me now leave our imaginary colleague and talk about musicologists. The literary and dramatic merits of the play have been widely debated, and I can surely not contribute to this discussion. But musicologists have, in writing but in talking even more, taken an essentially critical position. The point is this, I believe: *Amadeus* involves the depiction of Mozart as a thoroughly ludicrous figure who is nevertheless able to compose incredible music— although only his enemy, the composer Antonio Salieri, recognizes it. Obviously, the play is not about the historical Mozart but uses him as a metaphor for the concept of the genius, the man loved by God; and Salieri for the hard-working, competent musician who is not a genius and therefore feels betrayed by God. Some musicologists who were put off by the play said that history was falsified, but there are other works of fiction about Mozart (e.g., Mörike 1855; Pushkin [1831] 1938; Davenport 1932), partly about the mystery of his death, and they are not usually the subject of heated criticism. The critical view of *Amadeus* has, I suggest, other bases. Mozart was made to look ridiculous, the kind of person who could not possibly be taken seriously as a great master of music. The response was similarly heated when Beethoven, in a psychoanalytical study, was made to look weak, impotent, petty (Sterba and Sterba 1954). The Music Building denizens are concerned about the *kinds* of persons to whom they have accorded the great-master status, but they have not resolved certain dilemmas. Are great composers great souls, and does the music come from divine inspiration, or are they just excellent technicians? Is it better to be a genius who comes to his accomplishments effortlessly or someone who achieves by the sweat of his brow? Who should properly be loved by God? In some societies the matter has been resolved. In Madras I was told, "Tyagaraja was such a great composer *because* he was such a holy man;" and a Blackfoot composer received his songs directly from the supernatural, a source above criticism.

Development and Recapitulation: The Great Masters

In real life, these two themes are mixed and intertwined; let me briefly develop and eventually recapitulate them, returning to the ethnography of the Music Building and the centrality of the "great masters"—a dozen or so figures who are the deities of the culture. As geniuses, they exist on a different plane from other musicians. In the symphonic and chamber repertory, their works occupy some 65 percent of performance time, a bit less in piano and choral concerts. An elite within a segment of musical culture already elite, they stand out because they wrote only great music, and when they did not, it must be explained. Beethoven's works are accorded universal status as masterworks, and when a *Wellington's Victory* appears, special excuses have to be made: He didn't mean it, was playing games, composed the work only for money. Although there are borderline composers, for those individuals not in this group, one or two major works are regarded as masterworks while the rest are essentially ignored.

The great masters wrote great music, but opinion is sometimes divided on the basis of their personalities. The music of Richard Wagner, a man with tremendous ego and little regard for his fellow humans, so one is given to understand, is disliked by many for precisely that reason. Richard Strauss, an occasional Nazi sympathizer, was widely ignored as a composer. J. S. Bach's obviously profamily attitude has helped his music to be extolled, while Chopin's slightly outré lifestyle, Tchaikovsky's homosexuality, and Schumann's psychiatric history have lowered their status a bit. To the denizens of the Music Building, music lives in their conception of the principal units of musical thought—the persons of the great composers.

In musicology as well, the selection of research topics often revolves about a person; one is a "Mozart scholar," "Bach scholar," "Liszt scholar." Successful research on a minor composer depends to a considerable extent on the scholar's ability to show relationship to or influence from or upon a member of the great-master elite. The coherence of the corpus of creations by a composer is a paramount issue to scholars. To know the person who composed a piece is to know the most important thing about it. To find a new piece by a great master can give you the musicological equivalent of the Nobel Prize. To learn that a piece "by" Beethoven is actually by Friedrich Witt would today get you on the front pages of the *New York Times*. Such a piece, a bit like the song dreamed by two Blackfoot visionaries, is somehow no longer the same piece if Beethoven did not write it. And that it be truly a *piece* on its own terms, without excessive relationship to others, represents another value of the Music Building: the great importance of innovation.

The Music Building is in North America, but its denizens don't worry that the great masters are not Americans but, indeed, largely ethnic Germans. Their concept of art music is supranational, more so perhaps than in the case of visual art or literature. The emblem of this concept is the use of a single notation system which enables musicians who cannot speak to each other to play in the same orchestra. (This is not so everywhere; note the many systems operative in Japanese traditional music.) Furthermore, there is a universal terminology, derived from Italian, which has only recently begun to give way to national vernaculars. Why it should be Italian, in a repertory dominated by Germans, moves us to another guiding principle of Western art music, that of the musician as stranger. Deep in the roots of European culture is an ambivalence about music, suspicion of it, a belief that somehow the musician, often a strangely behaving person who can perform incredible feats, is in league with the devil. The musician is permitted, even required, to be a strange, unconventional person, wear his hair long, speak with an accent, be absent minded. The mad, inexplicable genius, perhaps; but he may also be thought to have a deviant lifestyle, to be a habitual drunkard, drug addict, debtor, homosexual, womanizer, but then also a foreigner. It is, I suggest, the idea of keeping music at arm's length that results in a foreign terminology for music, motivates denizens of the Music Building to be so much attracted to foreign teachers, and causes orchestras to seek foreign conductors (while never promoting, say, the first clarinettist to that post).

And so, while Austrians make much of *their* Mozart, and Germans of Beethoven, nations throughout the world, including some where their works have rarely if ever been heard, put their likenesses on postage stamps.

II. Andante: Mythological Variations
Theme: The Myth of Beaver

Our Martian observer has noted a number of guiding principles, foremost among which are hierarchies headed by a pantheon of great masters. If they are the deities, their character may be explained by myths widely told, if not rationally believed. Can one gain important insights into musical culture from the reading of myths? It is an approach well established in anthropology, and ethnomusicologists have begun to join it. Steven Feld, in *Sound and Sentiment* (1983), builds the interpretation of an entire musical culture on a single central myth about a boy who became a bird. Could one show the Music Building's system of ideas about music as the function of a mythic duel between Mozart and Beethoven? Let me show you what I mean by recalling an important myth of the Blackfoot people.

It concerns the interaction of a human family and the figure of the beaver, who is a kind of lord of the part of the world below the surface of the water, a sort of underworld. A great human hunter has killed a specimen of each animal and bird, and their dressed skins decorate his tent. While he is hunting, a beaver comes to visit his wife and seduces her, and she follows him into the water. After four days she returns to her husband, and in time gives birth to a beaver child. In Blackfoot society, such an affair would have been severely punished, but the hunter continues to be kind to his wife and particularly to the child. One day the beaver visits the wife again and, expressing pleasure at the way his child is treated, says that he wants to give the hunter some of his supernatural power as a reward. He asks for certain ritual preparations to be made and then visits the hunter. They smoke together and then the beaver begins to sing, song after song, each song containing a request for a particular bird or animal skin. The hunter gives the skin and in return receives the song. At the end, the hunter has received the songs of the beaver and their supernatural power—and with them the principal ritual of Blackfoot religion. (See Ewers 1958:168–69 for a more detailed account.)

This myth imparts many important things about Blackfoot music. Here is a brief summary. Songs come to humans and exist as whole units, and they are learned in one hearing. They are objects that can be traded, as it were, for physical objects. The musical system reflects the cultural system, as each being in the environment has its song. Music reflects and contains supernatural power. It is something which only men use and perform, but women are instrumental in bringing its existence about. Music is given to a human who acts morally, gently, in a civilized manner. It is the result of a period of dwelling with the supernatural, after which a major aspect of culture is brought, so in a way it symbolizes humanness and Blackfootness, a role that music has in some other Native American myths. Music has specific roles and functions and is used in a prescribed ritual. There is more, despite the fact that this is not specifically a myth of the origins of music.

Two Variations: Myths of Mozart and Beethoven

The mythology of the Music Building has more characters, and facts and fancy are intertwined in its stories. Yet they are myths in the sense that they explain complex reality to the ignorant and the young. We now hear a native consultant telling about his childhood in a family of denizens of the Music Building, though on another continent. He hears an attractive piece of music and is told it "is" Mozart, and, in bits of pieces, learns this: Mozart was a young boy with incredible talent and ability; no one could explain his feats. He composed without much in the way of lessons. His father took him to show him off to the royalty of Europe, but he seemed not to appreciate these advantages and eventually got along badly with his father. Later he tried to make his living as a composer but was always poor. He was not appreciated in his own city of Salzburg, and also not very much in Vienna; only in the somewhat foreign city of Prague was he understood. Very important: He could compose without trying, his music came full-blown into his mind and had only to be written down. He could hear a piece of music and play it back unerringly by ear, and he was a superb improviser. He had a ribald sense of humor. He was disliked by his rival Salieri and died very young, a mysterious death. When he was terminally ill, someone came to ask him to write a requiem, and he had the notion that it was for his own funeral but died before he could finish it. His accomplishments were the result of some kind of supernatural power; thus the great attention to his mysterious death. He was born a genius—a traditional European notion, related to social immobility and the belief in elites. (And indeed, Mozart is, I think, held in even higher esteem in Europe than in North America, as his kind of life fits better into the older, European notion of the relationship of art and life.)

Mozart, a composer whom a child could understand. But there is a second variation, as the informant soon hears about another composer, his music better for older people: Beethoven. He was a different kind of person; like his music, difficult, hard to get along with. In various ways, he was quite the opposite of Mozart. As Mozart had a mystery about his death, Beethoven had one about his birth; was he Dutch, German, maybe exotic, and was he aristocratic or lower class? He had a dark and brooding look. He suffered greatly, was frequently disappointed, never found the right woman, and of course there was the tragedy of his deafness. His music didn't come easily, you could tell he had to work hard to write it, you had to work hard to listen to it. His humor was ponderous. But he is said to be the man who "freed music" (from the likes of Mozart?). He had no children, but a nephew on whom he doted but who disappointed him.

For adults, the myth is elaborated: Beethoven, the master of serious music, had a hard life; his deafness dominates our idea of him. He worked hard, sketched his works for years before getting them right, is seen as a struggler against many kinds of bonds—musical, social, political, moral, personal. He is thought to have seen himself as a kind of high priest, giving up much for the spiritual aspects of his music. He was a genius, but he had to work hard to become and be one. It is perhaps no coincidence that he has been, to Americans, the quintessential great master of music—for this is, after all, the culture in which hard work was once prized above all, labor rewarded; the culture in which you weren't born to greatness but were supposed to struggle to achieve it.

These are the myths that this native informant pieced together in early years; they correspond, I believe, in general nature if not in detail to those perceived by that part of society that is involved with this music, the denizens of the Music Building. The two composers represent complementary values, they are the opposites in a Lévi-Straussian diagram, and they reflect the tensions that are the subject of the debates airing the most general issues of art and life.

Of course, speaking now as a musicology professor, I know that these two men were not all that different in their work habits, that Mozart was a workaholic and an innovator and did some sketching, while Beethoven was not just a grind and a firebrand. The point is that in looking at the popular conceptions of a population of musicians, ferreting out myths from various sources, we can learn about the relationship of the musical system to the rest of culture.

And so, as the Blackfoot beaver myth shows us important things about the way Blackfoot people conceive of their songs, the ideas we—today—have about Mozart and Beethoven reveal some of the values of our musical culture. Genius must suffer. There is conflict between inspiration and labor and between consistency and innovation. The great composer has supernatural connections or is a stranger. Music is mysterious; its great practitioners come, in some sense, from outside the culture. The "composers" are the main units of musical thought and recognition. Their configuration illuminates major structural principles of Western music and society such as hierarchy and duality.

III. Menuetto Scherzando: Reaching beyond the World of Music

The special nature of the Mozart-Beethoven relationship has been recognized in fields outside music, and as the role of the minuet is to move the symphony into the world of normal life, we now make brief forays into the realms of the psychological, culinary, and literary.

First Minuet: Becking's Curves

Carnatic musicians in Madras, looking with interest at the foreign musical culture of the West, said to me, "We have our trinity of great composers, Sri Tyagaraja, Syama Sastri, and Muttuswami Dikshitar, just as you have your trinity," meaning Haydn, Mozart, and Beethoven. But I would like to argue that dualism is a more significant guide to the conceptual framework of the Music Building and its cultural context. Mozart and Beethoven are presented as emblems of the two ends of a continuum not only by the myth-makers; they have been so recognized by musicologists for a long time.

Take, for example, a now largely forgotten work by Gustav Becking, *Der musikalische Rhythmus als Erkenntnisquelle* (1928). Becking had the idea that you could understand and interpret the fundamental musical character of a piece, a composer, a repertory, a period, perhaps even a culture if you listened to the appropriate music and allowed your hand or arm to beat time in the air rather naturally and without inhibition. From this kind of action he developed a series of typologies known as the Becking curves. He groups these into two categories and shows that they cluster about the contrast between two major figures, Mozart and Beethoven. He is, incidentally, clearly uncomfortable with a third category which he felt obliged to establish as an afterthought, whose model is Bach; he would rather show Western music as bipolar. And so he sees the classical-music system as essentially opposition between monistic and dualistic, spiritualist and materialist, idealistic and naturalist motivations.

Becking may just have been idiosyncratic, but the denizens of the Music Building do divide the world into sets of pairs: The major-minor dyad and the divisions of vocal and instrumental, sacred and secular, traditional and new, art music and everything else are major taxonomic modes. The sonata form, most central to the art-music tradition, is an exercise in dualism. Mozart and Beethoven as opposites have a strong hold, and the thought of musicians and even of scholars seems to be oriented toward pairing: Leoninus-Perotinus, Ockeghem-Obrecht, Peri-Caccini, Cesti-Cavalli, Handel-Bach, Schubert-Schumann (but also Schumann-Mendelssohn), Liszt-Chopin, Verdi-Wagner (but also Wagner-Brahms), Smetana-Dvořák, Bartók-Kodály, and Schoenberg-Stravinsky, all of them partaking of some of the kinds of contrasts that the Mozart-Beethoven paradigm presents.

Trio: A Matter of Synesthesia

To some music lovers, Mozart is the "sweet composer." His creations have a certain seamlessness. Perhaps one reason virtually all of his music is so easy to recognize after a few seconds is that nobody else pursues quite the same logic in moving from one thing to the next. Our Martian observer, ready for some fun after two heavy movements, takes new directions that lead him to a Viennese cookbook, some sweetshops, and a collection of telephone directories.

In the cookbook, an extremely comprehensive work by Alice Urbach (1936), the name of Mozart appears with some prominence: two dishes, similarly named Mozartkrapfen (p. 233) and the diminutive Mozartkrapferln (p. 308) appear, both with chocolate, marzipan, and pistachios. The sweetshop yields a product by now widely dispersed in North America: *Mozartkugeln,* or "Mozart balls," if you will. The originals, manufactured in Salzburg, are really round, while the most widely distributed ones, from Germany, sit on a flat bottom like conventional chocolates. But American confectioners now also manufacture Mozart balls, naming them thus despite the lack of the portrait on the wrapping.

By now clearly hooked by these superlative sweets, our Martian observer also discovers that there are sweetshops or *Konditoreien,* in several Austrian towns, also in New York and San Francisco, Toronto and Vancouver, and probably elsewhere, all named for Mozart. None for Beethoven, a laboring meat-and-potatoes composer perhaps, who has only a restaurant in San Francisco and the Beethoven Piano Movers in New York. The Viennese cookbook had no Beethoven entry, none for Haydn, also none for other great musical residents of Vienna such as Schoenberg, Brahms, the various Strausses. Only Franz Schubert has his own dessert of Krapfen (Urbach 1936:232). Needless to say, there is no Beethoven, Wagner, or Bruckner candy. The reader is smiling; they are great composers, to be sure, but not sweet.

In *The Anthropology of Music,* Alan Merriam devotes a chapter to synesthesia, the "experience of an associated sensation when another sense is stimulated," as Seashore stated it in 1938 (Merriam 1964:86). Merriam, I have to confess, does not make a convincing case for the usefulness of this concept in intercultural musical studies, but perhaps this is because he did not take the sense of taste sufficiently into account. Why is Mozart a composer of "sweet" music? It is sweets, and particularly chocolate, that "go down easily," provide no obstacles. Perhaps most among the music of the great masters, Mozart's gives the impression of ease, flowing naturally, moving without obstacle. Because it was, so the listener believes, composed that way, by a composer who wrote easily, didn't have to labor, was able to turn a sometimes frivolous face to the world while creating. To Mozart, people now often think, composing must have been "a piece of cake," or, if you will, "easy as pie," or perhaps "like taking candy from a baby."

As suggested by Urbach, a second composer whose music fits this description is Franz Schubert, who incidentally loved eating and drinking and is said to have composed, so full of ideas was he, on the back of a menu while waiting to be served. (What does this tell us about the speed of Viennese waiters ca. 1820?)

Second Minuet: Big Is Beautiful (Or Great Is Great)

It is the personality myth supported by the "sweetness" of Mozart's music that permits us today to make Mozart the subject of lighthearted yet admiring parody such as P. D. Q. Bach–Peter Schickele's *A Little Nightmare Music* and *The Stoned Guest*, and indirectly the inexplicable title of Sondheim's waltz-dominated *Little Night Music*. Mozart did it to himself in his "Musical Joke" and other works. But if the Mozart-Beethoven opposition is symbolized in the trivialities of candies and desserts, it is also emblematic of the fate of humanity in the largest picture.

That thoroughly despicable protagonist of Anthony Burgess's *A Clockwork Orange* (1963), Alex, has a curious side to him—his love of classical music and particularly of "Ludwig van," as he puts it, who at times thunders through the book and Kubrick's film with his Ninth Symphony, as if reminding the characters that they have abandoned decent, civilized existence. And at the end of another Burgess novel, *The End of the World News,* fifty survivors of a planetary collision zoom into the future in a spaceship to the sound of Mozart's "Jupiter" Symphony (Burgess 1983:386).

Mozart and Beethoven are there, with their largest ("greatest"?) works. The concept of musical value in Western art-music culture is closely associated with size. We use the word "great" to mean "excellent." A composition student striving for an advanced degree must ordinarily present a "large" work (meaning long and for large ensemble). European composers who did not try their hand at large orchestral works have a hard time making the great-master circle, and in the period 1730–1900, most composers felt obliged to make serious attempts. It was as if the musical world were saying, "To be a proper composer, you may write solo, piano, vocal, and chamber works, but you must write at least *some* symphonies and concertos, and an opera or two." The musical profile of many, many composers fits this model, and the exceptions such as Wagner and Verdi wrote more, not fewer, grand works.

In identifying the greatest works of the masters, all but the *most* sophisticated turn almost automatically to the long works written for large ensembles—symphonies, operas, oratorios, and masses. Modernizing societies in Asia and Africa usually understand very well that to the Western social establishments, beautiful is big, and in striving to preserve their musical traditions act accordingly, creating symphony orchestras and large ensembles of traditional instruments as quickly as possible.

Many musicians, if asked to identify Beethoven's most valuable work, would name the Ninth, and Burgess and Kubrick symbolize the values of Western culture, which the plot places in jeopardy, by this masterwork. In many ways, it is also Beethoven's biggest work. The "Jupiter," Mozart's largest symphonic effort, is presented literally as the final climax of the world's music. To Burgess, as to many, Beethoven represents worldly achievement, and Mozart the gift of the otherworldly.

IV. Finale: What Does Our Music Tell Us about Ourselves?
Adagio: Cultural Performances in Iran

This eighteenth-century symphony of a paper ought to close, as did Mozart's "Prague" Symphony, no. 38, with a brief virtuosic wave of fanfares to hail the Viennese classicists as well as ethnomusicological method. Instead, it succumbs to the academic's standard temptation to move through new and serious themes to a perhaps-inconclusive ending, more perhaps like Brahms's Fourth; but at least I do promise to end, like Brahms, in the majestic C major. The adagio introduction takes me to Iran, where it is particularly clear that fundamental values of a culture can be extracted from music, and especially from the kind of music that qualifies as "cultural performance." That is a term which is widely used by anthropologists to identify music, theater, pageant, and sports events in which a society abstracts for itself and others its governing principles, showing itself and others its uniqueness (Singer 1972:56–58). Examples may range from Native American intertribal powwows to performances by the Vienna State Opera.

In Iran, the classical-music system was re-created ca. 1900, as it were, in a form compatible and competitive with, and also in some ways similar to, Western classical music (Nettl 1987:5–9, 160). The *Radif,* the basic repertory of Persian music which is the basis for improvisation and composition, was fashioned into a structure similar to other grand designs of Iranian culture, such as the grand designs of carpets, Ferdowsi's *Shahnameh* (the national epic of Iran) and other composite works of poetry, and the principle of empire. But the *Radif* also took on similarity to major Western musical masterworks, such as the *Art of Fugue,* and at the same time imitated the grand design of musical theory as an internationally valid Western theoretical system. This characteristic and other features—Western instruments, notation, newly created large ensembles, and more—all made renditions of this music "cultural performances" in which the national character of Iran, its association with the international system centered in the West, and the Middle Eastern cultural basis were all combined.

It stands to reason that a musical system like this, even if not thoroughly understood by many Iranians, could show in detail certain values that were important to the culture at large. They include these: hierarchy—guidance provided directly from a central authority—balanced by the importance of human equality in Islam; individualism and the associated values of surprise and unpredictability; and the importance of introductory behavior in formal events (Nettl 1978).

Suppressing the desire to illustrate in detail or to examine the validity of this methodology, I would like to ask instead whether the *large* performances in the Music Building, of *great* works by *great* composers, by the *largest* ensemble—the symphony orchestra—further illuminate for insiders as well as our Martian observer the importance of the great-master concept in the art music of Western culture. With this concept as the main theme of our rondo, brief episodes comment on the taxonomy of music as revealed by costume; on the orchestra as metaphor of the factory, political organization, and colonial empire; and on the role of the great composers such as Mozart in concert programs.

Rondo: Three Orchestral Episodes
Clothes Make the Musician

Having seen several ways in which the hierarchical taxonomy of music of the denizens of the Music Building is expressed, our Martian observer notes that performers dress differently for different kinds of music. The relative status of repertories and genres or of musical events is expressed in, among other things, the dress or costume of performers and even of the audience. In the concert halls at the Music Building, classical-music concerts are ordinarily performed by musicians in tuxedos (or tails) and evening dress. Bands wear uniforms derived from military usage, but in recent years concert bands have tried to boost their status by sporting tuxedos. Big-band jazz is played in uniform trousers and blazers. New-music concerts, however, are performed by groups of people who dress rather casually (turtleneck sweaters are often featured) and avoid identical outfits. Choruses, ordinarily composed of unpaid amateurs (who sing with a paid orchestra), wear robes to associate themselves with the unpaid but religiously prestigious church choirs. The few professional choruses in North America often revert to tuxedos. Early-music concerts are often performed by musicians in Renaissance or medieval costumes. At rock concerts, musicians have a totally idiosyncratic kind of dress. Concerts of non-Western music are performed in non-Western dress, despite the fact that the performers may be Americans, or Asians who use Western dress every day. In country music, musicians perform in work clothes or in spectacular costumes ultimately derived from them. The audiences usually do not, of course, precisely follow the performers, but there is significant correlation. At symphony concerts, virtually all men wear jackets or suits; at jazz concerts, sweaters are preferred. The hierarchical structure of musical life, correlating to some extent with the class structure, is evident throughout.

Reflection of Cultural Structures

In the history of Western music, the standardization, maturity, and eventual expansion of the symphony orchestra as well as of its internal organization correlate with the development of European industrialization. The symphony orchestra of Haydn and Mozart coincides with the beginning of factories, and as the industrial system grew, the orchestra added first clarinets, then trombones, tubas, piccolo, English horn, bass clarinet, saxophone, euphonium, piano, organ, a vast array of percussion, divided string sections, and you know the rest. Also added was the practice of unison bowing and other kinds of uniformity under a time-beating conductor who was not also playing keyboard or first violin. A hierarchical substructure developed; the third-desk violist is supposed to be better, or to have more seniority, than the player sitting one desk back. The first-chair performers of the sections are department heads of a sort. And the concert master, whose main visible role is to preside over the tuning up of the orchestra (actually led by the first oboe), is a kind of factory foreman keeping things in shape for the management. There is also the matter of specialization in scoring, a growing practice until ca. 1890–1910, when huge orchestras were used but all or most instruments played together only a tiny percentage of the time. And note the labor-management relationship of orchestra and conductor, management being relatively invulnerable except to revolution. The parallels can be carried to interesting lengths, though of course there are many ways of interpreting them. But it is attractive to think of the orchestra as a kind of factory for making music which gradually adopted the refinements and efficiencies developed in the industrial world.

A further parallel comes from the colonialist counterpart of the industrial revolution: the plantation workers of the orchestra directed by a native headman for the foreign management. (We have already noted the widespread employment of foreign conductors in the late nineteenth and twentieth centuries.)

But the orchestra is also a kind of army and reflects a structure found in the military domain of culture, a structure that in turn closely reflects important parts of the Western social structure. The conductor is the general, his baton of military origin. He gets credit for victories, is listed on the album cover, takes the bows, but risks little from the audience, as he can't be heard. (His enlisted soldiers tell jokes: "Have you ever heard a conductor's baton play out of tune?") The occupants of the first chairs are officers, with a certain amount of authority over their troops—one of whose main tasks is to march (i.e., bow and finger) in unison, mainly for the appearance of discipline. There is little democratic discussion; the conductor decides, one does not vote on tempo, and at most the orchestra may rebel and remove the conductor. But actually there is rarely much hope of that, as the orchestra may be an army of mercenaries whose conductor can barely speak their language and has little sympathy for their culture. He may be comparable to many eighteenth- and nineteenth-century generals (who, throughout the world, were often Germans). He may be the most successful version of the cultural tradition of the musician as cultural or even racial outsider, and he is often permitted or even expected to be eccentric, sporting long hair, strange dress, and a foreign accent and leading a strange life. It is a pattern that continues to maintain itself despite the vast degree of culture change in the Western world's last several centuries.

Program Patterns

If the orchestra is a kind of factory or plantation for producing great music or an army for exhibiting perfection on the parade ground, it is principally in the service of the great masters. The content and structure of programs shed light on the significance of hierarchy and the hegemony of great masters. In the 1940s, a concert program of a symphony orchestra typically had this structure: (1) an overture or introductory piece, possibly by a Baroque composer, usually played by a smaller section of the orchestra; (2) the pièce de résistance, a symphony by a great master; (3) after the intermission, flexibility—a piece of twentieth-century music, or possibly a concerto; (4) a lighter number or group. The spot after the overture clearly seems the most exposed, as latecomers would miss the overture and as the intermission—which was an obligatory and essentially social event without which a classical concert can hardly be tolerated—would signal the beginning of a denouement.

Incidentally, other standardized concert traditions have their own patterns which similarly suggest guiding musical and social principles. In Carnatic music, the principal section, the improvised ragam-tanam-pallavi, begins just after the midpoint, although there is usually no intermission. In Persian classical music, the central section, the improvised *Avaz*, appears in the very center of the full-blown performance.

The well-known book by John Mueller, *The American Symphony Orchestra* (1951), narrates the history of programming practices of orchestras up to about 1950. Some 40 percent of the playing time of symphony orchestras was devoted to four composers—Beethoven, Brahms, Tchaikovsky, and Mozart, who were almost invariably the composers of the pièces de résistance. There are no precise figures for recent decades, but while no doubt in North America the mentioned degree of standardization has been softened, the hierarchical structure of the programs has been maintained and the great masters occupy the top (i.e., the pre-intermission) spot and provide the "great" (i.e., the longest) pieces.

Coda: The Great Masters and the Expression of Cultural Values

In this system of Western culture that produces wonderful music, what are the principles and values that underlie it and that it expresses? We see intriguing concepts such as genius, discipline, efficiency, the hierarchical pyramid of musics and composers, the musician as stranger and outsider, the wonders of complexity, the stimulus of innovation, music as a great thing with metaphorical extensions. But, we are forced to suggest, we also see dictatorship, conformity, a rigid class structure, overspecialization, love of mere bigness, and more of that kind, all explicitly or by implication extolled. Why do the denizens of the Music Building love so well a kind of music that grows from principles which they would probably dismiss as fountains of virtual brutality? One may counter that the analysis is faulty, that instead of conformity there is cooperation, instead of authoritarians there are leaders. Or one may argue that the kind of a social structure described, for all its undesirable aspects, is essential for the proper performance of music by the great masters, that in order for music of such an incredibly elite character as that of Mozart or Beethoven to be created and performed, one must simply sacrifice independence and personal opinion, must undertake an incredible amount of discipline and accept dictates of an elite, wherever they lead. But these counterarguments have a hollow ring. The ethnomusicologist from Mars has discovered questions but is far from providing definitive answers.

In trying to present things that you already know from possibly a different perspective, I have tried to look at the culture of the Music Building as many ethnomusicologists have tried to look at cultures foreign to themselves. If what I have said makes sense, then the established methods of musical ethnography, for all their variety, may be validated. If the reader from the world of the Music Building says "Sure, but so what?" ethnomusicologists may have to accept that the societies with which they conventionally work may be saying this as well. If I have trivialized or grossly misinterpreted, this essay may indeed serve as a critique of the methods of our field.

And so, in my role of ethnomusicologist, I am not sure how to reconcile technically and spiritually supreme musical accomplishment, by master composers who are presented as great human beings who have lived the good life, with values of an essentially negative character. Even so, I continue to be convinced that musical concepts and values can in the end be illuminated through the study of cultural values. Speaking, however, in my other role, as the native informant of this study, I have to say that when I hear Mozart's works, I am inclined to think that there is really only one composer.

WORKS CITED

Becking, Gustav. 1928. *Der musikalische Rhythmus als Erkenntnisquelle.* Augsburg: B. Filser.

Burgess, Anthony. [1963] 1981. *A Clockwork Orange.* New York: Ballantine.

———. 1983. *The End of the World News.* New York: McGraw-Hill.

Cameron, Catherine. 1982. "Dialectics in the Arts." Ph.D. diss., University of Illinois.

Davenport, Marcia. 1932. *Mozart.* New York: C. Scribner's Sons.

Ewers, John. 1958. *The Blackfeet, Raiders on the Northwestern Plains.* Norman: University of Oklahoma Press.

Feld, Steven. 1983. *Sound and Sentiment: Birds, Weeping, Poetics, and Song in Kaluli Expression.* Philadelphia: University of Pennsylvania Press.

Kingsbury, Henry. 1988. *Music, Talent, Performance: A Conservatory Cultural System.* Philadelphia: Temple University Press.

Merriam, Alan P. 1964. *The Anthropology of Music.* Evanston: Northwestern University Press.

————. 1967. *Ethnomusicology of the Flathead Indians.* Chicago: Aldine.

Mörike, Eduard Friedrich. 1855. *Mozart auf der Reise nach Prag.* Wien: Schroll.

Mueller, John. 1951. *The American Symphony Orchestra: A Social History of Musical Taste.* Bloomington: Indiana University Press.

Nettl, Bruno. 1978. "Musical Values and Social Values: Symbols in Iran." *Journal of the Steward Anthropological Society* 10, no. 1:1–23.

————. 1987. *The Radif of Persian Music: Studies of Structure and Cultural Context.* Champaign: Elephant & Cat.

————. 1989. *Blackfoot Musical Thought: Comparative Perspectives.* Kent, Ohio: Kent State University Press.

Pushkin, Alexander. 1938. *Mozart and Salieri.* Trans. R. M. Hewitt. Nottingham: University College. Originally published as *Motsart i Salieri* (1831).

Sakata, Hiromi Lorraine. 1983. *Music in the Mind.* Kent, Ohio: Kent State University Press.

Shaffer, Peter. 1980. *Amadeus.* New York: Harper and Row.

Singer, Milton. 1972. *When a Great Tradition Modernizes.* New York: Praeger.

Sterba, Edith, and Richard Sterba. 1954. *Beethoven and His Nephew.* New York: Pantheon.

Urbach, Alice. 1936. *So kocht man in Wien!* Vienna: Verlag der Zentralgesellschaft für buchgewerbliche und graphische Betriebe.

NINE

Hierarchical Unity, Plural Unities: Toward a Reconciliation
Richard Cohn and Douglas Dempster

Within the arts and humanities, a canon is widely understood to be an authoritative collection of "texts" with privileged status. A more abstract and less common conception understands a canon to be a law, rule, or principle governing the acceptable limits and internal constitution of some domain of activities or artifacts. To define a canon, in this sense, is to seek mastery over the apparently bewildering diversity of some domain by discovering some implicit, unifying principle—to reduce the many and much to one and little. For music theory, where generalizing about musical "texts" is a defining activity, the latter and etymologically prior sense of *canon* is more appropriate, and thus guides our treatment of the theme of this volume.

The principal and most persistent canon governing our Western aesthetic is that successful works of art, including the "masterpieces" of Western art music, exhibit unity, coherence, or "organic" integrity. Music theory upholds this canon in its seminal commitment to the presupposition that musical unity is to be found not "exposed on" the complex, sometimes bewildering phenomenal "surface" of a composition, but rather "hidden in" some "underlying" structural simplicity. Contemporary music theory has tended toward an even more specific version of this canon of "underlying simplicity": the underlying structure that unifies the surface complexity of music is hierarchical. Such a claim is specific enough to be testable, and the point of our paper is to test this canon of underlying hierarchical structure. Ultimately we argue that it yields an incomplete vision of musical unity, a conclusion which leads toward a reassessment of the more general canon of "underlying simplicity."

The essay begins by attempting to clarify the formal nature of hierarchies,

This paper has benefited from suggestions of John Rahn and Robert Morris, based on their readings of earlier versions.

to speciate three different ontological types of hierarchies, and to raise a question of scope with respect to the claim that music is hierarchical. The core of the essay examines the Schenkerian conception of unity in tonal music, perhaps the most sophisticated and powerful account of musical structure for which hierarchical status is claimed. After reviewing the theoretical basis for the claim of hierarchy, we probe the Schenkerian treatment of motivic relationships, in order to show that in analytic practice this basis is substantially undermined. The essay concludes by examining the potential for alternative conceptions of musical unity that preserve the advantages of hierarchies while simultaneously providing a theoretical basis for the realities of Schenkerian practice. We consider the case for complex networks (following the work of Meyer, Narmour, et al.), suggest some refinements to it, and consider how such a view encourages relocating musical unity on the compositional "surface" itself, rather than in some "underlying simplicity."

Part I: What Does It Mean to Say That Music Is Hierarchical?

Becker and Becker say it most generally: "Music is hierarchical" (1979:7). But what is a hierarchy, more exactly? Such claims also raise questions of scope: what things or features are being so characterized when we say that "music" is hierarchical? We begin by disambiguating some of these basic concepts.

The term *hierarchy* has several senses. A common usage refers to an arrangement of elements into ranks of relative power or status. This is a relatively weak use of the term, since it can only assert the very general relations of above, equal to, and below. A claim that music is hierarchical may mean only that musical events may be ranked by significance (Narmour 1983–84:197). Most hierarchical approaches to music have the more ambitious aim of precisely specifying the function of each event within a composition understood as a system of events, and it is this sense which will be the focus of this study. In order to clarify the formal sense of the term, we borrow a definition from systems science that is unnecessarily strict for our purposes; we will eventually loosen its boundaries so as to encompass a wider set of phenomena.

Initially we define a *hierarchy* as any relation among absolutely disjoint sets and/or individuals. A collection of sets and/or individuals is *absolutely disjoint* just in case every individual that is a member of the collection, or a member of a member of the collection, and so on, appears exactly once in the collection. The following somewhat more formal definition recursively defines hierarchical sets in terms of sets of individuals, which trivially satisfy this requirement.

> X is a *hierarchical set* if and only if
> > i) X is a set of all and only individuals, or
> > ii) there is some set Y such that
> > > a) X is a partial partition of Y, *and*
> > > b) Y is a hierarchical set.[1]

Accordingly, the following are all hierarchical sets:

> A = {a,b,c};
> B = {{a,b}, {c,d}};
> C = {a, {b,c}, {d, {e,f}}, g}

but the following are not:

> D = {{a,b}, {b,c}};
> E = {a, {{b,c}, {c}}}.

In order to provide better traction for intuition, hierarchical relations can be schematically represented by means of tree diagrams, defined as follows in Knuth 1968 (305):

> a finite set **T** of one or more nodes such that there is one specially designated node called the *root* of the tree, root **T**, and
>
> the remaining nodes (excluding the root) are partitioned into **m** $\geq$ 0 disjoint sets $\mathbf{T_1}, \ldots, \mathbf{T_m}$, and each of these sets in turn is a tree.

Schematic representations of our five preceding examples are given in Example 1. The root node is at the top of each diagram; the nodes at the bottom are called "terminal nodes." A property of tree structures is that all nodes are immediately subordinate to no more than one higher-level node. Thus only the first three of these diagrams are trees.

The Unique Connection Principle is an important corollary of the condition of absolute disjointness. This property holds that every element or node in a hierarchy is connected to every other element or node by exactly one path (Morris 1987:236). It is significant that this property is shared by a purely linear structure. Note, for example, that it is impossible to move circularly through a tree: any move is either toward or away from a given node, but never both toward and away from at the same time. By contrast, in a two-dimensional grid, such as a street map, there are multiple ways to travel between any two points. Consequently, a hierarchical structure preserves

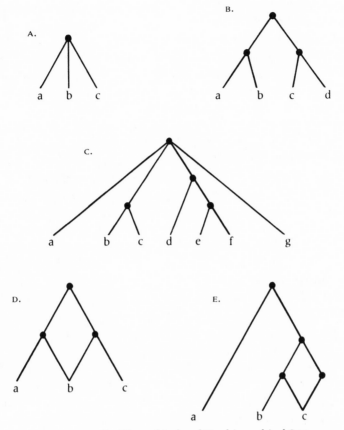

EXAMPLE 1. Hierarchical and Nonhierarchical Sets

some of the simplicity inherent in a single dimension, yet at the same time is capable of capturing some of the depth of relations in multiple dimensions.

Ontological characteristics also differentiate types of hierarchies. Our definition characterizes an *inclusion hierarchy,* where only the terminal nodes denote concrete individual elements or events; higher nodes are increasingly general groupings or classifications of those very same elements. Thus, in the tree, each concrete element is represented, as such, exactly once. Examples include Chomskian models of sentence structure, and the division of flora and fauna into orders and their subordinate families, genera, species, and races.

Although all tree diagrams display hierarchical relations, not all such relations are inclusional in nature. For example, many bureaucracies and corporations are structured along hierarchical lines of authority, yet, ontologically speaking, they are *robust hierarchies,* because concrete individuals are denoted by every node of the hierarchy. The root of a robust hierarchy (e.g., the chairman of the board) is no more nor less concrete than its terminal elements (e.g., the worker with no supervisory responsibilities).[2]

A *representational hierarchy* constitutes a third type that combines features of both inclusion and robust hierarchies. In a representational hierarchy, each node denotes a concrete individual, but each nonterminal node also denotes a representational relation that is inclusionary in character. Most university faculties are organized representationally: each departmental faculty selects a chair, who continues to serve as a member of the department but also sits on a council of chairs. A multilevel structure based on such relations resembles an inclusion hierarchy in that all elements appear at the lowest level, but also resembles a robust hierarchy since the elements at all levels are concrete individuals.

Another important distinction is suggested by the contrast between static and dynamic systems.[3] Although our discussion so far has been oriented toward a static conception of hierarchy, one could adopt a more dynamic interpretation by conceiving the hierarchy as "unfolding" in stages, either in time or in some less tangible dimension, such as compositional or auditory cognition. In a dynamic version, subordination is normally posited in operational terms: a subordinate node is "generated" or "derived from" its immediately superordinate node by means of some specifiable operation. Like most metaphors, these terms may be apt in some domains but not others (e.g., the idea of a manager generating employees is literally true only in a family business). Nonetheless, they can be applied, more or less intuitively, to any hierarchically structured system.

For any dynamically conceived hierarchy, there can, in principle, be almost as many different types of operations as there are nodes. However, hierarchical characterizations of complex phenomena are heuristically valuable only when derived, level by level, from the *recursive* application of a relatively small set of operations. In this way a formal system has the capacity to describe an indefinite set of phenomena, such as the members of a musical style or a natural language, by finite means (see Lerdahl and Jackendoff 1983:6).

Although all hierarchies may be viewed dynamically, as generative systems, the converse is not true. In the most general sense, to generate an entity is to specify precisely its position within a system of operations or relations, whether such a system is hierarchical or not. For example, a two-dimensional matrix, although perhaps generated algorithmically, is not hierarchical since it fails the test of the Unique Connection Principle.

Even if we are clear about what sense of *hierarchy* we apply to music, we must still contend with the problem of scope. When we say that music is hierarchical, what exactly do we mean to denote by *music?* First, is hierarchy supposed to be a property of any and all musical events, or are there limitations, of culture, of style, of the skill of the composer, etc.? Second, is hierarchy a property of musical events in themselves, or is it some fact about our cognition of music, or is it merely an analytical bias that an analyst may or may not choose to adopt? Third, and perhaps most important for subsequent considerations, if a piece of music is hierarchical, are we to assume that the piece itself, as some kind of independent substance, has an independently hierarchical form, or are we to assume that its hierarchical form is only one of many simultaneously possessed, equally important structural attributes, each revealed, perhaps, by different analytical biases? As we venture, in what follows, into Schenkerian efforts to understand musical unity in terms of hierarchical structure, we must remain alert to questions of scope.

Ideally, the sheer range of the distinctions outlined above demands a broad and extensive survey of music-theoretical and ethnomusicological scholarship that would attempt to situate hierarchical claims within these varying parameters. Our present goal will be, more narrowly, to examine the hierarchical claims of the Schenkerian approach to tonal music in the Western classical tradition. It is only through focusing on a single theoretical tradition that we can hope to approach the desired level of critical depth in the current forum. Our choice of Schenkerian theory results not only from its privileged position in the current community of music theorists, but also from our conviction that this position is justified by the insights that the theory brings to the study of tonal systems in general and individual compositions in particular.

Part II: The Hierarchical Interpretation of Schenkerian Models

Are Schenkerian models of tonal music really hierarchical? If so, in what sense? This section demonstrates that, given the proper interpretation of the concept of prolongation, Schenkerian models of voice-leading are correctly understood as hierarchical.[4] In Parts 3 and 4, we consider whether this implies that tonal compositions themselves are, in some sense, uniformly hierarchical.

The assertion that the Schenkerian view of tonal music is hierarchical depends on the coordination of three independent subclaims: that it views tonal compositions as systems, that these systems are rooted, and that they are absolutely disjoint. The first two are relatively uncontroversial. To say that a composition is a system is to say that all of its parts are linked in some way, that no part "exists independently of the whole." This conceit is at the foundation of all organicist theory, and Schenker's organicism pervades virtually every page of his mature writings.[5] Similarly, there is no doubt that Schenkerian analyses are rooted, although there is minor disagreement as to whether the root of the system is located in the tonic triad itself or in the slightly more complex "fundamental structure," or *Ursatz* (Snell 1979:34–35; Schachter 1981:124–25).

Somewhat more problematic is the condition of absolute disjointness, requiring immediate subordinacy of each node to exactly one other node. Schenkerians implicitly adopt, at different times, two conflicting ontologies, which correspond roughly to the distinction made above between representational and inclusional hierarchies. The disjointness condition is more palatably satisfied in inclusional than representational hierarchies. These two views agree that the events represented by the terminal nodes are concrete objects which take the form of notes in a composition, but differ over their relationship to nodes at higher levels.

The representational view holds that a musical unit is dominated by one of its constituent events (i.e., a pitch with temporal and registral location in the score), which is promoted one level upward in the hierarchy. As William Benjamin puts it, proponents of this view "specifically identify states in their higher-level models with literal piece states" (1982:45). Higher-level and terminal events differ in relative structural importance, not in kind. By relating the concept of prolongation to the traditional concepts of embellishment and diminution, Schenker appears to adopt a representational outlook (Schenker [1935] 1979:93–106). Embellishments are applied to actual pitch-events, rather than to abstract categories of events. If prolongations literally have the status of particularly complex diminutions, the implication that they are part of a representational hierarchy is inescapable. Further incentive to construe Schenkerian hierarchies representationally is provided by the uniform set of symbols used to depict events and relations at all locations in the model, and by the resemblance of these analytic symbols to those used in the score on which the model is based (cf. Keiler 1978).

However, the representational outlook, with its robust ontology, forces an unhappy dilemma upon the analyst: hierarchical well-formedness cannot be preserved without making arbitrary judgments at every turn. Consider one of the most elementary of Schenkerian operations, a neighbor figure such as D–E♭–D. Which of the two D's is prolonged, and thus which should be promoted to the next-higher structural level? The representational view forces a choice here, since it considers the two D's as separate events, and absolute disjointness in a hierarchy forbids subordination of E♭ to both simultaneously. Yet choices of this kind feel arbitrary and are in the spirit neither of our own intuitive understanding of neighbor figures, nor of Schenker's understanding of them via his graphing technique. A similar problem arises in equally fundamental passing motions. Theorists who have adopted a representational view have been forced either to make such choices (Deutsch and Feroe 1981; Lerdahl and Jackendoff 1983), or to abandon the claim of strict hierarchy (Snell 1979).[6]

This dilemma is avoided by adopting an inclusional attitude toward objects of prolongation. According to this view, nonterminal nodes represent abstract classes of events, such as scale steps (*Stufen*), which control the spans that contain the concrete events of the piece—the pitch-events that inhabit the terminal nodes—without being literally equivalent to any of them.[7] Thus none of the three constituents of a neighbor motion D–E♭–D *is* more nearly the prolonged event; all are contained in it. Similarly, a passing motion prolongs an abstract triad, rather than any particular pitch-class, pitch, or attacked note that represents that triad. By treating the constituents of the span as equally subordinate to the prolongation that controls the span, the absolute disjointness of the hierarchy can be preserved. The inclusional ontology thus has the virtue of maintaining the hierarchical status of the model without imposing a series of arbitrary choices. At the same time, adoption of this view extracts a price: the relationship of prolongation to the traditional concepts of diminution and embellishment—and consequently to species counterpoint—must be viewed as metaphorical and heuristic rather than formal and literal (cf. Cook 1989; Agawu 1989).

Part III: The Role of Extra-Hierarchical Entities and Relations

Having demonstrated the circumstances under which Schenkerian models may be taken as hierarchical, we now explore a potential implication of this claim that is much broader: that the compositions themselves are hierarchical. It has frequently been pointed out that, although Schenkerian models offer explanatory accounts of pitch-events and their relations to one another, they have little to say about the duration of events and their metric position; about texture, density, and timbre; about patterns of surface figuration and motivic relationships; about conventions of form and topos; and about the setting of texts. Although some information about some of these "design" aspects is included in some Schenkerian graphs, none of them is a necessary component of such a graph. Yet, with the possible exceptions of text, texture, and timbre, all are defining features of compositions, to the extent that their alteration constitutes an alteration of the identity of a musical work. The claim that compositions are hierarchical requires not only that the traditional disciplines of harmony, melody, and counterpoint be synthesized into a single model, the prolongational hierarchy (as Schenkerian theory has successfully done); it also requires that extra-prolongational features be accommodated to that hierarchy without undermining it.

Carl Schachter and John Rothgeb have pointed out that the omission of extra-prolongational features from prolongational models does not in itself constitute evidence that they cannot in principle be subsumed by such models (Schachter 1976; Rothgeb 1978). Indeed, they show substantial evidence that the process of constructing prolongational models relies tacitly on extra-prolongational features, and that the models themselves can lead to important insights about these other areas of compositional structure and design. But a strictly hierarchical view of musical structure demands not only that prolongational models *can* be shown to contribute to an understanding of extra-prolongational parameters. It demands that the fundamental structure, and the transformations upon it, be the *sole* source of such understanding. In short, it demands a principle of prolongational priority, whereby extra-prolongational features are generated directly from and are logically determined by the prolongational hierarchy (which is itself generated solely from the fundamental structure). A corollary of this principle is that generation must be unidirectional: the prolongational hierarchy is not conversely constrained, controlled, or generated, even in part, by extra-prolongational features.

That Schenker himself believed in the absolute priority of prolongational relationships seems beyond doubt. Axiomatic pronouncements such as "[Organic structure] is determined solely by the invention of the parts out of the unity of the primary harmony" (Yeston 1977:39) and "The fundamental structure . . . is the mark of unity and . . . is the only vantage point from which to view that unity" (Schenker [1935] 1979:5) abound in Schenker's mature writings. His more specific claims about individual parameters also attest to this view: "Orchestral colors . . . are subject to the law of the whole" (ibid.:7–8). "All rhythm in music comes from counterpoint, only from counterpoint" (ibid.:15).

The principle of prolongational priority continues to be echoed in the writings of contemporary Schenkerian scholars. For example, Rothgeb asserts that harmony and voice-leading "provide the *syntax* which *makes possible* the expression of those associations and other relationships which we call content" (1978:35) and that "it is not merely that harmony and counterpoint allow us to understand the other musical dimensions; rather it is through harmony and counterpoint that those other dimensions are able to take on any aesthetic significance whatsoever" (ibid.:36). Similarly, Schachter has argued that analysis of rhythm "is dependent upon" and "is bound up with" and thus "must be compatible" with the analysis of pitch (1976:290, 311), while Charles Burkhart and Rothgeb have made roughly parallel assertions concerning motivic connections: they are "indissolubly wedded" to harmony (Burkhart 1978:167) or "inextricably bound" to the theory of structural levels (Rothgeb 1983:40).[8]

To be sure, the language cited here allows for some flexibility in interpretation. For example, the invocation of compatibility, and the metaphors of wedding and binding, leave open the possibility of mutual dependency, such that the constraint of the prolongational hierarchy upon the interpretation of extra-prolongational features may be symmetrically balanced by a set of constraints running in the opposite direction. This suggests the possibility of a somewhat more flexible attitude, which requires compatibility, conformance, negotiation, or reinforcement between prolongational and extra-prolongational relations without specifying absolute control of one or the other. Indeed, this principle of prolongational compatibility is strongly suggested when Rothgeb proposes that a paper entitled "Design as a Key to Structure" might be complemented by a paper entitled "Structure as a Key to Design" (see Yeston 1977:93).

Yet it is not clear that Schenkerians are unilaterally committed even to the weaker principle of prolongational compatibility. For example, Schachter asserts that "conflicts between durational and tonal groupings can be of crucial importance in shaping a musical idea" (1980:330), hinting that the role of prolongational hierarchies is not to marshal all compositional relationships to a uniform interpretation, but rather to provide a basis for chronicling the play of the surface details with or against the context provided by "the structure" (cf. Cook 1989:129). William Rothstein acknowledges a similar conflict between "large-scale tonal motion" and "the evident layout of phrases and periods," and he argues that *"both* aspects must be acknowledged in a full description of the work's form" (1989:104). When he recasts this conflict in terms of "inner form" (which he equates with "that which operates powerfully but less obviously") and "outer form" (which "lies on the surface"), he directly acknowledges the possibility of conflict between the prolongational structure and other relationships that lie outside of that structure.[9]

Such acknowledgements implicitly represent a challenge to the central Schenkerian tenet that the fundamental structure is the sole source of organic structure and compositional unity, and thus to the hierarchical view of compositions. At the same time, they imply a move toward a conception of musical structure as an intersection or confluence of various independent systems, whose interaction is systematically indeterminate (although possibly determinable *ad hoc* in specific instances). Such a conception has long been advocated by Leonard B. Meyer and some of his followers, who hold that the prolongational hierarchy is, at best, one of many nonreducible analytic perspectives, each of which contributes to compositional unity (Meyer 1973; Narmour 1977; Gjerdingen 1988). Such affinities may be surprising, since the work of Meyerians has been strenuously rejected by Schenkerians.[10] It must be stressed, however, that these affinities exist only at the grossest metatheoretical level. There is still a fundamental antipathy between the two camps over what parameters may be in conflict. In particular, the Meyerian resistance to the synthesis of melody and harmony in a single model is fundamentally irreconcilable to even a modified Schenkerian view.

In any case, our survey of attitudes toward the relationship between prolongational structure and extra-prolongational features attests to an absence of consensus among modern Schenkerian scholars on this very crucial metatheoretical issue. In the following section, we show evidence that this unacknowledged absence of consensus symptomizes an unacknowledged but deep rift between theory and practice that has long been present in Schenkerian scholarship.

Part IV: A Case in Point: The Schenkerian Treatment of Motive

We now refine our inquiry further, by focusing careful scrutiny on Schenker's conception of thematic structure—in particular his utterly original concepts of motivic parallelism and concealed repetition, which are the source of some of his most fascinating insights into the coherence of individual compositions. This choice of focus is motivated in part by the abundant and distinguished scholarly literature on the subject,[11] but also because, of all of the compositional features not encoded into a prolongational hierarchy, it is thematic relationships to which Schenker most clearly attributes organic and unifying potential. This attribution is presented most clearly in paragraph 254 of *Free Composition*, where Schenker writes that "repetitions [are] the prime carriers of synthesis . . . the masters based their syntheses mainly upon such relationships" ([1935] 1979:100), but it can also be found in different forms throughout his mature writings.

If motivic relationships are unity-conferring, and all unity emerges from the Ursatz, it follows that motivic relationships must be subsumed by the prolongational hierarchy. In order to demonstrate that this is so, Schenkerians have focused attention on the way that the prolongational hierarchy constrains the definition of motive. In contrast to traditional theory, where motives normally consist of contiguous pitch-events, the components of Schenkerian motives need not be contiguous on the surface. They cannot, however, be selected willy-nilly from disconnected branches and levels of the prolongational tree, but must constitute a unified hierarchical subset of that tree. Ordered sets of pitches must be verified by, and thus depend upon, the prolongational hierarchy in order to achieve their status as motives. Charles Burkhart posits the principle as "the melodically particular arises from systematically defined constants" (1978:146), while John Rothgeb similarly writes that "proposed thematic relationships must bear scrutiny in the light of the Schenkerian theory of structural strata" (1983:42; see also Beach 1989).

This dependence has epistemic consequences for the analytic discovery of underlying structure: the process of reduction should be unaffected by the analyst's interest in revealing motivic connections. Rothgeb states: "A Schenkerian approach encourages the discovery of relationships (possibly unexpected) by 'reading through' diminution to underlying shape, but with the restriction that the 'reading' process must be informed by principles that are independent of any specific configuration one may believe 'ought' to be present" (1983:41; cf. Schachter 1982:16 and Beach 1989). In the process of executing these discovery procedures, the analyst recognizes no motives or motivic relationships, as such. Writes David Beach, "Recognition of motivic repetition is a byproduct of analysis" (1989:6).

While this view is internally consistent, and implementable in principle, in analytic practice Schenker and Schenkerians are not prepared to adhere to such strict structuralist procedures (cf. Keiler 1978). As in other empirical domains such as psychology and linguistics, strictly circumscribed discovery procedures can severely limit the capacity to generate interesting analyses. In his analysis of a Handel suite, for example, Schenker used his knowledge of the foreground content to guide his decision about the composition's background structure, invoking motivic considerations to tip the analytic balance toward one of two otherwise equally well-formed reductions (Burkhart 1978:170). In his analysis of a Haydn sonata, the desire simultaneously to bring out motives in the bass and the upper voice led Schenker to an otherwise peculiar decision to ignore the resolution of a dominant-functioning 6/4 chord.[12] Similarly, Beach 1983, after modeling the development of a Mozart quartet by invoking harmonic and voice-leading considerations alone, suggests an alternative reading generated by motivic concerns.

This crack between theory and practice can be sealed by abandoning the demand for discovery procedures confined solely to prolongational considerations. This need not be a large sacrifice, since Schenkerians elsewhere acknowledge that "Schenkerian theory contains no prescriptions whatsoever regarding what 'can' and 'cannot' be done in 'reducing' a piece to its harmonic-contrapuntal structure" (Rothgeb 1978:28) and are willing to accept a certain amount of circularity in their reductive procedures (Schachter 1981:132). The alternative would be to force a more vigilant introspection on analytic process and to accept the relative poverty of the ensuing results.

Another rift is revealed through examination of the identity conditions on Schenkerian motives in light of the principle that all parts must maintain "constant contact" with higher levels of structure (Schenker [1935] 1979:18). A consistent application of this principle logically demands that motives not only be conceived as sequences of notes or intervals, but also bear structural descriptions that indicate the relative status of the events in relation to one another. For example, the identity of a neighbor figure depends not only on the existence of a particular sequence of pitches or intervals, but also on the structural inferiority of the interior event to the exterior ones.

Nonetheless, Schenkerian motives are frequently identified merely as strings of pitch-classes or intervals, or as spans to be filled by stepwise motion, without regard for relative stability and dependency relations among the constituents of those strings. For example, a descending 4-line could describe the motion between the root and fifth of a triad; a filled third with incomplete upper-neighbor prefix; or a filled third with lower-neighbor suffix. Structurally, these are quite different situations; it is only on the surface that they appear similar. By calling each of these situations 4-lines, one runs the risk of legitimating such "apparent" relationships.

Schenkerian analytical practice reveals that the problem is not due merely to incomplete or abbreviated labeling conventions. For example, a Beethoven minuet contains two versions of the pitch-class sequence A♭–B♭–A♭–G–A♭ that bear quite different structural descriptions: in one instance, the interior A♭ prolongs those at the exterior; in the other, it acts as a structurally inferior passing tone (Burkhart 1978). Nonetheless, Schenker considers this "motive" as an agent of unity. In a different Beethoven minuet, Ernst Oster points to F–E♭ as an element of continuity, even though at first F is upper neighbor to E♭ (as $\hat{6}$–$\hat{5}$ in A♭), but subsequently E♭ is lower neighbor to F (as $\hat{3}$–$\hat{2}$ in D♭) (Yeston 1977:58–59). In these instances, Schenkerians overlook "underlying" structural differences, instead relating motives on the basis of "mere" surface similarities. Such situations are difficult to reconcile with the principle of prolongational priority.

This breach between theory and practice can again be mended by placing stronger controls on analytical practice and forgoing some potentially compelling results. The alternative to such austerity is to modify theoretical principles, but this time the price is much higher, since it requires relinquishing a number of cherished ideals: for example, that all unity stems from the Ursatz; that structure fully determines the interpretation of the surface; and that compositions are hierarchically structured and closed systems.

Yet these principles may be difficult to retain in any case, because the assertion that motivic relationships are subject to the principle of prolongational priority is beset with yet another problem which is more foundational. This third problem resides in the distinction between *entities* and *relations*. Schenkerians effectively demonstrate the correlation between motivic and prolongational entities; but unity results not from these entities per se, but from the relationships they bear to one another. If motivic relationships fail to correspond to prolongational relationships, then they cannot fully depend on the prolongational hierarchy. Correspondence, in this context, requires overwriting of lines of communication already present in the prolongational hierarchy, rather than creation of new, more direct connections, which would subvert the hierarchical status of the system by violating the Unique Connection Principle. A voice-leading model is hierarchical precisely because it fulfills this condition to the letter. Each new line of motivic connection would constitute a second path between the so-related events, and a system containing even a single pair of events related by two different paths is no longer strictly hierarchical.[13]

In the case of "nesting," where one of the related motives is subordinate to the other (see Burkhart 1978:151), overwriting occurs and the integrity of the hierarchy is not threatened. But hidden repetitions also "make possible . . . the organic connections of distant points" (Schenker [1935] 1979:132). If voice-leading transformations succeed in unifying an entire composition by demonstrating that all of its events are connected via their mutual connection to the Ursatz, why should "organic connections of distant points" require hidden repetitions? One can only speculate that such connections are more direct than prolongational connections. The language used by Schenkerians to characterize such relations—for example, in terms of enlargement, contraction, "seed and harvest" (Burkhart 1978:168–69)—corroborate this speculation, implying a direct transformational relationship between pattern and copy. This attitude is repeated in more recent literature: for Rothgeb (1983), the copy "derives from" or "grows out of" the pattern (44); the statement "engenders" its variant (45); "the seeds of the motivic events . . . lie . . . in bar 3" (55). Similarly, in many Schenkerian analyses (e.g., Forte 1980) the motivic content of the piece is generated from the opening measures, not from the Ursatz.

The crux of the matter is this: if all events in a composition are generated from the Ursatz, but some events are also generated from earlier events via motivic transformations, generation cannot be hierarchical.

This third argument suggests that, to rescue motivic relationships for the principle of prolongational priority, Schenkerians would have either to confine their motivic relationships to those which involve nesting (surely an undesirable restriction) or to demonstrate that, in spite of the direct transformational implications in their language, non-nested motivic relationships actually do overwrite or displace extant relationships in the prolongational hierarchy (as implied by Snell 1979). This latter contingency would require a radical reconstruction of the nature of prolongational and motivic relationships (and the language by which they are described), which would sacrifice a considerable amount of analytical power, even so. For example, the applicability of linkage (Rothgeb 1983), which relates events that are surface-contiguous but structurally remote, would become greatly weakened.

Part V: Alternative Conceptions of Musical Unity: Some Speculations

Each of the three problems outlined in Part 4 illustrates that the principles of Schenkerian theory frequently do not accord with analytic practice. In principle, unity is fully determined by the prolongational hierarchy; but in practice, unity is produced by motivic relations that cut across and override that hierarchy. In principle, "the fundamental structure . . . accompanies each transformation in the middleground and foreground, as a guardian angel watches over a child" (Schenker [1935] 1979:18); but in practice, motivic unity often relies on association of surface shapes detached from the transformations that yield them. In principle, motivic relationships must emerge as a by-product of voice-leading reduction; but in practice, voice-leading reductions are molded in part to optimize motivic relations. These tensions reflect the plural demands of motivic unity and prolongational priority, which are not always in accord in Schenker's world. When they compete, theorists must choose whether to sacrifice claims about motivic unity in individual compositions—regardless of how salient or powerful these claims might be—or to compromise the principle of prolongational priority and thereby abandon the claim that tonal music is exclusively hierarchical.

On the one hand, to sacrifice analytical power is ultimately to diminish interest in a theory, which acquires legitimacy by leading to compelling readings of individual compositions. On the other hand, abandonment of a comfortable metatheoretical home compels a search for new quarters. If Schenkerian analytical practice does not faithfully adhere to a hierarchical paradigm, what paradigm does it fulfill?

We begin by considering the general concept of *network,* of which a hierarchy is a distinct subspecies (Narmour 1977; Gjerdingen 1988). A network consists of any system of nodes which are connected, so that at least one path may be traced between any pair of nodes within the system. As we showed in Part 1, a network which adheres to the Unique Connection Principle and which is rooted also qualifies as a hierarchy. Any network can be transformed into a hierarchy by specifying a root and expunging connections until the Unique Connection Principle is fulfilled; thus a network always contains one or more hierarchies as a subset. Conversely, if a hierarchy loses its status by the addition of extrahierarchical connections between its events, it still retains its status as a network. This last consideration is particularly appropriate to the present study, since it accords well with our characterization of Schenkerian analytic practice.

Networks have the advantage of liberating analysis from the vast number of constraints imposed by hierarchies and thus encouraging certain salient and powerful analytic claims that are suppressed or disabled by a purely hierarchical stance. In their tolerance of multiple cross-relations and over-determination of individual events, they are able to capture the richness that we often sense in those events. At the same time, in the absence of any further limitations, networks are too general to be of much use as paradigms of musical structure. Without imposing limits on the type or number of inter-relationships, without providing an apparatus for exploring the possible impacts these relationships have on one another, without distinguishing between strong and weak, structural and incidental, networks threaten to be more complex than the surfaces they purport to explicate. In themselves, networks fail to satisfy our critical urge both to acknowledge and to master phenomenal complexity by discovering some underlying structural simplicity that specifies the contribution of every individual element. Abandoning the hierarchical home for unconstrained networks threatens theorists with a nomadic life of promiscuous pluralism, indeterminacy, or chaos.

What seems to be in demand is a paradigm of musical structure which encourages minimization of relationships without demanding uniformity; which is capable of distinguishing between structural and incidental, at least in part; and which seeks relatively simple accounts of apparently complex phenomena, without confining generativity to a single source. The remainder of this essay sketches a view of musical structure as a network resulting from a set of generative operations that are intertwined yet independent of one another, and investigates some of the benefits that accrue from such a view, both music-analytically and aesthetically.

The concept of *product network,* briefly introduced by David Lewin in his recent book *Generalized Musical Intervals and Transformations* (1987), provides an example of how such a paradigm might ideally look, although Lewin's discussion is confined to several brief examples that merely hint at a formal characterization (204–6; 236). Lewin introduces product networks as one of three ways to generate a fragment of parallel organum (Example 2a). The first method begins by generating the harmonic perfect fourth, which is then transposed by the melodic intervals of the tune (Example 2b). The second method begins by generating the tune from its first note, then transposing up a perfect fourth to yield the upper voice (Example 2c). Although both of these essentially hierarchical methods generate identical results, each carries with it an implication that either melody or harmony is conceptually prior. This assignment of priority may or may not be appropriate, depending on the music being modeled. The product network, offered as a third mode of generation, makes it possible to avoid privileging one of these dimensions: the melody of the passage and the harmony of a perfect fourth act as coequal generators. The organum is the product of the two operands. As shown in Example 2d, a product network is

a)

Principalis:

Organalis: Nos qui vivimus, benedicimus Do-mi-no,

b)

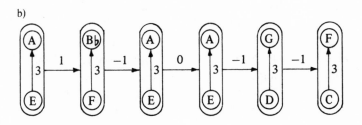

c)

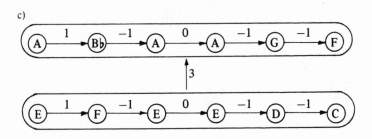

d)

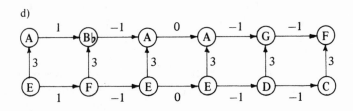

EXAMPLE 2. Generating Parallel Organum (from Lewin, *Generalized Musical Intervals and Transformations* [1987])

represented visually by a two-dimensional matrix, with each event linked both vertically, with its harmonic mate, and horizontally, with its melodic neighbors.

By locating each individual pitch-event at the intersection of the independent operations, Example 2d illustrates that paradigms exist for modeling music which are simultaneously generative (in the sense of precisely specifying each event) and nonhierarchical. It further suggests how easily products may be overlooked in favor of hierarchies, since any structure generable by a product network can also be generated by one or more hierarchies (cf. Knuth 1968:309). Yet the example is limited to a very specific set of relationships of very small dimensions. Although we are unprepared to generalize this scheme, the following examples suggest that the product-network paradigm opens some fruitful directions for tracing the interaction of a prolongational hierarchy with motivic, thematic, or figurational relations in tonal music.

1. Rothgeb 1987 analyzes the opening three measures of Brahms's Fourth Symphony as a set of neighbor figures prolonging $\hat{5}$ over a tonic pedal. The same passage may be viewed as a series of descending thirds, with octave transfers. A strict hierarchical view takes these two characterizations to be in competition, insisting that one is an incidental (and perhaps therefore irrelevant) by-product of the other.[14] Our proposal views the passage as a product of the two characterizations, and perhaps even as a unique solution to the problem of intersecting these two generative schemes. Maintaining the mutual independence of the two characterizations makes available a double fund of properties which may be artificially detached and presented in isolation from each other. In this movement, Brahms takes advantage not only of the potential of the neighbor figure to be presented independently of the descending thirds (see Litterick 1987), but also of the potential of the descending thirds to occur independently of the neighbor motion (as in measures 190–192).

The example suggests that, whenever Schenkerians trace non-nested motivic relations, they are in fact viewing compositions as products of the prolongational hierarchy and some more loosely defined scheme of motivic generation.

2. A product network could capture the relationship between intrameasure figuration and extrameasure voice-leading in a figuration prelude, such as the first two preludes from Book I of J. S. Bach's *Well Tempered Clavier*. Schenker's exemplary graphs of extrameasure motion in these preludes suggest no reason why each measure of the C-major prelude contains an upward arpeggiation in relatively closed spacing, while each measure of the

first half of the C-minor prelude bears an inward arpeggiation, in relatively open spacing, with the inner pitches ornamented by a lower neighbor.[15] Figuration plays an obvious role in unifying these pieces, in the sense that the figuration which Bach chooses for his first measure generates the choices he makes for subsequent measures. Yet the surface figuration in these pieces apparently varies independently of the voice-leading structure. If the extra-measure voice-leading schemes in these pieces select, in some way, for particular intrameasure figuration, no one has yet shown how. Whereas a strictly hierarchical view is capable of deriving the figuration from the voice-leading, it must do so cumbersomely, proceeding measure by measure. Because the figuration-deriving operations for each measure would occur independently of one another, the obvious surface parallelisms among them would be rendered incidental. Because of the absence of parallels between figurational patterns and higher-level motions, there would be no hierarchically sanctioned top-down (nesting) parallelisms by way of compensation. There are two advantages to considering the composition as generated coequally by its linear graph and its figurational scheme, so that each individual event is a product of top-down generation from the Ursatz and left-to-right generation from the figuration of the first measure: it is more efficient (since the figuration need not be generated separately for each measure) and more productive (since the analysis recognizes the surface figurational parallels).

3. Viewing compositions as cogenerated by voice-leading designs and metric/figurational schemes enables proper credit to be given to the influence of inter-opus topical and stylistic conventions on the construction and experience of compositions.[16] In a Turkish march, a chorale, a minuet, or a call to the hunt, a hierarchical view makes no place for the impact of any source outside of the fundamental structure and its transformations. Yet topical conventions, which can subsume conventions of meter, tempo, duration, and figuration into a higher-level construct, are clearly generative, in the sense of guiding specific compositional decisions which in turn promote unity for performer or listener. This point may have intra-opus implications as well. Note, for example, that topical conventions may vary independently of a voice-leading paradigm, as in a set of variations or a suite;[17] but also that voice-leading paradigms may vary independently of topical conventions, as in a set of German waltzes. By locating compositions at the intersection of voice-leading paradigms and topical conventions, the product network values the unifying potential of movement along either of the two axes.

One might respond to these examples of product networks by remarking that they do not yield especially profound or subtle music-analytic insights. But a moment's reflection will suggest why this is so: the generative and unifying roles of surface figuration and of topos have always been recognized. Music theory's increasingly subtle outlook on prolongational relations has not driven these more obvious surface relations from view. The product-network paradigm merely states explicitly what has been implicit all along.

Nonetheless, acknowledgement of the appropriateness of the product network as a paradigm of music-analytic activity has consequences both for Schenkerian theory and, more broadly, for our conceptions of musical unity in general. There are two implications within the relatively narrow domain of Schenkerian theory. Although analysts of tonal music are encouraged to continue searching for an ultimately uniform source encompassing as many unifying parameters as possible, their failure to discover such a source in a given composition becomes more tolerable. Acknowledging Schenkerian analyses to be product networks also has an important impact on how Schenkerians view their role within the larger universe of the analysis of tonal music: they need not consider Ursatz organicism to be in competition with other modes of generation.

The potential implications of product networks for our conceptions of musical unity are more extensive. The image of a composition as a product of logically independent operations is dissonant with our desire to provide a relatively simple unifying basis for surface complexity. Instead, such a conception promises more diversity and greater complexity "beneath the surface" of a complex musical event, and perhaps even threatens to deepen the cognitive mysteries behind our ability to achieve a coherent appreciation of such complex aesthetic phenomena. Reconsidering our commitment to uniform hierarchies thus exerts pressure toward reassessing more fundamental canons of musical unity. The concept of product networks suggests that, instead of thinking of a complex musical surface as unified by an underlying structural simplicity, we consider the musical surface as a *solution* to the compositional problem of mutually satisfying the demands of several sets of independent formal operations. In other words, the compositional surface is something like the intersection—perhaps even the unique intersection—of several formally independent compositional parameters. (In principle, this intersection could be uniformly hierarchical, in cases where multiple parameters are related by inclusion; but in practice, such cases are difficult to discover.)

What is most potentially unsettling about this view is that the apparently complex musical surface is reconceived as the basis of a composition's unity. It is the surface that "holds together" underlying diversity by providing a compositional solution to multiple and disparate demands of harmonic, contrapuntal, motivic, and rhythmic operations. To be sure, this surface unity cannot be formally appreciated without first appreciating the underlying parameters impinging on that surface. Consequently, musical comprehension seems best served not by neglecting underlying structure, but rather by shuttling between the surface and underlying compositional parameters. The surface reveals both *what* underlying parameters are compositionally active and *how* they coordinate to generate the surface.

This view may be less unsettling if compared with a familiar phenomenon outside of the realm of music. Why do we value puns and double entendres? Surely not because of their underlying semantic simplicity; by definition, puns have multiple semantic readings. Yet puns are neither disunified nor incoherent. We appreciate good puns because diverse underlying meanings are simultaneously active within the uniform syntax and context (i.e., *surface*) in which they appear. And they are not only active, but interactive, because two (or more) semantic readings can be mutually informing, causing a re-appreciation of either meaning in light of the other. It is this possibility of dynamic interactivity between independently generative agents that makes product networks appropriate paradigms for capturing the relations between prolongational hierarchies and motivic relations or other extrahierarchical parameters.

From a philosophical viewpoint, turning musical organicism on its head has two very attractive aspects. First, analysts are frequently accused of neglecting what is musically valuable when they listen "beneath" the surface interests of a piece. This objection is disarmed by a product-network conception of musical unity, which draws our attention, and the analyst's, back to the surface of the piece as the ground of its unity.

Second, the concept of a composition as a product of multiple intersecting constraints has some appealing cognitive implications. Composers may in some way select a compositional "seed" which they systematically transform into a well-formed hierarchical sequence in accordance with a small menu of prolongational operations. A performer may in some way seek to project these relations between underlying "kernel" and complex surface, and a listener may in some way seek to discover them. But we are dissatisfied with so tidy an image of musical cognition. We intuitively find it more appropriate to imagine the composer, performer, or listener juggling and coordinating, in the many ways available, the multiple influences of diverse compositional parameters, as dictated by nature, convention, and invention.

Although such intuitions can ultimately be verified only by cautious empirical enquiries into the creative psychology of musicians and listeners, we suspect that they are widely shared. For an illustration, reconsider Example 2a from the viewpoint of the performer. A singer can minimally execute the higher part, following Example 2b, by tuning the initial interval with his partner and then simply singing his melody, ignoring the string of harmonic relationships so produced. He can also execute the part, following Example 2c, by immediately producing a perfect fourth above each note that his partner sings, while ignoring the line he himself is producing in the process. Either of these hierarchical methods will succeed in "generating" the passage. But unless the singer is simultaneously attending both to his line and to the harmonies he is forming with his partner—that is, fitting into the two-dimensional matrix of Example 2d—we are unlikely to consider the performance "musical."

𝄐

Although unity and coherence are surely important canons of musical and music-analytic value, acting alone they are insufficient to distinguish masterworks from well-formed exercises in species counterpoint. The search for plural unities, over and above the unity certified by prolongational hierarchies, attests that music theorists are equally committed to a second, independent canon, which may best be characterized as *richness*. If this commitment is often tacit, perhaps it is for fear that richness can be captured only at the expense of unity: the open-minded adoption of many disjunct analytic perspectives is tantamount to having no unified vision at all. We have suggested reason to believe that, although basically independent of each other, the canons of hierarchically generated unity and richness are not in competition, but coordinate to produce musical and music-analytic values. Just as plural unities interact to generate events that constitute a musical composition, and condition their interpretation, so also plural canons interact to generate, and condition the interpretation of, the products and activities which constitute the music-analytic discipline.

NOTES

1. X is a partial partition of a set Y if and only if:

For some sets P and Q
   i) P ⊂ X and Q ⊂ Y
   ii) P is a partition of Q
   iii) X − P = Y − Z (X − P denotes the complement of P in X)
And every partition of a set X is automatically a partial partition of X.

2. Our formal definition of hierarchy, which was designed for inclusion hierarchies, would need to be revised to accommodate robust hierarchies. Such a revision, though unproblematic, is inappropriately technical and lengthy for the current forum.

3. All systems are susceptible to both static and dynamic interpretations; this dichotomy is more a choice of orientation than an absolute typological distinction. See Whitehead 1948.

4. That Schenker, who died in 1935, does not appear to have explicitly invoked the concept of hierarchy in his writings is hardly surprising, since strict, formal hierarchies attained prestige in academic circles only via post-war research in linguistics and cybernetics. The convergence in Schenkerian theory of this twentieth-century structural paradigm with the nineteenth-century tradition of German idealist philosophy, a convergence that began in the 1950s, surely makes one of the more fascinating unwritten chapters in the intellectual history of music theory.

5. The relationship of Schenker's organicism to a broader intellectual tradition has been well documented in a number of sources, including Solie 1980 and Pastille 1985.

6. Proctor 1989 shows that the representational interpretation of Schenkerian hierarchies can result in misconstruals of Schenkerian theory on the part of its critics.

7. For a clear exposition of an inclusional view of prolongation, see Proctor 1978, chap. 2; Keiler 1983–84: 213–15; Komar 1988. Komar appears to assume that a Schenkerian prolongation is representational but recommends an inclusional ontology (for the higher levels of structure only) as a revision of that view.

8. These views are reiterated, using similar language, in Beach 1989.

9. See also Narmour 1977:104–6; Laskowski 1980:57.

10. Rothgeb 1978 is a particularly impassioned critique, but Narmour in particular has been attacked throughout the Schenkerian community.

11. Recent contributions to this literature are summarized in Beach 1989.

12. See Schenker 1926:47 (*Anhang*), measure 8 (reproduced in Yeston 1977:43, example 2.2). The motives in question are the arpeggiation upward to D, and the bass neighbor figure F–G♭–F. The simultaneous retention of D in the upper voice and F in the bass results in an implied extensive prolongation of a 6/4 chord which never resolves. (The dotted line from D♭ at measure 9 in Yeston's edition is a printer's error not found in the original German edition, where it more logically emerges from the D at measure 8.) Schenker's own discomfort with this solution is reflected in the middleground graph (Schenker 1926:46; Yeston 1977:42), where the 6/4 disappears entirely in favor of events which the foreground graph claims to be subordinate to it.

13. This argument elaborates a specific suggestion of Peel and Slawson 1984 (290) and has been more generally anticipated by Narmour 1977 and Gjerdingen 1988.

14. Thus Rothgeb (1987:210) writes that "the idea that the theme . . . consists of (seven) descending thirds . . . contains not the smallest grain of truth."

15. Schenker's most comprehensive treatment of the C-major prelude may be found in Schenker [1933] 1969:36–37; the C-minor prelude is analyzed in Schenker 1926:85–91. In the latter, Schenker finds motivations for Bach's occasional alterations of the figurational patterns (91), but not for the form of the original pattern itself.

16. The interaction of topos and voice-leading is a concern of Agawu 1987.

17. The 1710 treatise of Friedrich Erhardt Niedt shows how a single thorough-bass can generate a variety of Baroque dances, depending on the topos with which it is combined (Niedt 1989:163–78).

WORKS CITED

Agawu, V. Kofi. 1987. "The First Movement of Beethoven's Opus 132 and the Classical Style." *College Music Symposium* 27:30–45.

———. 1989. "Schenkerian Notation in Theory and Practice." *Music Analysis* 8:275–301.

Beach, David. 1983. "A Recurring Pattern in Mozart's Music." *Journal of Music Theory* 27:1–30.

———. 1989. "Schenkerian Theory." *Music Theory Spectrum* 11:3–14.

Becker, Judith, and Alton Becker. 1979. "A Grammar of the Musical Genre Srepegan." *Journal of Music Theory* 23:1–44.

Benjamin, William. 1982. "Models of Underlying Tonal Structure: How Can They Be Abstract, and How Should They Be Abstract?" *Music Theory Spectrum* 4:28–50.

Burkhart, Charles. 1978. "Schenker's 'Motivic Parallelisms'." *Journal of Music Theory* 22:145–75.

Cook, Nicholas. 1989. "Music Theory and 'Good Comparison': A Viennese Perspective." *Journal of Music Theory* 33:117–42.

Deutsch, Diana, and John Feroe. 1981. "The Internal Representation of Pitch Sequences in Tonal Music." *Psychological Review* 88:503–22.

Forte, Allen. 1980. "Generative Chromaticism in Mozart's Music: The Rondo in a minor, K. 511." *Musical Quarterly* 66:459–83.

Gjerdingen, Robert. 1988. *A Classic Turn of Phrase: Music and the Psychology of Convention.* Philadelphia: University of Pennsylvania Press.

Keiler, Allen. 1978. "The Empiricist Illusion." *Perspectives of New Music* 17:161–95.

———. 1983–84. "On Some Properties of Schenker's Pitch Derivations." *Music Perception* 1:200–228.

Knuth, Donald. 1968. *The Art of Computer Programming.* Menlo Park: Addison-Wesley.

Komar, Arthur. 1988. "The Pedagogy of Tonal Hierarchy." *In Theory Only* 10, no.5:23–28.

Laskowski, Larry. 1980. "Symmetrical Design and Its Relationship to Voice-leading." *Theory and Practice* 5:57–65.

Lerdahl, Fred, and Ray Jackendoff. 1983. *A Generative Theory of Tonal Music.* Cambridge, Mass.: MIT Press.

Lewin, David. 1987. *Generalized Musical Intervals and Transformations.* New Haven: Yale University Press.

Litterick, Louise. 1987. "Brahms the Indecisive: Notes on the First Movement of the Fourth Symphony." In Michael Musgrave, ed., *Brahms 2: Biographical, Documentary and Analytical Studies.* Cambridge: Cambridge University Press.

Meyer, Leonard B. 1973. *Explaining Music.* Berkeley: University of California Press.

Morris, Robert. 1987. *Composition with Pitch-Classes.* New Haven: Yale University Press.

Narmour, Eugene. 1977. *Beyond Schenkerism: The Need for Alternatives in Music Analysis.* Chicago: University of Chicago Press.

———. 1983–84. "Some Major Theoretical Problems concerning the Concept of Hierarchy in the Analysis of Tonal Music." *Music Perception* 1:129–99.

Niedt, Friedrich Erhardt. 1989. *The Musical Guide.* Trans. Pamela L. Poulin and Irmgard C. Taylor. Oxford: Clarendon Press. Originally published in three volumes, 1700, 1710, 1721.

Pastille, William. 1985. "Ursatz: The Musical Philosophy of Heinrich Schenker." Ph.D. diss., Cornell University.

Peel, John, and Wayne Slawson. 1984. Review of Lerdahl and Jackendoff 1983. *Journal of Music Theory* 28:271–93.

Proctor, Gregory. 1978. "The Technical Bases of Nineteenth-Century Chromatic Tonality." Ph.D. diss., Princeton University.

———. 1989. Review of Gjerdingen 1988. *Intégral* 4:171–200.

Rothgeb, John. 1978. Review of Narmour 1977. *Theory and Practice* 3.2:28–42.

———. 1983. "Thematic Content: A Schenkerian View." In David Beach, ed., *Aspects of Schenkerian Theory.* New Haven: Yale University Press.

———. 1987. Review of *Brahms and the Principle of Developing Variation,* by Walter Frisch. *Music Theory Spectrum* 9:204–14.

Rothstein, William. 1989. *Phrase Rhythm in Tonal Music.* New York: Schirmer Books.

Schachter, Carl. 1976. "Rhythm and Linear Analysis: A Preliminary Study." In Felix Salzer, ed., *Music Forum,* Vol. 4. New York: Columbia University Press.

———. 1980. "Rhythm and Linear Analysis: Durational Reduction." In Felix Salzer, ed., *Music Forum,* Vol. 5. New York: Columbia University Press.

———. 1981. "A Commentary on Schenker's *Free Composition.*" *Journal of Music Theory* 25:115–42.

———. 1982. "Beethoven's Sketches for the First Movement of Opus 14, No. 1: A Study in Design." *Journal of Music Theory* 26:1–22.

Schenker, Heinrich. 1926. *Das Meisterwerk in der Musik.* Vol. 2. Munich: Drei Masken Verlag.

———. 1969. *Five Graphic Analyses.* New York: Dover. Originally published 1933.

———. 1979. *Free Composition.* New York: Longman. Originally published as *Der freie Satz* (Vienna: Universal Edition, 1935).

Snell, James L. 1979. "Design for a Formal System for Deriving Tonal Music." M.A. thesis, SUNY Binghamton.

Solie, Ruth A. 1980. "The Living Work: Organicism and Musical Analysis." *Nineteenth Century Music* 4:147–56.

Whitehead, A. N. 1948. *An Introduction to Mathematics.* London: Oxford University Press.

Yeston, Maury, ed. 1977. *Readings in Schenkerian Theory.* New Haven: Yale University Press.

TEN

A Lifetime of Chants
Katherine Bergeron

On a flyer distributed by the Liturgical Press in Collegeville, Minnesota (one of the principal liturgical publishers in the United States), a modest type-written letter advertises a new collection of Gregorian-chant recordings, commemorating the 1987 sesquicentennial of the Abbey of Saint Peter in Solesmes, France—home of the Benedictine monks who devoted their lives to the study of this music over a century ago.[1] Underscored in red, the following line announces the offer:

Tune your inner ear to the CHANTS OF A LIFETIME

It's a mixed message. While the page, with its visual field of black and white and red, recalls the timelessness of a religious institution and its texts (the Missal, the Lectionary), the command pleads the urgency of the moment. Playing on the typical extravagant rhetoric of the advertiser, the announcement presents a product whose lasting value is established in the accompanying letter. "Dear Friend," it begins,

> As you are acutely aware if you listen to radio today, *music has many forms*. They range from the melancholy to the hyper-active, from the simple to the complicated, from country to grand opera, and from the ridiculous to the sublime. In short, they reflect the tastes of a variety of people. But they have one thing in common: They are short-lived—if you count in centuries.

The opening pun on *chance* evidently spells out something quite different: far from a one-time-only proposition, the chants sold here reflect the essence of tradition; they are a great value because they have endured for centuries. As age-old music, they are certain to bring every listener, as they did the monks themselves, a lifetime of musical fulfillment.

182

THE LITURGICAL PRESS
St. John's Abbey — Collegeville, Minnesota 56321 — 612-363-2213

Tune your inner ear to the CHANTS OF A LIFETIME

Dear Friend,

As you are acutely aware if you listen to radio today, music has many forms. They range from the melancholy to the hyper-active, from the simple to the complicated, from country to grand opera, and from the ridiculous to the sublime. In short, they reflect the tastes of a variety of people. But they have one thing in common: They are short-lived--if you count in centuries.

Only one form of music seems to have outlasted its critics--it might have had some!--and become truly universal in its appeal: Gregorian Chant.

Some people feel the key to the charm of Gregorian Chant lies in its simplicity (but it is a simplicity that is deceptive, lying only on the surface). Others claim its appeal can be attributed to its calm religious character (but many "non-religious" people also find chant appealing). Still others claim the listening pleasure of chants rests in the "masculine" sound (but feminine voices intone chant as beautifully as do male voices).

Whatever the reasons--and there are many more than given here--chant is a tonic to a broader range of listeners than any other type of music. For THAT reason we continue to add to our selection of chant recordings. Some of the major titles described below have been on our lists for a long time, but they continue to sell as new listeners are introduced to the richness, the serenity, and the purity of chant. So, read on...and tune your inner ear to THE CHANTS OF A LIFETIME.

SUNDAY VESPERS AND COMPLINE--Monastic Choir of St. Peter's Abbey, Solesmes, France; directed by Dom Jean Claire
This and other recordings of the Solesmes Abbey Choir are from a series commemorating the 1987 sesquicentennial of the raising of St. Peter's to the status of an abbey. This Compline service includes the tolling of the great bell of Solesmes; the chant here expresses a tenderness that reduces even a great cathedral to the intimacy of a chapel.

7413 Stereo LP, or 7415 Stereo cassette, $8.95

FEASTS OF OUR LADY--Monastic Choir of St. Peter's Abbey, Solesmes, France; directed by Dom Jean Claire
From the first Salve to the last antiphon, Regina Caeli, the chants presented here elegantly express the filial affection with which the Church honors the Virgin Mary.

7428 Stereo LP, or 7429 Stereo cassette, $8.95

FIGURE 1. Advertisement, *The Liturgical Press* (1987)

Tu(r)ning the Ear

But the advertisement bears further consideration. For its opening
lines also suggest that these timeless Gregorian chants be measured against
less permanent ("short-lived") music according to a more precise scale of
values, evident in the very first words on the page: "*Tune* your inner ear."
This phrase, too, like the "chants" that follow it, engages a pun, a double
allusion, a (possible) slip of the tongue: "tune your ear" seems to emerge,
imperceptibly, from "turn your ear." Indeed, the letter's first sentence encourages the allusion. In its appeal to a commonplace activity, the sentence
forces a reading that joins both signs together, suggesting precisely what we
do "if we listen to the radio today": we *turn* the radio dial; we *tune* a station.
The play between turning and tuning thus seems to define a play of the
short-lived, a play whose ideal instrument is the radio.

It's the ear that makes a difference. The ear inserts itself into the play between signs, throws the proposition off balance (even here where the object
is the inner ear, the locus of balance), and hence directs us to a different result, one unimaginable on the radio: the music of a lifetime. In a sense, the
radical difference between the ear and the radio reinforces the distinction
between chant and the short-lived. For the radio is (as John Cage realized)
the perfect locus of "chance." With the radio we relinquish control over
what we hear: the more we try to bring the radio to conform to our expectations (by tuning in different channels, turning it on and off), the more our
listening is transformed into a kind of chaos. Amidst limitless possibilities for
tuning and re-tuning, there is no order: the radio does not tell us how to
discriminate.

A very different sort of instrument, the ear (especially the inner ear) is sen-
sitive; it cannot be tuned by the same kind of distracted gesture with which
we search, unsuccessfully, through fragments of static and words and tunes,
for the "right" station, the song that will satisfy. Here we must perform a far
more critical, more discriminating adjustment, one that can be carried out
only with *discipline*. In tuning the ear we do in fact turn the ear, with all the
self-control that such a move implies. We take heed; we reform our expectations; we bring our ear *in line*. And so we rule out a seemingly endless range
of competing and ever-changing musics—we turn away from the radio, in
other words—to tune in the one music that never changes, music that for
one hundred and fifty years has been sung according to the discipline known
as the Solesmes method.

This essay, like the advertisement, plays on that discipline. So it is per-haps significant that I begin with a pun, that playful (and stubborn) figure of *un*disciplined writing.[2] For the pun, especially in this context, cannot remain unruly for too long. In my reading of it, I impose discipline; I make the pun conform to the conventions of The Scholarly Essay (I render it important, useful). Merely a gimmick within the advertisement (corny or, what is worse, in poor taste), the pun now becomes legitimate, precise. I make it work for me.

The Solesmes monks, I would argue, were in very much the same position around the middle of the nineteenth century in undertaking their first stud-ies of Gregorian chant: they too needed to discipline what presented itself as an essentially undisciplined corpus. Indeed, by the 1860s, when the Bene-dictines began to turn their own ears toward the chant, the Gregorian revival was already well underway in France.[3] The discovery of two important manuscripts from the ninth and eleventh centuries, and the subsequent publication of a new, modern gradual for the diocese of Rheims based on one of these sources, had inspired a flurry of activity in monasteries and libraries across the country among free-lance clerics seeking similar fortune. In Ger-many, too, the establishment of the *Allgemeiner Cäcilienverein* in 1868 institu-tionalized a growing interest in plainchant and sacred music, an interest that eventually brought about, under the direction of Franz Haberl, the publica-tion of the much contested neo-Medicean antiphoner in 1878. In this charged and fertile atmosphere of renewal, where manuscripts and editions were multiplying, the Benedictines entered the fray; guided by their founder Dom Guéranger, they sought to make their own mark on the chant. They hoped, in short, to bring order to this melodic body within an ever-growing—and ever more confused—mass of editions and manuscripts. Like the pun, the unruly chant presented the possibility of too many realizations, too many meanings. Its domestication by the monks of Solesmes hence can be read as a sign of their discipline, an index of scholarly "method." In what follows I offer a critique of such methods.

History and Discipline

It was in the years between 1880 and 1910, a time of intense scholarly activity at Solesmes, that the new Gregorian discipline began to emerge sys-tematically in the work of the abbey's principal scholars: Dom Joseph Pothier and his student Dom André Mocquereau (see Pothier 1880 and Mocquereau 1889, 1908). Histories of Solesmes often focus on the second half of this thirty-year period as the era that witnessed, under the influence of the younger Dom Mocquereau, the most significant advances in the discipline. Not surprising, perhaps, for this was a time when history itself, and its offshoot musicology, were emerging in their own right, as disciplines founded on new rules, orderly methods: in a word, on standards that promised scholars a new sort of control, and hence a new sort of influence.[4]

Such standards were nowhere more evident than in Mocquereau's "school" at Solesmes, an "incomparable instrument" for Gregorian learning organized after 1889.[5] It was with scientific, not strictly monastic, discipline that he and his rigorously trained staff of monks labored to become legitimate scholars: to remove Gregorian studies from clerical isolation, from scholarly eccentricity; to release the chant into the wider world of the professional historian. According to at least one follower of Solesmes, Mocquereau's methods had the desired result. The theorist Jules Combarieu, reporting as early as 1896, observed enthusiastically that "[under Dom Mocquereau and his staff] the science of Plainsong has become, as it were, *secularized.*" By applying, as he put it, "principles of the historic method" to the sacred song the monks had elevated their musical studies to the level of a science—an inspiration, Combarieu adds, "for which the world cannot be too grateful" (Combarieu 1897:179, quoted in Cagin and Mocquereau 1904:22).

The new, "secular" science of plainsong appeared to address the Vatican far less than it did the newly burgeoning Academy: it was not so much Rome as the *world* that benefited from this achievement in Gregorian science. Combarieu clearly approved of the way the Church's sacred tradition of song was being overhauled, analyzed, and restored according to new historical principles. In a long declamatory passage, he elaborates:

> [the Solesmes monks] have become grammarians, scholars and philologists, paleographers and photographers in order to restore the Gregorian tradition in all its purity, and to defend this tradition against all scepticism. . . . They have published in phototypical facsimiles about three hundred passages in manuscript proving that the unity of the liturgical chant was preserved for a thousand years from its origin: they have applied the principles of comparative grammar to the study of these documents; [and] they have analysed them in an artistic and literary spirit so as to make their original beauty felt and appreciated. (Cagin and Mocquereau 1904:22–23)

It is Combarieu's final judgment, however, that points to the most compelling aspect of these Benedictine achievements: the Solesmes research, he concludes, "opens to the general history of music a future which promises to be fertile in results" (ibid.).

This idea that history might have a "future" reveals an important motivation for the development of the new French science. What had once been the *"general* history of music" was now being conceived as something more specific—as Music History, a viable part of the Academy, whose status and whose very future depended on the work of Music Historians like Dom Mocquereau. Gregorian-chant studies were being professionalized, "disciplinized," as Hayden White would say, according to new standards of historical investigation (indeed, they would soon be legitimized with a new, professional name: *musicologie*).[6] Such "disciplinization" had obvious political implications, separating music historians from other scholars, defining and protecting a distinct territory, a "field." And that turf was protected not so much by a set of facts as by, to borrow White's terms again, a "set of negations": the field was defined, in other words, by repression. For it was only in being controlled, prevented from doing certain things, that disciplined historians could then "claim the authority of discipline itself for their learning" (White 1987:62).

What exactly did Music History deny these would-be authorities? For one thing, it prevented the possibility of speculation, of imagination, what Dom Mocquereau called *fantaisie*—fantasy or "fancy." Discipline in music history came from self-control, from hard facts, from verifiable, scientific evidence. And Dom Mocquereau's critical school took that to mean something very specific: an exhaustive study of the Gregorian neumes, those last traces of the true chant tradition. The general introduction to his *Paléographie musicale* of 1889—a monumental work that sought to present the complete collection of manuscripts containing chant in ultramodern photographic facsimiles— reflects this preference for order, outlining the differences between the manuscript and the treatise as sources for scholarly inquiry:

> Faced with a more or less obscure, more or less isolated [treatise],
> a text which the author did not believe to need explaining to his
> contemporaries, but which would have to be formulated for us in
> clearer, less technical terms, or interpreted by other texts, one's
> imagination [*fantaisie*] could easily be given free rein; but it is not
> so easy to abuse the facts furnished by the neumes. (Mocquereau
> 1889:24)

In this testimony the historian's imagination is not simply discouraged, it is declared an outright abuse: to give fancy "free rein" is flagrantly to reject responsibilities, especially as the historian now had at his disposal photographs that "furnished facts" about real neumes, facts that were neither "obscure" nor "isolated." Mocquereau's judgment bears witness to the negations or repressions of his discipline, because it devalues a certain type of historical investigation, namely, the reading of treatises—presenting their interpretation as an inevitable product of invention. The treatise (like the pun with too many meanings) is in effect ruled out. The political significance of this action is all too apparent. For in negating treatises as legitimate "sources" for the study of Gregorian chant, Dom Mocquereau negates the one tool that most scholars actually had at their disposal; and at the same time he establishes original manuscripts as the only viable means of study. It should come as no surprise that in 1889, when the *Paléographie musicale* first appeared, the Benedictine monks of Solesmes had perhaps the single largest collection of Gregorian manuscripts, both in photographic and calligraphic reproductions, of any "school" or monastery in Europe. The scriptorium was, in a word, stacked.[7]

But of course it was not enough simply to have the manuscripts. The disciplined historian needed to be able to evaluate them critically, to wrest from them the secret of Gregorian melody. He needed a method. And Dom Mocquereau's school had one: a complex, scientific apparatus, a "laboratory" that promised certainty and precision. In a detailed monograph about his critical school, Mocquereau defended his method at length, marking out first—in the manner of a true disciplinarian—what it was not:

> The critical study of neums and of notation derived from neums may be pursued in two ways.
> The student may confine himself to examining a series of manuscripts on a given point one after the other, and thus *mentally* achieve a result which can be definitely accepted. But what is such a proceeding worth? What guarantees does it offer beyond the conscientiousness and ability of the worker? How can such a sporadic examination yield a sound means of classification and comparison, without which it is impossible to arrive at a conclusion, and to give the grounds of one's decision with certainty and precision . . . ? And even if a person of extraordinary abilities could do this, how, after all, could a single, isolated individual answer every challenge with evidence at every moment? In a word, whence could be produced the critical apparatus of his edition? (Cagin and Mocquereau 1904: 29–30)

Mocquereau's rejection of the purely mental process seems to resemble in some measure his self-control and repression of *fantaisie*. For to proceed through a series of manuscripts with nothing more than eyes and a memory as a guide was to run the risk of error; indeed, Mocquereau would go so far as to say that "such a proceeding is, at bottom, domestic dilettantism" (ibid.:30). The words smack of the very things the monks were not: they were not dilettantes (and they were, needless to say, *not* domestic). Within the same passage, in fact, Mocquereau makes this clear: "We are strict with ourselves, opposed to mere approximations, eager for light . . . and for precision."

The Solesmes scholars could promise such precision by means of a completely new vision of the repertory, presented in extensive "synoptical tables"—a scholarly apparatus that imposed order on the manuscripts, capturing them in an enclosure, a field of writing, controlled by the scholar's gaze. The tables made the melodies visible, legible—with the different versions arranged on the page so that all variants could be seen at a glance. As Dom Mocquereau described it:

> One of us gets the manuscripts with the Romanian signs, and copies once for all from left to right, on as many horizontal lines as there are manuscripts to be ransacked, the whole reading of the Christmas Alleluia, just as they give it. He takes care to write the neums widely apart and arranges the corresponding groups beneath one another in a perpendicular row. Thus he has a vivid presentation of them in order [and] in separate rows, enabling him to follow from top to bottom the various possible vagaries of the neum.
>
> When the table of this first group of manuscripts has been drawn up the compilation of the second . . . is begun on the same plan as the first. (Cagin and Mocquereau 1904:42)

In such a precisely organized, segmented space, it became possible to control the individual scholar's work, and thus to control the details, the notational idiosyncrasies, of each manuscript.[8] The ultimate aim, of course, was to control history—to trace, as Mocquereau put it, "the history of a neum . . . either in its persistency or variations or corruptions" (ibid.:31). For history, according to this vision, was written in the neumes themselves. Indeed, the new Solesmes discipline, devoted to discovering this original truth, left little room for other types of historical discourse, especially for anecdote or biography; the neumes alone were to tell the true story of the chant—pure, unembellished, free of fantasy. And with Saint Gregory (along with other so-called historical figures) apparently repressed, ruled out of this space where only handwritten figures counted, the *bio*graphical aspect of history seemed

Table I

	Version B.	Version A.	Version D.	Version X.		1.2.3. 4. 5. 6.7.8.9.10. 11. 12.13.14.		
					Liber Gradualis. Solesmis. 1895.			
					Alle.lú. ia.		
A	4				Brit. Mus. Eg. 857. fol 5' XI.th cent		℣. Hic est discipulus.	Acquitanian, Metz, etc., mss.
B		1			Laon. ms 239 X.th cent		℣. Dies sanctificatus	
C				1	Paris Bibl. Nat. Lat 1132. fol. 11' XI.th c.		℣. "	
D	14				Montpellier École de Méd H.159. XI.th c. p. 100.		℣. " "	Franch, Norman and English mss.
E		1			Cambrai 75 fol 40' XI.th c.		℣. Vidimus.	
F				2	Chartres. 130 (148) fol. 50. X.th XI.th c.		℣. Dies sanctificatus.	
G		2			Saint Gall. 359. p. 42 IX.th X.th c.		℣. Hic est discipulus.	St. Gall and German mss.
H	2				Saint Gall. 376 p. 103. XI.th c.		℣. "	
I	13				Bamberg. A.II.54 fol. 8 A.D. 1002-1024.		℣. Video caelos.	
K		3			Modène. Est. XI.c.6. fol 4' XI.th XII.th c.		℣. "	
L	34				Paris. B.N. Lat. 10508. fol 47' XII.th c.		℣. Dies sanctificatus.	Mss with staff
M		1			Bruxelles. Bib roy Tilio 1172. XIII.th c. fol. 13		℣. Iustus non conturb.'	
N				5	Marseille Abb. S Madeleine. XII.th c. fol. 3'		℣. Dies sanctificatus.	
O				3	Paris. Ars. lat 112.157. fol. 75 XVII.th c		℣. Hic est sacerdos.	
P					Grad. Cartusianum fol 27. Cod. Rosenthal (München) XII.th c		℣. Dies sanctificatus.	
Q					Grad. S.O. Praedicatorum. p. 33 Tournai 1890		℣. " "	
R					Grad. Romanum Paris. Lecoffre 1860 p 34		℣. " "	
86 =	67	8	8	3	Liber usualis. Editio Solesmense Tornaci 1904.			

FIGURE 2. Synoptic Table of the Christmas Alleluia (Solesmes)

190

to disappear into the purely graphical. Fables were replaced by tables. Hence Mocquereau's scientific method distinguished itself again from conventional studies, disowning, in the name of history, most existing criticism as plainly "undisciplined."[9]

Manuscripts and photographs and charts thus became, it would appear, political tools—weapons with which the monks could maintain their newly defined historical field by force, fending off skeptics, alarming those who had no adequate form of protection. Indeed, the whole of Solesmes musicology, whose orderly methods have in part formed the basis for our modern discipline, seemed to involve motives which appear to us (from our position of historical distance) more blatantly political than we could ever imagine our own scholarly intentions to be. The monks sought to win favor not simply within the Academy, but at the Vatican—to have their scholarship *officially* recognized over that of other historians competing for similar materials and similar results. And they planned to succeed. Dom Paul Cagin, Mocquereau's close friend and colleague in the Solesmes school, relates (with no obvious display of humility) the following story in 1904:

> Last year a German doctor of music came to consult Dom Mocquereau in our place of exile about a work which he thought of taking in hand. When face to face with the master and his pupils, at the sight of the number of manuscripts at their disposal, of their wonderful apparatus for study, and of the use they were making of it, he went away in some sort discouraged, saying that it was impossible to follow them in such a path, and that they had such a start, such an organization, and such resources, that it was impossible to prevent their being everywhere and always ahead. (ibid.: 25)

Of course, we all know the end of the story: the Solesmes monks came out ahead. Their comprehensive, scientific method—overwhelming in its organization, its resources, its apparatus—carved out for them the future that Combarieu had envisioned, because it left even the most serious scholars behind, "discouraged." When "face to face" with the Solesmes laboratory, one had no choice but to recognize its authority. Rome, too, eventually saw the light that Mocquereau's school had been so eager to cast on the chant, a light that clearly reflected back on Solesmes. In 1904 the newly ordained Pope Pius X entrusted the monks with the publication of the new Vatican edition, expressing confidence in their ability "to restore to the Church the unity of her traditional chant, as the science, the history, the art, and the dignity of liturgical worship would demand."

𝄡

This final accomplishment brings us back, in a sense, to where we began. For it was through this historic act that the name of Solesmes became
officially and universally associated with Gregorian chant—the music that
represented, as it were, the Church's lifetime. Acknowledged now by Rome,
Solesmes could set the standard. The very historical methods with which the
monks sought to remove the chant from clerical isolation eventually re-
turned it to the Church, restored; the discipline that brought the monks recognition within the secular science of history won them official recognition
from the Vatican: Holy Mother Church and Historical Science seemed, at
least in this one canonical act, to share some basic values.

But they did not share the same authority. As specialists, as true historians
of the chant, the monks (and especially Mocquereau's *atelier*) claimed an authority that the Church did not have—authority that, as should be obvious
by now, was measured in terms of their discipline, their historical self-
control. From this vantage point, the Church's decision to bring the chant
restoration to an end with a single judgment, even when this judgment was
favorable to the monks, posed more than a slight problem. For one of the
things that history would always deny the historian, especially the disciplined historian, was closure. The pope's Motu Proprio of 1904, however,
proclaimed unequivocally, through the authority of its own speech act, that
the case was closed: the period of study could cease now that the chant was
officially complete. While Dom Mocquereau obviously respected this papal
privilege—indeed, benefited from it—he also stood apart from it. In the end
he remained a true disciple of history; he had no choice but to project his
work, his school, into the future. And so in that very same year he wrote of
the imprudence of offering the Solesmes editions in a final form, adding the
unlikely disclaimer that "in fifty years' time we may hope to obtain such a
result, but not today" (Cagin and Mocquereau 1904:35).

Not today, indeed. So much of Mocquereau's authority as an historian
seems to be invested in these words: not today. The phrase becomes, in a
sense, a clear sign of his discipline. But it is also a sign of his resistance to that
other, more central authority that judged the restoration complete. To look
at Rome's reaction to his words is to understand the idea of "discipline" in a
broader, more political context. Dom Mocquereau could not maintain such
a position of resistance with impunity. And it is a story often repressed in
histories of the restoration that a year after his appointment to the Vatican
Commission (the committee that was to oversee the publication of this

newly restored tradition in official, Vatican books) he, along with his entire Solesmes school, was fired.[10]

It was, of course, the only practical solution. The monks of Dom Mocquereau's school proved again and again unwilling to defer to their apparently less qualified colleagues on the commission; and those commissioners, needless to say, were wary of allowing the Solesmes experts to have so much control—to become, as one member expressed it, "the authoritative source for the total Gregorian practice of the future" (Wagner 1960:16). The chant had to remain securely within the jurisdiction of the Church. A much awaited communication from the Vatican finally made this clear, decreeing that the Holy See would now "take under its authoritative and supreme protection the special edition of the liturgical books . . . , leaving at the same time a free field for the studies of scholars competent in the Gregorian discipline" (see Hayburn 1979:270). The Church protected her chant by putting its scholars out to pasture. And while "disciplined" studies, such as those undertaken at Solesmes, were not actually prohibited by this new pronouncement, they were definitively relocated—moved (along with the scholars who performed them) to some "free field," a scholarly Siberia whose remoteness ensured that the chant's integrity could not be threatened.

Mocquereau's scholars were, in effect, disciplined by the Church for being disciplined historians. The Church, after all, had her own standards to maintain. Like history itself, she expected a certain discipline from its practitioners, a certain kind of orderly conduct—in a word, obedience. The conflict between the Vatican Commission and Mocquereau's school thus reflects a conflict of disciplines, largely in the form of a dispute over rights of ownership. Both the commission (representing the Church) and Mocquereau (representing history) claimed control over the chant, yet each wanted exclusive control. Indeed, how could each guarantee a future for the chant without jealously guarding it in the present?

Such a question leads us to consider a final, more specialized meaning of the word *discipline,* one which carries some significance for our story: "discipline" is, of course, training in the art of war.[11] Certainly such training implies the protection of things: of rights, of property, of individuals and principles, of discipline itself. Yet it also implies, like the rigid training undergone by that skilled army of Benedictines in the name of Gregorian science, a protection of the future, the lifetime of "tomorrows"—which is the meaning of Dom Mocquereau's "not today."

Notes

1. I am grateful to Lenore Coral for sharing this advertisement with me.

2. For a more extensive reading of the pun and its significance, see Culler 1988.

3. Emerson 1980 provides an excellent summary of the different branches of this restoration throughout Europe from its earliest stages in the 1840s.

4. See Kerman 1984 for an analysis of the forces contributing to the development of musicology in the nineteenth century. My thoughts concerning the significance of Gregorian chant studies at Solesmes in this period were influenced by Hayden White's "The Politics of Historical Interpretation," which addresses larger questions of historiography and discipline (see White 1987).

5. Such hyperbole can be found throughout Norbert Rousseau's early history of this school (Rousseau 1910). The school, incidentally, was later removed to Appuldercombe on the Isle of Wight, where the monks sought refuge in 1901. Following the mandate of the newly organized Third Republic which effectively forced all religious orders from France by denying them the right to form community or to own property, the monks moved across the Channel and remained there until the 1920s (see Combe 1969).

6. According to the *Trésor de la langue française*, the earliest appearance of this term can be traced, interestingly enough, to a course on plainchant taught by Pierre Aubry in 1901.

7. For a more detailed consideration of the significance of photography in the emerging Gregorian science, see Bergeron 1989, chap. 3.

8. Foucault's account of the serialization of the labor force at the end of the eighteenth century fits nicely with this picture of the Solesmes scriptorium. Compare his analysis of the factory:

> It was a question of distributing individuals in a space where one might isolate and map them. . . . Production was divided up and the labour process was articulated on the one hand, according to its stages or elementary operations, and on the other hand, according to the individuals, the particular bodies, that carried it out: each variable of this force—strength, promptness, skill, constancy—would be observed, and therefore characterized, assessed, computed and related to the individual who was its particular agent. Thus spread out in a perfectly legible way over the whole series of individual bodies, the work force may be analysed in individual units. (1979:144–45)

The control of the individual scholar was thus accomplished by his implication in a network, a field of surveillance.

9. As Frank Kermode would maintain, such a shift of critical emphasis is characteristic of all reforms organized around the preservation of a canon. His discussion of biblical criticism, in particular, strikes a tone with the present observation about Solesmes: "In disowning the authority and the tradition, Reform showed how it is possible to alter the relation of center to margin. What mattered now were the words on the page. . . . The original text, by virtue of its divine inspiration, was *sui ipsius interpres*" (1985:77).

10. It should be pointed out that Mocquereau's former teacher, Dom Pothier, sat at the head of this committee, a fact that suggests the possibility of more complex

motivations for the decision. In this case, the conflict might be viewed simply as a problem of the disciple speaking out against the master. (For a brief reflection on this dilemma of the discipline see Derrida 1978:31–32.) Yet the "higher" authority that Mocquereau's school threatened was, I would claim, twofold: it included, so to speak, both Mother (as Church) and Father (as Pothier).

11. This sense of the term is corroborated, remarkably, in a passage from *L'Oblat* (1903), a novel by that inimitable *fin-de-siècle* decadent, J. K. Huysmans. The protagonist Durtal, having undergone—like Huysmans himself—a conversion at (of all places) Solesmes, ruminates on the particular brand of monastic discipline he finds there. Consider the passage's central metaphor:

> How, indeed, would it be possible to realize Solesmes as a whole, the solemnity of its services and the glory of its chant, without that serried mass of monks? How, if not with a hand of iron, *can one control an army of nearly a hundred men,* whose assorted tempers, by ever rubbing together, cannot fail to be warmed? Discipline therefore must be, and as strict, nay, even stricter in a monastery than in a camp. (Emphasis added. Huysmans [1903] 1924:4)

WORKS CITED

Bergeron, Katherine. 1989. "Representation, Reproduction, and the Revival of Gregorian Chant at Solesmes." Ph.D. diss., Cornell University.

Cagin, Dom Paul, and Dom André Mocquereau. 1904. *Plainchant and Solesmes.* London: Burns and Oates.

Combarieu, Jules. 1897. *Études de philologie musicale.* Paris: Picard.

Combe, Pierre. 1969. *L'Histoire de la restauration du chant grégorien d'après des documents inédits.* Solesmes: Abbaye de Solesmes.

Culler, Jonathan, ed. 1988. *On Puns: The Origin of Letters.* Oxford: Basil Blackwell.

Derrida, Jacques. 1978. "Cogito and the History of Madness." In *Writing and Difference.* Trans. Alan Bass. Chicago: University of Chicago Press.

Emerson, John A. 1980. "Western Plainchant: Nineteenth-Century Restoration Attempts." In *The New Grove Dictionary of Music and Musicians,* vol. 14, 827–30. New York: Macmillan.

Foucault, Michel. 1979. *Discipline and Punish: The Birth of the Prison.* Trans. Alan Sheridan. New York: Vintage.

Hayburn, Robert Francis. 1979. *Papal Legislation and Sacred Music.* Collegeville, Minn.: The Liturgical Press.

Huysmans, J. K. 1924. *The Oblate.* Trans. Edward Perceval. New York: E. P. Dutton. Originally published as *L'Oblat* (1903).

Kerman, Joseph. 1984. "A Few Canonic Variations." In Robert von Hallberg, ed., *Canons,* 177–95. Chicago: University of Chicago Press.

Kermode, Frank. 1985. *Forms of Attention.* Chicago: University of Chicago Press.

Mocquereau, Dom André. 1889. "Introduction générale." In *Paléographie musicale,* vol. 1. Solesmes: Imprimerie de St. Pierre.

———. 1908. *Le Nombre musical grégorien, ou rhythmique grégorienne.* Tournai: Desclée.

Pothier, Dom Joseph. 1880. *Les Mélodies grégoriennes.* Tournai: Desclée.

Rousseau, Norbert. 1910. *L'École grégorienne de Solesmes.* Tournai: Desclée.

Wagner, Peter. 1960. "The Attack on the Vatican Edition; a Rejoinder." *Caecilia* 87:10–44. Originally published as *Der Kampf gegen die Editio Vaticana* (Graz, 1907).

White, Hayden. 1987. "The Politics of Historical Intepretation: Discipline and De-Sublimation." In *The Content of the Form: Narrative Discourse and Historical Representation,* 58–82. Baltimore: Johns Hopkins University Press.

ELEVEN

Epilogue: Musics and Canons
Philip V. Bohlman

Plurals/Pluralities/Pluralisms

It's getting harder and harder to talk about "music" in the singular these days. Just about everywhere we look, music is proliferating, multiplying to become "musics," as if some unchecked population explosion had occurred. There may well have been a population increase (or at least the recognition of a population that is many times larger than previously imagined) but it is unlikely that this alone is responsible for the transformation from singular to plural. Instead, it may be that we have refined our census-taking methods, which keep on turning up new musics as they ask more difficult questions.

Many musicologists may find themselves uncomfortable with the defiant plural; some may nervously chuckle about what they regard as a clumsy-sounding cluster of sibilants; there may even be a few who long for the hegemony of the German *die Musik,* the definite article staving off all onslaughts against the authority of the singular. But musics are among us. They have been for quite a while, and they are here to stay. Bearing witness to this plurality and pluralism of musics is yet another plural: the canons so variously construed and constructed by musicology itself.

That *canon* means different things to the essayists in this book is obvious and perhaps was not all that unpredictable. That *music* means different things to the essayists is also obvious, though the sullying of more than a few usual assumptions about the nature of the phenomena we comfortably call "music" was not necessarily predictable. Musicology, too, has many different faces in this book. It is probably not the case that most of the authors would claim to be, first and foremost, a musicologist. Surely, music theorists and ethnomusicologists are also musicologists, and many are quickly rankled if accused of not *really* being musicologists. But musicology does mean different things to them, which in turn plays a significant role in determining what they understand musics to be and how they go about engaging in the praxis of disciplining music. Musicology, at least as represented in this volume, might have been better off or truer to its practitioners had we pluralized it as well, perhaps in a subtitle like "Musicologies and Their Musics." Getting used to "musicologies" would probably be no more difficult than getting used to "musics."

The encroachment of plurals into the disciplining of music also bespeaks a reality that is far more serious than simply the play of words. To the extent that musicologists concerned largely with the traditions of Western art music were content with a singular canon—any singular canon that took a European-American concert tradition as a given—they were excluding musics, peoples, and cultures. They were, in effect, using the process of disciplining to cover up the racism, colonialism, and sexism that underlie many of the singular canons of the West. They bought into these "-isms" just as surely as they coopted an "-ology." Canons formed from "Great Men" and "Great Music" forged virtually unassailable categories of self and Other, one to discipline and reduce to singularity, the other to belittle and impugn. Canon was determined not so much by what it was as by what it was not. It was not the musics of women or people of color; it was not musics that belonged to other cultures and worldviews; it was not forms of expression that resisted authority or insisted that music could empower politics.

Disciplining music was an act of domesticating music, making it our own and commanding it to be docile. Rather suddenly, however, the other musics were asserting their presence. It was harder to ignore African-American music or the role of women in the formation of music cultures throughout the world. More peoples demanded that musicology take stock of their musics and their canons. The musicologies of this volume, as well as future assessments of musics and canons, were inevitable. They've been with us for quite a while now.

The Quintessentially Canonic Discipline

Very few of musicology's endeavors fail to exhibit some investment in canons and canonizing. Whatever else one might say about the scholarly study of music, one has to say that musicologists through their diverse activities are in the business of defining musics, delimiting their internal patterns of coherence, and identifying their relations with some sort of external order, all of this to communicate to others the importance of musics as diverse forms of human expression. Implicit in such general musicological endeavors are other activities considerably less neutral and objective in their communicative function: arbitrating tastes; performing evaluation *qua* valuation; specifying favorites—what's good and what isn't; excluding and evading the noncanonic.

Quite simply, musicologists are engaged in making choices, usually at the behest of others, thereby establishing authority. Given the vast number of musical repertories and potential musical experiences, musicologists are responsible for choosing a few and then justifying those few for others not in the business of cultural arbitration. Creating canons and buttressing them is indeed a normative task for musicologists.

The development of musicology as a discipline has been coeval with the increased need to make decisions about appropriate canons and to arbitrate tastes for the reception of those canons. A distinct body of broadly musicological writings—historical, theoretical, critical, and anthropological—began to emerge in the eighteenth century at approximately the same moment at which European society began to carve out niches for more musics than those of an immediate time, place, and function—that is, music tempered by the tastes and contexts of the present and previous generation or so.[1] There was, so to speak, an historical imperative for canon formation; and early musicology responded accordingly, forming its first canons by adhering to historical criteria.

During the eighteenth century the role of music in European society became strikingly more historicist, and using the music of the past—recuperating that music and placing it in different contexts—became increasingly commonplace. Just as it was modish and modern to stage monster concerts of Handelian oratorios, so too could Forkel extend biographical treatment to J. S. Bach (1802) and Herder cobble together a construct like *Volkslied* to embody the historically sustained core of poesy (1779). These were different acts of canon formation, and they were, similarly, different forms of early musicology. Together, however, they contributed to the mapping of a European intellectual landscape that tolerated, for the first time, the cohabitation of multiple musics and multiple canons, as well as their unrestricted proliferation.

Musicology surely has even more canons and canonic perspectives today. There are the popular and the unpopular musics, the overly ripe and the inchoate genres. We are all familiar with musicological literature urging us to turn with new perspectives to the important works and the most influential composers—say, to reformulate the Mozart canon on the occasion of the two-hundredth anniversary of his death. In contrast, woefully neglected cultures and the correct targets for canonic affirmative action have also earned a presence in the musicological literature, though relatively few have yet to be formulated, much less reformulated, as canons. The curricula of music departments depend on the scaffolding afforded by the essential repertories and pedagogical pigeonholes—which is to say, the canons necessary for graduation and degree-granting. Entrance into the field demands familiarity with a central set of canons, even if, indeed, one chooses another set for one's "real" interests once entrance has been secured.

In short, musicology's history of disciplining music is inseparable from a history of canon formation and from a persistent dependence on canons. It could almost seem that the disciplining of music is synonymous with the formation of musicology's canons. As tautological as such claims may seem, they do serve to explain some of the apparent contradictions in the ways canons are traditionally regarded (Altieri 1983:41–43). They explain why the same canons are at once deified and scorned, why some musicologists concern themselves with building canons and others with tearing them down. It is, then, less of a contradiction that some measure of power accrues both to those who advocate central canons and to those who effectively seek to undermine the same canons, supplanting these with their own. If we compare by drawing an example from modern historiography, we might argue that the *annaliste* arrogation of everyday life is, in this sense, no less canonic than any other historian's attraction to kings and wars.

To say that musicology fundamentally engages in disciplining music by at once maintaining and challenging canons does not mean, however, that musicologists are all concerned with the same canons or that they go about forming canons in the same way. Quite the contrary, the field appears fairly tolerant of a vast number of canons. It may be true that the new Americanist and ethnomusicological canons have entered the scene during the past generation or so, but, despite initial moments of revolution, these canons, too, have increasingly come to play a role in disciplining music. After all, it is a simple fact of our political economy that most scholars of American music and most ethnomusicologists in academic positions hold those positions in music departments, as opposed to, say, American studies or anthropology.[2]

The essays in this volume examine different canonic perspectives that emanate from the disciplining of music and that converge on the discipline of musicology. In characteristic (i.e., historically persistent) fashion, the essays criticize some of musicology's canons and advocate others. They admit to the obvious, namely, that there are certain central canons but that these weren't always central and needn't be so in the future. But whether these canons will or will not retain any centrality depends on how musicology deems it appropriate to go about disciplining itself.

Canonic Authority and the Authorities of Canons

The concept of canon as commonly understood in musicology suggests both an object and the act of determining what that object is. Musicology maintains "music" as its object, but the different disciplines of musicology come to understand what music is in different ways. Accordingly, the object, "music," cannot be a single phenomenon; it cannot have universally sanctioned meanings. Linking musicologist to music are the many processes of identifying the diverse phenomena that constitute music and establishing the complex relations among its meanings.

The distinction between object and agency is therefore difficult to pin down; the two depend on each other. Out of this dependency grows an intrinsic relation between canons and their ability to generate a discipline. Canon, indeed, seems to possess a certain immanent power—an imperative and a concomitant ability to ascribe law and order to music—that yields discipline or, better, the discipline. Canon establishes authority, and that authority is understandably attractive to those who would discipline music.

It might be possible to describe canon in the singular as a principle or rule whereby a discipline is maintained. Even in the singular, canon exhibits a complicitous relation with certain ideologies (those that insist upon the need for authority or claim that music has a meaning in the singular) and political necessities (those that back up discipline with power).

Musicology's canons, it follows, have the potential to maintain the discipline of musicology and require some measure of loyalty from those who advocate them. The fact that musicologists traditionally thought of canon as a body of representative works should not disturb this relation too much, since these works are also the manifestations of political and ideological principles, such as greatness, genius, importance to a social group or class of society, etc. Further anchoring the concept of canon to a body of representative musical works is the notion that it is only by such works that a disciplined scholar is ruled: she aspires to success in *her field* by controlling *her music* more and more. The canon, therefore, governs the behavior of those within a discipline, proffering a measure of authority while acquiring more itself (cf. Bruns 1983).

Canon and discipline are therefore ineluctably bound, even though they are not the same. Their differences seem evident in what they are and how they are empowered to achieve status and stasis through authority. Couched in other terms, the canon is the performative; discipline is the performance. Canon is inevitably linked to texts, whereas discipline requires acts of deciding upon and interpreting those texts. The subsequent link is one that admits many texts—musics, for our concerns—and accordingly proliferates the possibilities for parallax readings.

The Texts of Canons

The fundamentally oral nature of music notwithstanding, musicology's canons arise from the field's penchant for working with texts. The language with which we realize our concern for canons is replete with a vocabulary that locates the discipline in questions of text and the understanding of text. We think of pieces of music as discrete texts, rendered so by the notation with which we study and represent music. We form these discrete texts into larger works: anthologies, genres, standard or core repertories, sometimes musical monuments. Even musics in oral tradition—say, folk song—enter the canon when they take their positions as texts alongside other texts that constitute a repertory unified almost exclusively by texts.[3]

Musicologists discipline these texts by creating yet other types of texts: music histories, dictionaries, journals, bibliographical indexes, field recordings, Schenker graphs. These texts further encode the canon, increasing accessibility to it and assuring scholars that, if they know the texts, they know the discipline. Although the essays in this volume address different canons, these are nonetheless textual in some way, at the very least because of the way they lend themselves to the diverse forms of ethnography and criticism we have mustered here. Texts are essential to the canonizing process because they replace the timeliness of music as an oral phenomenon with the timelessness of music as a textual ontology. To enter the canon of great works, a piece of music must "last," and how better to make it last than to transform it into a text? One can study and analyze a text, thereby controlling it and acquiring some degree of its power. To know the right musical texts is to pass the entrance exams and qualifying exams, to pay one's dues for entrance into the scholarly sanctum.

The timelessness undergirded by texts permeates and spurs the process of canon formation. "Reviving" musical works and "restoring them to their rightful positions" almost always require some moment of discovering texts—overlooked, in, say, an archive, monastery library, or Javanese court—and then interpreting them to rediscover the lost riches they contain. Accordingly, we determine precisely where their position in the canon will be. Working over repertories to find the "original text" and reframing this to give the assurance of authenticity animate the activities and intent of virtually all historical musicologists (Kenyon 1988). Music theorists and ethnomusicologists, too, look for original texts when determining fundamental formal principles of a piece, style histories, or tune families. Historians of theory and historical ethnomusicologists further refine the notion of text by reaffirming the role of words in the transmission of text. The potential to become classic accrues to music when its texts are revived and reframed. And what is a canonic work if not a "classic," that is, a work existing outside of history, a text whose meanings have value for any and every society?

It is, perhaps, because texts have come to symbolize canons that they have come also to exert such powers of suasion and control of the field. A practitioner of the musicological discipline, for example, stands to earn a healthy sum when she or he discovers and creates (by editing) a new text and then publishes it. Those in control of the canonic texts maintain a disproportionate degree of authority over the means of reproducing them in other textual formats (Clifford 1988:21–54). Actually, a rather complex constellation of institutions—editors, publishers, printers, archivists, librarians, critics, curriculum designers—may share this authority, even though the central texts eventually achieve their own canonic authority. The text, then, serves as the most visible evidence of a canon in the singular. It is the product wrought by disciplining. We may recognize it as "our music," "the notes," "die Musik an sich," or simply "the material we have to cover in a fifteen-week semester." A canon acquires the function of fixing and encoding some representation of music and serving as the vehicle for its own timelessness.

Processes of Canon Formation

The texts of canons are not simply givens, nor do they somehow form in a manner sui generis; rather, they follow from and depend upon processes of canon formation, on dynamic acts of disciplining. At their most basic level, acts of disciplining take the form of choices: including and excluding. More often, however, considerable valuation accompanies the formation of musicology's canons. Canon formation has various and distinct steps, for works do not acquire canonic status without acquiring the measure of timelessness that only a temporal process can afford. Canon formation, furthermore, depends on agents, at the very least the canonizer and the audience for which she creates a canon. More often than not, multiple agents assist in this process.

One of the initial gestures in creating a canon is determining how the proto-canon reflects some putative value from the past (see Morgan 1988 and Taruskin 1988). Perceptible in a work of music should be some model of the past, expressed as formal similarity, aesthetic context, or mythological purity. The classicisms, neoclassicisms, and neo-neoclassicisms of Western art music always rely on the past for some canonic model. Models are even more directly stated in the concepts conferred upon contemporary performances of Asian classical repertories, with oral proto-models not infrequently taking the form of modern texts that represent controllable repertories—for example, the *Radif* of Persian classical music (Nettl 1987). The canons of folk music employ age as a criterion, reflecting the belief that current folk song derives from an earlier, valorized model.

Processes of canon formation may also result from a conscious repudiation of the past. Modernism and postmodernism, structuralism and deconstructionism are no less appealing for their canonic authority, despite the consecutively staged strategy of repudiation that they entail. Rarely is the musical avant-garde slow in identifying its own canons. The history of Western music theory often appears to be a succession of repudiations, one theoretical system shoring up the weaknesses that a previous system failed to recognize. Indeed, attempts to repudiate canons without in some way proposing alternatives inevitably ring hollow and founder. The repudiator, in essence, fails to play by the right rules, but still enjoys the successes afforded by the game.

The next stage in the process of canon formation—though stages generally overlap and are often conflated—shifts temporal attention to the present and the future (cf. Taruskin 1988). In other words, there is an overt attempt to appropriate the past for use in the present, thereby preserving it for the future. This stage in forming a canon is necessary in order to render its texts timeless. Again, models of the past are important, and when real models are not present, surrogates and imaginary models will do just fine. More often than not, canons form from a sort of *bricolage,* the bits and pieces that together manufacture a model of who Josquin was or what an "old-style" Hungarian ballad must have been (Lévi-Strauss 1966 and Zetzel 1983). One society may even borrow its model from another, confiscating too the power that the model holds (cf. Anderson 1983). This means that a model need not have existed at all, for the option of creating one is always available in the process of canon formation.[4]

Finally, there is a stage in which the canon itself is replicated. The replication of the canon both fixes certain texts and legitimizes them by disseminating them so that they have a presence throughout the discipline. The texts appear to be canonic simply by dint of their omnipresence. Of course, their omnipresence also predisposes those not yet familiar with the canon to take stock of it. Those with the power to control the dissemination (i.e., the selling) of the canon do so with the tools available to them (see Ohmann 1983). The *New Harvard Dictionary of Music* is offered to the public at a price every musicologist can afford; can any musicologist, then, afford not to buy into such a canon, inscribing it in his footnotes and bibliographies (Randel 1986)? The *New Grove* is forever coming up with a deal that will make every musicologist want to have a copy on her bookshelves. Thus, all steps are taken to make sure that the new text appears as the embodiment of fundamental principles, without which a systematic treatment of music would be impossible. The new canon has formed.

Canonizers

Throughout this epilogue I have been stressing the decision-making process and the agents who animate it as essential to the disciplining of music. These agents, in essence, canonize by deciding what will enter canons and by undertaking the representation of canons as texts. Just as there was a certain orderliness in the stages necessary for canon formation, so too do we witness a wide array of quite specific agent types—musicologists and significant others—who participate in the canonizing process. From a social-scientific perspective I might even suggest that one way of understanding the field is to interpret it as a community of agents who discipline musicology in such a way as to make community life orderly and functional.

Those who engage in a particular act of canonizing usually do so intending to contribute a model to an existing mode of discourse in musicology. Music historians of the early nineteenth century extolled composers who would serve as exemplary "Great Men." Somewhat later in the century, "Great Men" diminished in importance as compared to repertories that justified an ineffably progressive impetus in history, whereby Hegelian paradigms started to pop up in great music. In these cases we witness two different types of canon, which accordingly attracted two different types of text, even when the unassailably canonic fitted both—for example, Beethoven, a great man who created great music. These two types of canonic ordering, moreover, characterized the disciplining of music in two different historical contexts.

Institutions, too, stand among the agents I am here calling canonizers. As societies for the historical performance of music, the study of "Oriental" cultures, and the collection of folk-song texts formed in the nineteenth century, so did their members forge new canons of music. The university and the conservatory, as venues for the daily disciplining of music, became prominent by the late nineteenth century. It became a measure of their power and influence to emphasize more and more the importance of certain canons over others. And surely record companies and music publishers are easily recognizable as institutions that would be impossible to imagine without the agents—musicians, musicologists, and businesspeople—who canonize music and earn their livings from it in the meantime. These institutions require texts and the individuals necessary for producing texts. Such individuals act on behalf of the institution, one step removed from ultimate responsibility, but perhaps more disciplined in their adherence to the models on which they rely.

The canonizers of musicology today are a more varied lot than their ancestors, and accordingly they have stimulated the proliferation of canons and musics. Still, the modern canonizers are no less concerned with the maintenance of models of scholarship and the implicit canons that result. Dictionary and encyclopedia editors make claims for their responsiveness to changing canons, while keeping many an older category intact.[5] Journals and journal editors maintain a variety of models, and some openly urge their contributors to explore new areas in their articles (for example, Temperley 1978); rarely, however, are journal editors free to effect any sort of radical change that would situate a journal at the vanguard of new directions in the field.

In whatever ways the canonizers of music engage in the process of canon formation, they do so effectively only when they wield some kind of power and maintain some basis of authority. Authority may rest in profound skill and boundless energy; it may result from the residence of an editorial office on campus. We must see in these factors a reminder that the essence of canon formation inevitably depends, for better or for worse, on possessing a considerable measure of authority. To function effectively as a canonizer, then, means that the musicologist can identify such authority and use it to the advantage of both personal canons and those of the entire discipline.

The agents of canon formation are generally identifiable from the ways in which they contribute to the authority a canon commands. Whether arbitrating taste is acquired or simply assumed, it affords the music critic considerable power. Politics in various manifestations inevitably accompany the maintenance and establishment of canons. These manifestations of politics may be as relatively innocuous as an internecine struggle to determine the course content of a university music-history sequence; or they may be as potentially career-making or -breaking as opening a publisher's doors to one canon while excluding another. For young scholars entering the field, their choice of canon often preselects the range of available career opportunities. Opting for American-music studies placed far more limitations on a young scholar in the 1970s than did a choice for Renaissance studies or Javanese classical music. The play of politics is also invested in the determination of which areas of study musicology will valorize—and at the expense of which other areas.

Musicology's Canons Today

That musicology's canons today are many and varied, that they must be plural and pluralistic, is abundantly evident in the range of essays in this volume. By no means do we mean to claim that this range is exhaustive; ideally, we would have preferred to bring even more musics and their canons into the debates begun within these pages, and we trust that others will in the future expand the discussions initiated here. It should be clear, however, that the range is intentionally not exclusive, which we believe is a sign that musicology is more inclusive today than it has ever been.

At the very least, the perspectives on musicology's canons in this volume signal a break from the compartmentalization of the field. The essayists blur the subdisciplinary boundaries between historical musicology, ethnomusicology, and music theory, and in so doing they challenge the very validity and meaning of those boundaries. Literary theory and historiography both contribute trenchantly to the understanding of the field. The classical and the contemporary, music close to home and music of the Other seem equally loaded with canonic potential.

It would seem, perhaps, that timeliness is retaking the place of timelessness, at least insofar as musicology is concerned. These essays are not so much preoccupied with value systems that ensure lasting qualities or meanings that transcend time; they ponder the reasons for classicism but stop short of privileging it. The essays ask whether there are voices to which we need to listen more carefully, musics whose canons we have yet to recognize. Indeed, these essays suggest a more pressing interest in the present moment, in the field as it currently endeavors to discipline itself. As a reflection of that moment, the essays are relatively unified in their attention to a disciplinary dialogue, an increased canonization of a multivoiced musicological discourse. We may yet grow comfortable with "musicologies"!

Inseparable from the formation of musicology's canons today are issues of reception, social structure, and community—in other words, the cultural context that canons reflect and in which they must survive. Without cultural reinforcement there would be no maintenance of canons. To some degree, this implies a sharing of power by canonizers and those whose musics lend themselves to modern study. The new canons demand reflexivity and the broadening of the community. The voices of new musics and new canons can only produce a more interesting community if, in fact, power is more evenly dispersed. We have long recognized that the canonic repertories of oral tradition are truly possible only if there is some community that keeps them alive by performing them. The social background of canon mainte-nance today exists as a complex community of professionals and nonprofes-sionals, those who keep a repertory alive and those who continue to go back to the concert hall to hear more. It is implicit in the political economy of modern music that, without those who purchase, read, study, and talk about musicology's texts, canon formation would at best be inchoate.

The cultural contexts of canon maintenance also suggest some important strategies for disciplining music. They allow one to identify and investigate canons in popular culture or in non-Western cultures or in societies without musical texts. Some strategies place canonic maintenance in the hands of the working class or the segment of society responsible for mass consumption. We begin to witness that other disciplines, in fact, have already been arguing forcefully for recognition of the impact of musical canons on other cultural domains, a notable example being the sweeping metaphor that the blues sig-nifies in African-American society (Baker 1984). The new contexts in which musics and canons arise suggest further that Marxist, feminist, or de-constructionist theories can contribute considerably more to the disciplining of music than the hegemony of previous canonic principles admitted. And they suggest that the sister disciplines constituting musicology—historical musicology, ethnomusicology, music theory, and music criticism—may not maintain canons or canonic approaches that are fundamentally different from one another, for they have, in fact, found ways to share in the same modern discourse.

It would be presumptuous to say that the musics and canons examined in this volume will provide the field with new ways of disciplining itself. But I think it is not inappropriate to say that the essays in the volume serve as wit-nesses to a refocusing of canonic perspectives. This refocusing, in turn, is not unrelated to the reestablishment of a more broadly based dialogue within musicology, a dialogue that has taken the form of increased interdisciplinary and intradisciplinary exchange. Musicology's canons are—so these essays and so the present historical moment indicate—changing. And as these canons change, as we come to welcome and celebrate their plural presence among us, so too does the disciplining of music change.

NOTES

1. Other Western disciplinary canons were also products of eighteenth-century thought and the ensuing development of scholarly fields. Charles Altieri locates the formation of a Western literary canon in that century, specifically with Samuel Johnson, whom Altieri calls "the canonical figure most useful for thinking about canons" (1983:41). Historians of anthropology frequently take the eighteenth century as the seminal moment for the birth of that field (see, for example, Boon 1982 and Fabian 1983). René Wellek argues for the inception of what we might understand as a modern historiography of canons. "The history of literary criticism between the middle of the 18th century and the 1830's is the period which most clearly raises all the fundamental issues of criticism that are still with us today" (1955:1).

2. This observation may seem self-evident until one realizes that most anthropologically trained ethnomusicologists (e.g., three of the four faculty members at the University of Washington, including the director of the School of Music, Daniel M. Neuman) teach in music departments. To my knowledge, no musicologically trained ethnomusicologist teaches on an anthropology faculty.

3. It is hardly coincidental that the best-known (and most canonic) English-language folk-song repertory, the Child ballads, is customarily referred to as the Child canon (Bronson 1959:xiii–xviii), or that Francis James Child himself, the canonizer, was primarily a philologist, a scholar of texts (see Child 1882–1898).

4. This concept of animating the process by assembling it from real and imaginary *bricolage* has been dubbed the "invention of tradition" (Hobsbawm and Ranger 1983).

5. The editors and editorial staff for the *New Grove Dictionary of American Music* (1986) took special pains to redress the lack of attention in many standard encyclopedias to vernacular, ethnic, and popular musics in the United States—and they unquestionably succeeded in large measure. Still, a tacit willingness to hang on to old canons is evident when one notes that the number of articles devoted to American organists is about equal to the number of those devoted to the music of all ethnic groups in the United States, in each case about one percent of the total.

WORKS CITED

Altieri, Charles. 1983. "An Idea and Ideal of a Literary Canon." In Robert von Hallberg, ed., *Canons*, 41–64. Chicago: University of Chicago Press.

Anderson, Benedict. 1983. *Imagined Communities: Reflections on the Origin and Spread of Nationalism*. London: Verso.

Baker, Houston A., Jr. 1984. *Blues, Ideology, and Afro-American Literature: A Vernacular Theory*. Chicago: University of Chicago Press.

Boon, James. 1982. *Other Tribes, Other Scribes: Symbolic Anthropology in the Comparative Study of Cultures, Histories, Religions, and Texts*. Cambridge: Cambridge University Press.

Bronson, Bertrand Harris. 1959–72. *The Traditional Tunes of the Child Ballads.* 4 vols. Princeton: Princeton University Press.

Bruns, Gerald L. 1983. "Canon and Power in the Hebrew Scriptures." In Robert von Hallberg, ed., *Canons,* 65–83. Chicago: University of Chicago Press.

Child, Francis James. 1882–98. *The English and Scottish Popular Ballads.* 5 vols. Boston: Houghton, Mifflin and Company.

Clifford, James. 1988. *The Predicament of Culture: Twentieth-Century Ethnography, Literature, and Art.* Cambridge, Mass.: Harvard University Press.

Fabian, Johannes. 1983. *Time and the Other: How Anthropology Makes Its Object.* New York: Columbia University Press.

Forkel, Johann Nicolaus. 1802. *Über Johann Sebastian Bachs Leben, Kunst und Kunstwerke.* Leipzig: Schwickert.

Herder, Johann Gottfried. 1975. *Volkslieder.* In Heinz Rölleke, ed., *"Stimmen der Völker in Liedern"* and *Volkslieder.* Stuttgart: Reclam. Originally published 1779.

Hitchcock, H. Wiley, and Stanley Sadie, eds. 1986. *The New Grove Dictionary of American Music.* 4 vols. New York: Macmillan.

Hobsbawm, Eric, and Terence Ranger, eds. 1983. *The Invention of Tradition.* Cambridge: Cambridge University Press.

Kenyon, Nicholas, ed. 1988. *Authenticity and Early Music: A Symposium.* Oxford: Oxford University Press.

Lévi-Strauss, Claude. 1966. *The Savage Mind.* Chicago: University of Chicago Press.

Morgan, Robert P. 1988. "Tradition, Anxiety, and the Current Musical Scene." In Kenyon 1988, 57–82.

Nettl, Bruno. 1987. *The Radif of Persian Music: Studies of Structure and Cultural Context.* Champaign: Elephant and Cat.

Ohmann, Richard. 1983. "The Shaping of a Canon: U.S. Fiction, 1960–1975." In Robert von Hallberg, ed., *Canons,* 377–401. Chicago: University of Chicago Press.

Randel, Don M., ed. 1986. *The New Harvard Dictionary of Music.* Cambridge, Mass.: Harvard University Press.

Taruskin, Richard. 1988. "The Pastness of the Present and the Presence of the Past." In Kenyon 1988, 137–207.

Temperley, Nicholas. 1978. "Editorial." *Journal of the American Musicological Society* 31, no. 1:1–2.

Weber, Samuel, ed. 1985. *Demarcating the Disciplines: Philosophy, Literature, Art.* Minneapolis: University of Minnesota Press.

Wellek, René. 1955. *A History of Modern Criticism, 1750–1950.* Vol. 1, *The Later Eighteenth Century.* London: Jonathan Cape.

Zetzel, James E.G. 1983. "Re-creating the Canon: Augustan Poetry and the Alexandrian Past." In Robert von Hallberg, ed., *Canons,* 107–29. Chicago: University of Chicago Press.

Contributors

KATHERINE BERGERON teaches at Tufts University. She is completing a book on the nineteenth-century Gregorian reform.

PHILIP V. BOHLMAN studies Jewish musical traditions in Europe and the Middle East and pursues research on the intellectual history of ethnomusicology. He teaches at the University of Chicago.

RICHARD COHN is Assistant Professor of Music at the University of Chicago. His articles on theoretical and analytical problems in twentieth-century music appear in *Music Theory Spectrum, Journal of Music Theory,* and *Journal of the American Musicological Society.*

DOUGLAS DEMPSTER teaches philosophy at the Eastman School of Music and the College of Arts and Science, University of Rochester. He spends much of his time thinking about problems in aesthetics, philosophy of music and music theory, and philosophy of language. He sometimes writes on these topics as well.

PHILIP GOSSETT is the Robert W. Reneker Distinguished Service Professor and Dean of the Division of Humanities at the University of Chicago. He serves as general editor of *The Works of Giuseppe Verdi* and the critical edition of the music of Gioachino Rossini.

ROBERT P. MORGAN is Professor of Music at Yale University. His *Twentieth-Century Music* was recently published by W. W. Norton.

BRUNO NETTL is Professor of Music and Anthropology at the University of Illinois at Urbana-Champaign. He is the author of *The Study of Ethnomusicology* (1983), *The Western Impact on World Music* (1985), and *Blackfoot Musical Thought* (1989); and he is co-editor of *Comparative Musicology and Anthropology of Music* (1991).

DON MICHAEL RANDEL is the Given Foundation Professor of Musicology at Cornell University. The subjects of his scholarship have included medieval liturgical chant, fifteenth-century French music and poetry, and Latin American popular music.

RUTH A. SOLIE is Professor of Music at Smith College and participates in the

Women's Studies programs there. She is co-editor (with Eugene Narmour) of *Explorations in Music, the Arts and Ideas,* an associate editor of *19th Century Music,* and the author of essays concerning music in the history of ideas, criticism, and feminist studies.

Gary Tomlinson is the John Goldsmith Term Professor of Music at the University of Pennsylvania. He has written on various subjects, including Monteverdi, music historiography, and nineteenth-century opera, and is currently completing a book entitled *Sounding Others: Studies of Music in Magical Culture, 1450–1650.* He was awarded a MacArthur Fellowship in 1988.

Index